CROSS-CULTURAL ENCOUNTERS ON THE
UKRAINIAN STEPPE:
SETTLING THE MOLOCHNA BASIN, 1783–1861

TSARIST AND SOVIET MENNONITE STUDIES

A publication series sponsored by the University of Toronto's Research Program in Tsarist and Soviet Mennonite Studies. The series includes research guides, source publications, and studies.

GENERAL EDITOR: HARVEY L. DYCK

RESEARCH PROGRAM IN TSARIST AND SOVIET MENNONITE STUDIES

The Research Program in Tsarist and Soviet Mennonite Studies at the University of Toronto was established in 1989 as an autonomous program within the University's Centre for Russian and East European Studies.

The program seeks to animate and promote scholarship in the field through the collection of sources, research, and publications. It also promotes international scholarly collaboration and assists individuals and institutions engaged in Mennonite studies in the former Soviet Union.

HARVEY L. DYCK, DIRECTOR
LEONARD FRIESEN, ASSOCIATE DIRECTOR
INGRID EPP, RESEARCH ASSOCIATE
JOHN R. STAPLES, SECRETARY

Cross-Cultural Encounters on the Ukrainian Steppe

Settling the Molochna Basin, 1783–1861

JOHN R. STAPLES

UNIVERSITY OF TORONTO PRESS
Toronto Buffalo London

Printed in Canada

ISBN 0-8020-3724-0 (cloth)

Printed on acid-free paper

National Library of Canada Cataloguing in Publication

Staples, John Roy, 1961–
    Cross-cultural encounters on the Ukrainian steppe : settling the Molochna
    basin, 1783–1861 / John R. Staples.

    (Tsarist and Soviet Mennonite studies)
    Includes bibliographical references and index.
    ISBN 0-8020-3724-0

    1. Molochnaya River Region (Ukraine) – Colonization – History.
    2. Land settlement – Ukraine – Molochnaya River Region –
    Cross-cultural studies.   3. Land settlement – Ukraine – Molochnaya
    River Region – History.   4. Land settlement – Government policy –
    Russia – History.   5. Steppes – Ukraine – Molochnaya River Region –
    History.   I. Title.   II. Series.

    DK508.9.Z36S73 2003   947.7'3   C2002-903531-7

University of Toronto Press acknowledges the financial assistance to its
publishing program of the Canada Council for the Arts and the Ontario Arts
Council.

This book has been published with the help of a grant from the Humanities
and Social Sciences Federation of Canada, using funds provided by the Social
Sciences and Humanities Research Council of Canada.

University of Toronto Press acknowledges the financial support for its publishing activities of the Government of Canada through the Book Publishing
Industry Development Program (BPIDP).

Contents

List of Tables

List of Maps and Figures

Maps

Figures

Acknowledgments

I have accrued more debts of gratitude during my years of research and writing in Canada, the United States, Russia, and Ukraine than I can ever properly repay. These acknowledgments only touch the surface.

I thank Professor Harvey L. Dyck (University of Toronto), my friend and mentor, who supervised the PhD thesis from which this book originated. His contagious enthusiasm and his dedication to getting it right remain a constant source of inspiration. Thanks as well to Professor Robert Johnson (University of Toronto), who introduced me to environmental history, to Professor James Bater (University of Waterloo), who helped me see history through a geographer's eyes, and to Professor Julian Dent (University of Toronto), for conversations that spanned centuries and disciplines, but never failed to enlighten.

To Ingrid I. Epp I offer a special thanks for helping me to decipher the mysteries of gothic German script, for sharing her unparalleled knowledge of the Braun Archive, and for countless insights into our mutual acquaintance Johann Cornies. Other friends, too, have provided intellectual stimulation, and more importantly, moral support, for which I am deeply grateful. I particularly thank Robert Austin, Harold Otto, Alexander Prusin, and Randal Smathers.

Alexander and Elena Prusin took on the tedious job of correcting my woeful Russian in footnotes and elsewhere. Kate Baltais and Harold Otto, copy-editors extraordinaire, went well beyond their mandate to correct my almost-random German spelling and grammar. Dr Ann K. Deakin of SUNY Fredonia's Department of Geosciences created the wonderful maps. The help and friendship of all of them is deeply appreciated.

From among countless archivists and librarians in Russia, Ukraine, and Canada who helped me along the way I must single out Aleksandr S. Tedeev, Director of the State Archive of the Zaporizhzhe Region, Ukraine. His professionalism, knowledge, and enthusiasm are unparalleled.

To Mom and Dad, Chuck, Michelle, Simon, Johnroy, Chucky, Anne, Steven, Richard, Christopher, Norah, Danielle, and Ashleen, I offer my undying gratitude for the sanctuary and distraction they provided during the years of hard work.

Finally, and most importantly, I thank Barbara, Duncan, and Emma. Without their love and support, it would not be worth the doing.

Note on Terminology, Orthography, and Transliteration

All of the primary subjects of this book were classified by the tsarist state as members of a single, legally defined social estate (*soslovie*): the 'state peasantry.' They were not, however, socially or culturally heterogeneous, and because this book is largely concerned with comparing their differences, it has been necessary to devise a means to label, and thus distinguish, the separate groups.

I identify the largest group of settlers by their Russian Orthodox religion, calling them 'Orthodox state peasants,' or 'Orthodox peasants.' These settlers came to Molochna from many different regions of the Russian Empire, and it has proved impossible to usefully distinguish them further as Russians, Ukrainians, or members of other ethnic, linguistic, or cultural groups.

Molochna was also home to two significant groups of sectarian Slavic peasants, whom I identify by the names of their sects as Doukhobors and Molokans. I use the commonly accepted English spelling 'Doukhobor,' rather than the Library of Congress transliteration 'Dukhobor.'

The Nogai Tatar Horde, who were Muslim, Turkic-speaking, semi-nomadic pastoralists, I simply call 'Nogai.' I have abjured the awkward Russian plural '*Nogaitsy*,' and the equally awkward anglicized plural 'Nogais,' opting instead to use 'Nogai' as both the singular and plural form.

The German-speaking Mennonites who immigrated to Molochna from Prussia, and the Lutherans, Catholics, and other Protestants who immigrated to Molochna from various German states, present a special difficulty. The Russian administration called them all 'colonists' (*kolonisti*), and I correspondingly use this appellation to refer to German-speaking settlers. I label the Lutherans, Catholics, and others collectively as 'German colonists,' or occasionally just as 'Germans.' The Mennonites I call 'Mennonites,' or 'Mennonite colonists.'

Ambiguity arises from the colonist habit of calling both their multivillage settlements, and their individual villages, 'colonies.' I avoid this problem by calling the multivillage settlements 'settlements,' and the villages 'villages.'

German-language documents written by Mennonite colonists provide a vital source of information for this book. Mennonites spoke their own unique dialect of Low German, but wrote most of their documents in High German. Some wrote with perfect spelling and grammar in beautiful gothic script; most did not. Deciphering intermixed Low and High German text in documents scribbled by poorly educated clerks has been one of my major research challenges. With the help of patient copy-editors I have attempted to put all German-language text into modern standard High German. Where errors in German spelling and grammar remain, I am of course solely responsible.

In transliterating Russian into English I have followed standard Library of Congress guidelines. I have, however, first converted the nineteenth-century Russian-language text into modern standard Russian spelling. The process of abbreviating lengthy Russian-language document titles has sometimes necessitated minor changes in grammatical structures.

Glossary of Russian Weights and Measures

arshin	71 cm or 28 inches
chetvert	Dry measure equalling 2.099 hectolitres or 5.95 bushels. Also land measure equalling one-half desiatina
desiatina	1.092 hectares, or 2.7 acres
funt	0.408 kg or 0.9 pounds
pud	40 *funty*, 16.32 kg, or 36 pounds
sazhen	2.13 metres or 7 ft
verst	1.067 km or .66 miles

Location of Molochna region – see regional maps 1–4 for details

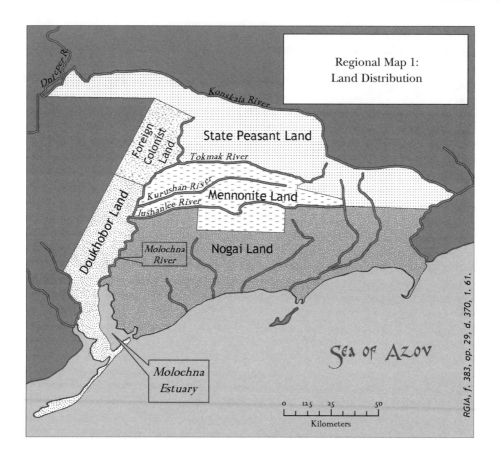

Regional Map 1:
Land Distribution

Dnieper R.

Konskaia River

Foreign
Colonist
Land

State Peasant Land

Tokmak River

Doukhobor Land

Kurushan River

Mennonite Land

Iushanlee River

Molochna
River

Nogai Land

Molochna
Estuary

Sea of Azov

0   12.5   25   50
Kilometers

RGIA, f. 383, op. 29, d. 370, 1. 61.

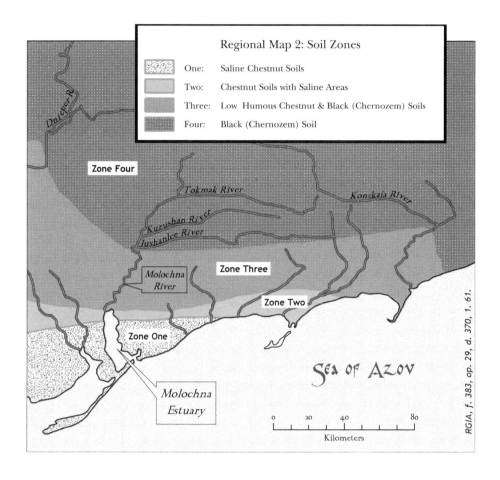

Regional Map 2: Soil Zones

One: Saline Chestnut Soils

Two: Chestnut Soils with Saline Areas

Three: Low Humous Chestnut & Black (Chernozem) Soils

Four: Black (Chernozem) Soil

Dnieper R.

Zone Four

Tokmak River

Konskaia River

Kurushan River

Iushanlee River

Molochna
River

Zone Three

Zone Two

Zone One

Molochna
Estuary

SEA OF AZOV

0   20   40   80

Kilometers

RGIA, f. 383, op. 29, d. 370, 1. 61.

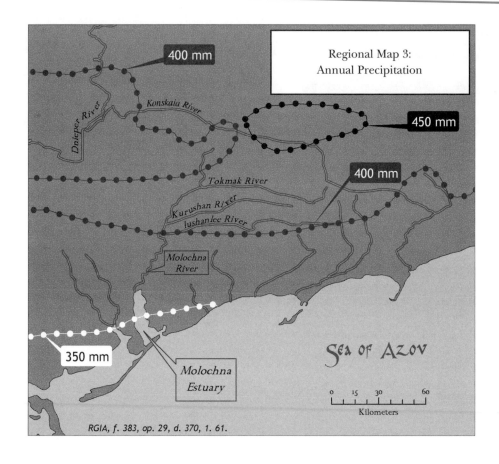

400 mm

Regional Map 3:
Annual Precipitation

450 mm

Konskaia River

Dnieper River

Tokmak River

400 mm

Kurushan River

Iushanlee River

Molochna River

350 mm

Ꞩєᴀ ᴏꜰ Azᴏᴠ

Molochna Estuary

0   15   30   60
Kilometers

RGIA, f. 383, op. 29, d. 370, 1. 61.

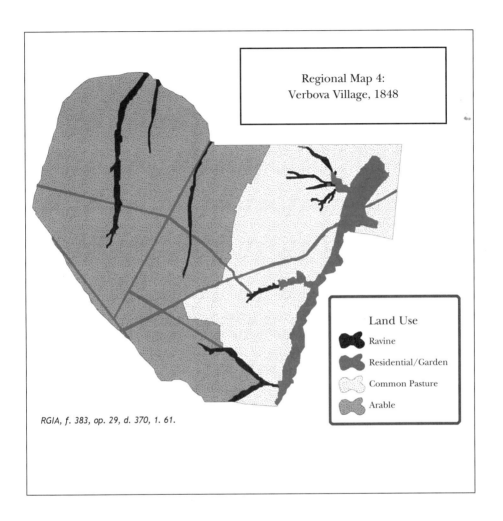

Regional Map 4:
Verbova Village, 1848

Land Use

Ravine

Residential/Garden

Common Pasture

Arable

RGIA, f. 383, op. 29, d. 370, 1. 61.

CROSS-CULTURAL ENCOUNTERS ON THE
UKRAINIAN STEPPE:
SETTLING THE MOLOCHNA BASIN, 1783–1861

Introduction

In 1848 an anonymous critic dismissed the agricultural success of Mennonites in New Russia on the grounds that 'the land of the Mennonites is, as I understand it, not steppe, but ... an *oasis on the steppe*.'[1] Years later a Mennonite described a different scene, recalling his grandmother's stories about helping to found the village of Gnadenfeld in 1835: 'They came to a barren steppe ... no tree, no bush, only tall, dry, bitter grass and prickly camel fodder grew on the dry, cracked ground.'[2]

Faced with common environmental, economic, and administrative conditions, why did the diverse groups of settlers in the Molochna River Basin of New Russia (now southern Ukraine) pursue sharply divergent paths of development? The starkly contrasting images captured in the above descriptions suggest four interlocking themes that form the foundations of an answer. First, human efforts transformed a near-desert into an 'oasis.' When Ukrainian peasants arrived in 1783 they found an isolated, uninhabited stretch of steppe land. Within fifty years, however, the Molochna basin was filled and overflowing, with villages dotting the shoreline of the river and up the banks of its tributaries, and countless attendant horses, cattle, and sheep pastured across the landscape in search of good grazing. By the mid-nineteenth century ploughed fields were replacing pastures while, here and there, villages had become towns, with textile mills, forges, and brick works to serve the bustling communities. This book examines the processes of colonization, the ways that people transformed their environment on the Ukrainian steppe frontier, and how, in turn, the people were transformed by the environment.

Second, perceptions of the environment on the frontier can be distinguished along cultural lines – Orthodox Christian Ukrainian settlers; sectarian Russian settlers; German-speaking Mennonite, Catholic, and

Lutheran settlers; and Turkic-speaking Muslim settlers (Nogai) – and these culturally distinct perceptions translated into distinct agricultural and social practices. To the semi-nomadic and pastoralist Nogai Tatars the 'barren steppe' was not barren at all, for Nogai were accustomed to eking out a living in an arid environment. The transformation of the Molochna basin from 'cracked ground' to 'oasis' required intensive methods of husbandry, and the social and cultural adjustments demanded by such adaptation would pose an enormous obstacle to Nogai prosperity. In contrast to Nogai, most settlers to Molochna brought with them agricultural systems largely suitable for grain production. They suffered catastrophic crop failures and desperate shortages until they learned to adjust their methods to less intensive forms of agriculture. In exploring these adaptive processes this book forms a comparative study of the ways that differing ethnocultural traditions effected different adaptive strategies to the common conditions of the steppe frontier of New Russia.

Third, perceptions notwithstanding, the environment itself placed fixed limits on human adaptation to life in the Molochna River Basin: low precipitation, indifferent soil composition, winter blizzards, and summer dust storms all represented constraints that would not yield to any tradition. By the 1830s animal husbandry dominated Molochna's agricultural economy, but before long livestock herds would overtax the natural carrying capacity of rangelands. Molochna's growing population demanded a growing economy, even if livestock herds could not keep pace. The fixed limitations of the environment, interacting with demographic growth and the growth of markets, pushed Molochna's settlers towards both crop agriculture and industrialization. These economic changes brought social upheavals that took the form of land repartition and economic stagnation in Ukrainian peasant communities, economic differentiation and a 'landlessness crisis' in foreign Colonist communities, a decline into poverty and dependency in Nogai communities, and the forcible exile of the Russian sectarian Doukhobors. The examination of the interaction of environment and society in this study constitutes an attempt to apply the methods of environmental history to our understanding of the expansion of the Russian Empire.

Fourth, perceptions of Russian policy differed between the state's centre and periphery. Administrative inefficiencies were created by disparities between the perceptions of central policy-makers, who thought they were administering an oasis, and settlers who had to marry central policy to the regional reality of arid steppe conditions. The state expected Molochna to grow grain and based its assessment of the inhabitants' economic condition on crop yields. As a result of this policy, while enjoying exceptional economic prosperity based on wool production, Molochna was for many years officially classified as a 'grain deficit region' eligible for tax reductions and grain subsidies. An examination of such specific instances of centre–periphery relations in the Russian Empire offers refinements to existing literature by highlighting the barriers that blocked effective administration and demonstrating that the settlers' ability to mould the state's authority to their own needs was a vital factor in their economic success.

These four themes depict the foundation on which all else in the development of Molochna was based. The allocation and use of land became the hub around which public life in Molochna revolved. Decisions about land were affected by a complex matrix of variables involving five broad categories: the environment, markets, population growth, administrative policy, and culture and tradition. Environment and markets limited land use; population growth and administrative policy limited land allocation; and culturally specific perceptions of justice and equity mediated reactions to the environment, markets, and population growth, as well as to administrative policy. Culture and tradition led the decision-making processes of Molochna settlers. Some decisions were bad ones and incongruent with one or another of the limiting factors. Consequently, some settlers sank into poverty and dependency or left the region altogether. Whether settlers were successful or unsuccessful, however, it is my central contention that in Molochna it was the settlers themselves – and not the state – who ultimately decided how they would adapt to the arid steppe of New Russia.

The Molochna River flows out of the Azov Uplands into the Azov Lowlands, terminating at the Molochna Estuary, a salt-water lake separated from the Sea of Azov by a narrow spit of land.[3] The Azov Uplands constitute the southern edge of the Ukrainian Crystalline Shield and form the watershed between the Dnieper River and the Sea of Azov. The uplands extend to approximately forty kilometres from the Sea of Azov, the transition point between uplands and lowlands lying roughly along the Iushanlee River. The lower reaches of the Molochna River mark the western border of the lowlands, which extend eastward along the shore of the Sea of Azov for 200 kilometres. A low ridge that rises some forty metres above the steppe parallels the Molochna River on its west bank, separating the Azov Lowlands from the Black Sea Lowlands to the west.

The transition from lowlands to uplands is not obvious to the naked eye, for the increase in elevation is small and gradual. The slightly undulating ground is occasionally dissected by shallow ravines and gullies. It rises to a maximum elevation of 307 metres above sea level eighty kilometres inland near the headwaters of the Tokmak River at the peak of the optimistically named Siniaia Gora (Blue Mountain). Beneath the surface there are, however, critical differences between the two areas. The uplands have chernozem topsoils approximately thirty centimetres in depth, with 4 to 6 per cent humus. While they are not as rich as the soils of the central Ukrainian steppe, they are very fertile. The lowlands have much less fertile chestnut topsoils, twenty centimetres in depth, with humus ranging from 3 per cent in the north to 0.5 per cent in the highly alkaline areas immediately bordering the Sea of Azov. The flood plain of the Molochna River forms a narrow ribbon of chernozem soils cutting across the chestnut soils of the lowlands.

In the twentieth century the entire region was intensively cultivated using chemical fertilizers, and this has left little contrast in vegetation between the two areas. When the first settlers arrived in Molochna, however, the difference must have been clearer.[4] The lowlands are wormwood steppe, characterized in their natural state by sparse growths of wormwood grass and, in places along the coast, salt-marsh grass. In contrast, the uplands are feather-grass steppe characterized in their natural state by a luxuriant growth of feather grass intermixed with timothy, spear, and broom grass, wild oats, wild rye, and wild wheat. To the first settlers the difference was crucial; all other factors being equal, the uplands allowed much higher agricultural productivity (see Map 2).

The uplands also benefited from higher levels of precipitation, a critical factor in the arid Molochna region.[5] On the coast of the Sea of Azov average annual precipitation was only 320 millimetres; this rose to 380 millimetres at the Iushanlee River and as high as 500 millimetres in the highest areas of the uplands (see Map 3). The difference is vital because most types of grain require at least 400 millimetres of annual precipitation, making arable agriculture a risky undertaking on the lowlands. This question of precipitation is far more complex than simple averages reveal, for the great inconsistency of precipitation from year to year and month to month is as important as total precipitation. As Figure 1.1 shows, annual precipitation at Ohrloff, on the border between the lowlands and the uplands, could drop to as low as 176

Figure 1.1   Annual precipitation at Ohrloff, 1841–1855

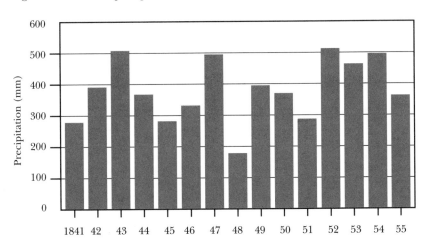

Source: 'Niederschlag der ... Regen und Schneemenge jahrliche,' *PJBRMA*, file 796.

millimetres and climb to as high as 512 millimetres. In the fifteen-year period for which records exist (1841–55), total precipitation fell significantly below the critical 400-millimetre mark eight times, resulting in serious harvest failures and fodder shortages. Even when precipitation was adequate it often failed to come at the time when it was most needed. Ideally, crops need water when they first germinate. In Molochna this means in March and April. However, recorded rainfall in this region was heavily concentrated in the months of May, June, and July (see Figure 1.2).

Inconsistent precipitation made groundwater particularly important. On the high steppe groundwater lay from thirty-five to fifty-five metres below the surface, making well-digging too costly to be practical. This sharply restricted viable settlement sites.[6] Well water on the flood plain of the Molochna River and the lower reaches of its three major tributaries, the Iushanlee, Kurushan, and Tokmak rivers, could be found at an average depth of 4.6 metres, while along the upper reaches of the tributaries at an average depth of 8.3 metres.[7] During years when precipitation was high this difference had no bearing on crop production, but during dry years the significance was enormous; crop yields on the lower flood plain averaged nearly twice those on the upper tributaries (see Table 1.1). The value that settlers placed on flood-plain land is

Figure 1.2   Average monthly precipitation at Ohrloff, 1841–1855

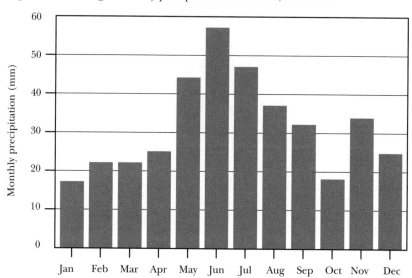

Source: 'Niederschlag der ... Regen und Schneemenge jahrliche,' *PJBRMA*, file 796.

vividly illustrated by the dispute that took place between the Doukhobor village of Troitskoe and the Mennonite village of Altona concerning which channel of the Molochna River formed the dividing line between their lands.[8] The original land survey simply defined the border as the Molochna River; however, at the bend marking the border the river had carved two channels. The protracted dispute launched in 1805, was finally decided in favour of Altona in 1828. This dispute – over a mere five desiatinas (approximately 5.5 hectares or 13.5 acres) of land – began at a time when there was significantly more unsettled than settled land in the region, and it reveals the crucial importance of the flood plain even in the earliest years of settlement.

The continental temperature pattern in Molochna, with its moderate temperatures and long average growing season of 180 days is far kinder to agriculture than the precipitation pattern is. Even in the hottest months of June and July temperatures seldom climb above the low twenties (Celsius) (see Figure 1.3), while the short mild winters mean that in most years livestock require fodder only from December to February, and some years it can graze on the steppe year-round. How-

TABLE 1.1
Relationship of crop yields to precipitation

| Year | Annual total precipitation (mm) | Crop Yields (output/seed ratio) | |
		Molochna and lower tributaries	Upper tributaries
1845	281	4.66	2.93
1848	176	4.21	2.28
1849	392	3.97	4.60
1854	493	5.65	5.99

Sources: 'Die Weitzen Ernte 1839,' 1840, *PJBRMA*, file 606, 12ob. 'Kurze Übersicht,' 1846, *PJBRMA*, file 110. 'Verzeichnis über den Ernte,' 1855, *PJBRMA*, file 1749, 1-1ob.

ever, on occasion the prevailing winds blowing out of the east would bring with them their own unique hardships for settlers. In winter, fierce blizzards with high winds and killing cold sometimes swept across the steppe, decimating livestock herds. Summers could bring week-long windstorms – known to settlers as 'black blizzards' – with hot, dry winds that stirred huge dust clouds and sucked the moisture from soil and plants, destroying unharvested crops, and sapping the nutritive value from fodder grasses.

The environment, often harsh and unforgiving, was the one constant in the lives of all Molochna settlers. For although environments are subject to change, and indeed, human habitation necessarily changes them, at any given time in Molochna all settlers experienced a virtually identical environment. This placed limits on the range of possible agricultural adaptations. The different ways in which settlers solved these common problems provides an entry point into the complexities of Molochna society.

In focusing on the reciprocal relationship of environment and society I have been heavily influenced by the work of environmental historians.[9] This relatively new field, sometimes called ecological history, has become increasingly influential in the past two decades. Donald Worster, one of its most respected practitioners, defines the task of the environmental historian as 'the discovery of the structure and distribution of natural environments of the past,' the study of 'productive technology as it interacts with the environment,' and the study of 'that more intangible, purely mental type of encounter in which perceptions, ideologies, ethics, laws, and myths have become part of an individual's or

Figure 1.3   Average monthly temperatures at Ohrloff, 1841–1855

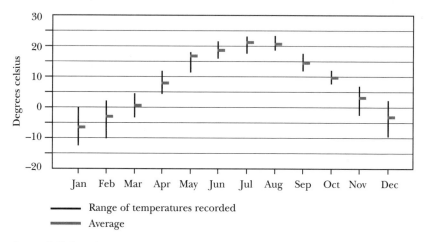

Source: 'Mittlern Temperatur in der Molotschna Mennoniten Kolonie Ohrloff,' 1855, *PJBRMA*, file 795, 1–12.

group's dialogue with nature.'[10] Notably, it is the environment itself that comes first in Worster's formula. For some environmental historians the environment alone is the historical subject, and for all of them the roles of natural history, biology, and ecological sciences are basic, although there is little agreement about where the balance between environment and society lies.[11] Wherever the dividing point is, it must be made clear from the outset that I make no claim to share this bias towards the environment as subject. Rather, it is the people who occupied the Molochna River Basin who are my subject. This is first and foremost a work of social history, although one that is more than usually cognizant of the interaction of its subjects with their natural surroundings.

Historiographic tradition offers little in telling the story of settlement and adaptation in Molochna. There are many historical monographs on various aspects of Mennonite history, including two histories of the Molochna Mennonite settlement. However, these are notorious for their silence on the subject of Mennonites' interaction with their neighbours.[12] Studies by historian David G. Rempel, anthropologist James Urry, and others have made important strides towards refining Mennonite history, but it nevertheless remains a history of the Mennonites alone, with little attention paid to the neighbours of the Mennonites and only passing mention of the environment.[13] Other German-speaking settlers in Molochna, as well as the sectarian Doukhobors, have also received attention in historical literature, but here too the broader story of their interaction with their neighbours and the environment remains untold.[14] My debt to all of these specialized studies will be apparent throughout this book.

The closest semblance to a regional history of Molochna is E.I. Druzhinina's four monographs on the history of New Russia.[15] Molochna only occasionally creeps into Druzhinina's account. More importantly, her allegiance to a Soviet model of historical development in which regional history serves to confirm the place of regions in the orderly development of the empire renders her work of little interpretative value. To cite but one example, Druzhinina claims that Mennonite settlers in Molochna 'comparatively quickly found their feet and became typical landlords.'[16] This statement grossly distorts reality. Druzhinina misses altogether the complexities of a Mennonite community that came to include landlords, tenants, factory owners, wage labourers, merchants, and craftsmen. Still, she provides a wealth of statistical data, from which I have borrowed liberally, and her notes are invaluable aids for locating archival sources.

The historiography of Molochna itself is meagre, but there is a significant body of work dealing with peasant history in general. It is important here to carefully define terms. All but a few hundred of the people in Molochna were 'state peasants' by legal estate (*soslovie*). In 1858 fully 40 per cent of Russia's rural population and 37.5 per cent of its total population were state peasants, but the immense void in the historiography of Russia on the subject of the state peasantry means there are few convenient definitions available to delimit just what is meant by 'state peasant.'[17] Juridically, state peasants were defined by the Code of Laws of 1832 as 'free rural dwellers,' and they possessed far greater freedoms than serfs did: 'Unlike serfs, they had civil and political rights. In common with other free classes, they took the oath at the accession of a new tsar. They were represented at consultative assemblies on the rare occasions when these assemblies met ... They had personal property rights and could undertake all manner of financial commitments. They could buy land, though not estates with serfs. Their children could enter universities. They could change their place of residence, become townsmen, and renounce their peasant status.'[18] Despite these rights there is a consensus among historians that, in their day-to-day life, state peasants were little more than the state's serfs, or, as Russian historian A.V. Aleksandrov phrases it, they were 'the peasantry ... that lived under state feudalism.'[19]

The most important study of the state peasantry is N.M. Druzhinin's seminal book *The State Peasantry and the Reforms of P.D. Kiselev*. Druzhinin provides an exhaustive account of the administrative structures governing the state peasantry and the reforms overseen by Kiselev and the Ministry of State Domains starting in 1838.[20] However, Druzhinin does not find – or even look for – any significant distinctions between state peasants and serfs. Instead, he concentrates on their economic exploitation through unjust and corruptly administered fiscal programs. Records of administrative corruption, venality, and incompetence are common, and indeed, Druzhinin provides ample evidence that such problems were ubiquitous. Druzhinin never asks, though, where it was that the overburdened state peasants found enough money with which to pay so many bribes, nor does he look beyond aggregated economic statistics to ask about regional variations. Druzhinin's conclusions remain unquestioned in Soviet and Russian historiography – and studies of regions as diverse as Lithuania and Bessarabia claim to find no qualitative difference between state peasants and serfs.[21] The most extensive English-language examination of the state peasantry is George Bolotenko's 'Administration of the State Peasants' and it has most of the same shortcomings.[22] Although Bolotenko blames malign political and administrative practices rather than economic forces, like Druzhinin he treats the state peasantry as socially and regionally undifferentiated.

Druzhinin and Bolotenko do provide essential background, and I draw heavily upon their work to outline the administrative structures that applied to Molochna state peasants. However, the undifferentiated peasantry they describe bears little resemblance to the state peasants that I will describe here. Molochna settlers included industrialists, commercial farmers, merchants, craftsmen, farm labourers, and herders, all legally classified as state peasants. The findings of a study such as this, of an isolated river basin on the Russian Empire's southern frontier, can make no claim to be representative of the experience of all state peasants; they do, however, challenge the consensus that state peasants were simply undifferentiated 'state serfs.'

Although the subject of state peasants is underrepresented in the historical literature, there is a rich literature on peasants in general. Anthropologist Eric Wolf's widely accepted generic definition of peasants as 'rural cultivators whose surpluses are transferred to a dominant group of rulers' provides a useful starting point.[23] It should first be noted that this definition *excludes* pastoralists, and hence, at times, most Molochna settlers. However, it also, at times, *includes* most Molochna settlers, and the process of peasantization and de-peasantization is an important concern of this study. The second vital component in Wolf's definition is the transfer of surpluses to ruling elites. Surplus expropriation is an important factor in most definitions of peasants, for it is expropriation that is usually credited with keeping peasants at subsistence levels and preventing them from breaking out of their impoverished and economically stagnant condition.[24]

The most influential modern scholar of peasant studies is political scientist James C. Scott. Primarily concerned with the relationship between subordinate and superordinate classes, Scott is interested in defining the ways subordinates resist superordinates and in explaining how resistance mechanisms shape the larger societies shared by both groups. Scott focuses his research on peasants because it is in the extreme type of subordination experienced by peasants that he finds the subtleties of resistance most clearly exposed.[25]

As a by-product of his research Scott has found a particularly powerful tool for defining peasant perceptions of justice, showing that redistributive mechanisms in peasant communities should be understood, not as a product of an innately egalitarian ethic, but rather as a logical microeconomic system that has evolved to ensure subsistence under conditions of dearth. He calls the cultural embodiment of this peasant justice system a 'moral economy.'[26] The static nature of peasant societies over time is not a central concern for Scott, and for the most part he takes for granted the role of states and landlords as expropriators of peasant surpluses and thus as guarantors that the prerequisite condition of dearth remains present.

With its twin focus on peasant resource allocation and peasant resistance Scott's moral economy thesis has obvious applications to two of the great questions of Russian peasant history, the nature of the peasant commune and the role of the peasantry in Russia's revolutions. Consequently, Scott's thesis is widely employed in Russian peasant historiography, providing important insights into subjects as varied as serf estates in the early nineteenth century, migratory labour markets in the late nineteenth century, and collective farms in the mid-twentieth century.[27] In the process, the paradigm has undergone a subtle transformation. For Scott the central subject, resistance mechanisms, provides a window onto peasant society, but in recent Russian peasant historiography resistance itself has increasingly been seen as the dominant characteristic of that society. The danger here is that the circumstance prompting resistance – surplus expropriation – is taken for granted as a fixed value in a static model in which peasant culture is seen as less a culture of subsistence than a culture of resistance.

For my own purposes the static assumption of the 'moral economy' paradigm is problematic. The conditions of dearth that first shaped the moral economy of peasants in Molochna were not a product of expropriation, but of geographic isolation and environmental constraints. In the absence of state authority, ethnically and culturally distinct groups of Molochna settlers found broadly parallel solutions to dearth. By the time the state was able to penetrate the isolation of Molochna, local society as a whole seemed poised to break the constraints of peasanthood under the centrifugal force of economic differentiation and transform itself into a complex proto-industrial society of commercial farmers, manufacturers, craftsmen, and wage labourers.

To this point the Molochna case seems to support Scott's paradigm, showing that in the absence of state expropriations the redistributive mechanisms of the moral economy were eroding. However, when the state reasserted its authority the distinct ethnocultural groups that made up Molochna society suddenly diverged sharply from their common developmental path, some reverting to redistributive practices characteristic of the moral economy and others continuing along the path of de-peasantization. The moral economy paradigm, for all its value in explaining internal mechanisms of peasant society, has little utility in explaining such divergent reactions to a common experience of change in relationship to the state. In Molochna, peasants made self-conscious decisions about their relationship to the state, accepting or rejecting state directives to suit their own perceptions of justice and equity. It was not their relationship to the state that made them peasants or determined their path of development. Instead, decisions that the Molochna settlers made in reaction to demographic growth and changing markets under restrictive environmental conditions brought about the characteristics of peasanthood – and the erosion of those characteristics – *independent* of the subordination posited as necessary by Scott, Wolf, and others.

This monograph is based upon a wide range of archival and secondary sources. Nevertheless, Mennonite records play a central role throughout, and this requires a special note of explanation. Molochna provided a home to the largest settlement of Mennonites in the Russian Empire. Through their industry and innovation Mennonites played a key role in transforming Molochna into one of the most economically dynamic regions in the empire. This alone justifies the attention they receive. It is also justified by the fact that Mennonites were an unusually literate and observant group who left records of both their own history and (to some extent) that of surrounding peoples. The richness of these records is perhaps unequalled for any peripheral region of the Russian Empire in the nineteenth century.

Naturally, this exceptional source of material creates its own problems of interpretation. Mennonites recorded the world from the perspective of Polish/Prussian Anabaptist peasants, with all of the biases that this implies. Yet the Mennonite perspective has unique advantages, as well. Their high level of literacy and reputation for honesty led the Russian state to use Mennonites as agents of imperial colonization policy in Molochna, and thus they provide important insight into that policy. At the same time Mennonites were themselves the subject of colonial policies as the Russian state sought to incorporate them into the state peasant system. As principled defenders of a highly distinct world view, Mennonites frequently found cause to debate among themselves and with their imperial masters the merits of official policy, thereby providing invaluable insight into Russian regional administrative practices. Of unique importance in this regard is the Mennonite Johann Cornies who, by the time of his death in 1848, was arguably the most influential man in all of New Russia. Cornies influenced state policy throughout the empire, and consequently this fascinating individual is the subject of my particular attention.

This study proceeds chronologically. Chapters 2 and 3 examine the period from Russia's acquisition of Molochna in 1783 to the famine of 1833. Chapter 2 reviews the Russian state's policies towards colonization in New Russia. The extent to which the state had knowledge of the regional environment and the formal structures established to administer it are discussed. The state's goal for its peasants was the development of agriculturally self-sufficient nuclear villages, and separate policies were established towards each of the ethnocultural groups permitted by the state to settle Molochna – based on the state's assessment of the group's level of development as an agriculturally self-sufficient nuclear community. The agricultural adaptations made in the period before 1833 are described in Chapter 3. In the absence of an effective central administration, settlers created unofficial structures of self-administration, forging broadly parallel patterns of adaptation in response to common environmental and market conditions.

The period from the famine of 1833 to the harvest failure and live-stock epidemic of 1847–8 is examined in the next three chapters. Chapter 4 describes the 1833 famine and how it demonstrated dramatically to both settlers and the state that existing agricultural methods were inadequate to feed Molochna's growing population. The famine became a crucial impetus to both administrative and agricultural reforms, which in turn saw efficiency and standardization replace wardship as the central goals of the state. The exile of the Doukhobours from Molochna is detailed as a case study of how the settlers perceived land shortages, and how the state's lack of control in the region lent itself to the abuse of authority.

Chapter 5 analyses the economic adaptations that the colonists made between 1833 and 1848. Johann Cornies constructed a model of civil society based on a combination of the demands of state policy, Mennonite norms of justice and equity, and his own sophisticated understanding of environmental and market conditions. This model, conceived by Cornies by the early 1820s and refined by experimentation on Nogai Tatars in the late 1820s and early 1830s, was applied rigorously to Mennonites and to a lesser degree other foreign settlers and Orthodox state peasants in the late 1830s and 1840s. The resulting economic growth helped mitigate the social tensions that had grown out of differentiation in Mennonite society.

Orthodox state peasants developed their own solutions to the problems of overcrowding and land shortages. These are examined in Chapter 6. Poor peasants used the state's renewed interest in Molochna to apply their definitions of justice and equity in land distribution, forcing the introduction of land repartition. As a consequence the Orthodox peasants' path of economic development diverged sharply from that of foreign colonists, and the peasants sank into economic stagnation.

Chapter 7 addresses the period 1847 to 1861, recounting the harvest failure and livestock epidemic of 1847–8 and showing how they helped to consolidate the transformation to arable husbandry that saw the amount of arable land in Molochna pushed to its natural limits. Interlocking economic developments in Mennonite and Nogai society pushed both groups to the brink of crisis, and this ultimately became a significant catalyst for both the Nogai exodus to Turkey in 1861 and the Mennonite landlessness crisis of the 1860s. The landlessness crisis is the final event examined in this study.

Contrary to conventional wisdom, for state peasants in Molochna, expropriation either by landlords or the state played no necessary role in their socioeconomic development. Rather, as the Molochna settlers showed, the state was ill-equipped to administer its own periphery, leaving peasants to accept or reject the centre's demands on their own terms. The results, whether peasantization or de-peasantization, were a product of ethnocultural conceptions of justice and equity that owed little if anything to the official world of St Petersburg.

CHAPTER TWO

Colonization and
Administrative Policy

In 1822 the Russian Ministry of Internal Affairs granted a group of state peasants from Chernigov guberniia permission to resettle in Tavria guberniia. When the peasants arrived to inspect their newly allotted land they reacted with dismay, angrily advising the civil governor of Tavria that they 'utterly refuse to settle at the assigned spot for the following reasons ... (1) [It] is on the very borders of Rubenovska and Serogozska [villages], and if they settle there, it will lead to disputes without end; (2) In all of the allotted lands ... the only hay meadows are located [on the spot designated for the village], and if they use this area for the village, they will not have any hay; (3) There is insufficient well water at that spot.'[1]

The words of these disgruntled peasants reveal important characteristics of the Russian colonization process. First, it was controlled and administered by the state. The state assigned the peasants preselected land and even designated the location of their village on that land. The peasants, however, were not simply helpless subjects of the state. They were permitted to send an advance party to inspect the land, and when it proved unacceptable they did not merely protest – they *refused* to accept it. Moreover, they did so in terms that implied (correctly, as it would turn out) that they had a real say in the matter.

Second, there is a clear implication that these were *litigious* peasants, for they took it for granted that land located too close to other villages would be the subject of 'disputes without end.' This implied litigiousness is confirmed by the countless disputes that clogged guberniia land survey offices in Simferopol and Kherson. These peasants operated within a system that gave them rights that they were aware of and busily (altogether too busily, the land surveyors must have thought!) employing for their own benefit.

Yet there is a contradiction here, for had the peasants truly been part of a fully integrated system, surely there would have been no cause for 'disputes without end.' The land had been surveyed, the borders defined, the maps drawn, and that should have been that. But it was not. From experience peasants knew that the state could not be relied upon to come to their aid when drought, cold, locusts, and other disasters disrupted their lives. Beyond the realm of state authority and administrative decrees, settlers were doing their own surveys and defining their own borders.

This chapter details the state's policies for the colonization of New Russia and records demographic growth in the Molochna region. It also describes the official systems by which Molochna was administered before 1838, arguing that the paternalistic state viewed Molochna settlers as wards, allotting them land and establishing administrative organs based on its assessment of (1) their ability to feed themselves, (2) their potential to contribute to the state's welfare, and (3) their potential to enhance or threaten the state's security. This description of official policy will serve as a backdrop to the descriptions in Chapter 3 of the unofficial, self-administered systems the settlers established in the Molochna River Basin.

Colonization Policy and Demographic Overview

The Russian Empire absorbed the Molochna River Basin on 8 April 1783 when Catherine II proclaimed Russia's annexation of the Crimean Khanate. The Ottoman Empire formalized the annexation by treaty on 9 January 1784, and in February 1784 Catherine incorporated the former Khanate into the Ekaterinoslav guberniia of the New Russian krai as Tavria oblast. It became Tavria guberniia in 1803.[2]

Settlement of the Russian steppe was sequential, with Cossacks constituting the first wave, followed by the establishment of fortified military towns, which secured regions against Tatar raiders and permitted peasant agriculturists to settle. Such peasants came, sometimes with the approval of the state, sometimes at the command of their landlords, and sometimes illegally, as fugitives from either state or landlord.[3] This sequence applies generally to Tavria guberniia, but important variations make the area a special case. To begin with, Tavria was the final frontier in Russia's push to the Black Sea, and with its occupation there was no longer free land to the south to provide a continued outlet for excess population. Moreover, the Crimea, unlike much of the steppe, had a permanent, sedentary population with claims on land not easily ignored by newcomers. Finally, the territory was acquired by a state – and an empress – gripped by a passion for planning.

Catherine II's policies were 'populationist,' based on physiocratic notions of population as the basis of national wealth.[4] Colonization proceeded in accordance with the March 1764 'Plan concerning the distribution of state lands in the New Russian province for their settlement,' with settlement open to 'people of any status' as long as they moved legally.[5] This qualification had important implications, for no settlers were free to move without state permission; consequently, immigration was officially a controlled process.

New Russia experienced a flood of immigration in the last third of the eighteenth century, but the Molochna region was little affected.[6] When P.S. Pallas, a German naturalist and explorer, passed through in 1794 he saw a vast rolling plain occupied only by wandering tribes of nomadic Nogai Tatars, who had arrived in 1792.[7] A 1797 map of the region shows only four Orthodox peasant villages and ten Nogai villages.[8] Large-scale settlement began in 1802 when Doukhobor sectarians began arriving. They were followed in 1803 by the first foreign settlers, while large-scale Orthodox immigration began in 1805.

The state planned immigration to the Molochna region, but the planning left much to be desired. The tsar's Land Survey Department, based in Simferopol, allocated the land. The department worked without accurate survey equipment and subjected most of the region to only the most cursory inspection.[9] Its job was to allot Orthodox and sectarian peasants fifteen desiatinas of 'useful' (*udobnyi*) land per male soul. Mennonites were to receive sixty-five desiatinas per family, and other German-speaking settlers were to receive sixty desiatinas per family. 'Useful' land specifically included 'farmsteads and commons, gardens and threshing areas,' while excluding 'rivers, streams, ravines, marshes, ponds, roadways, gullies, and other places altogether unsuited to crop- and hay-raising.'[10] Notably lacking were specific instructions on soil quality, precipitation, or access to water. In effect, the Land Survey Department treated land as simple area, undifferentiated in its productive capacities and easily adaptable to human needs.

Demographic growth in the region is difficult to trace, because the Molochna River Basin did not conform to the borders of formal administrative districts, while even formal borders were poorly defined and sometimes changed as a matter of administrative convenience. In 1842 the state redrew the boundaries of the uezds in Tavria guberniia in reaction to the growth of the region's population, and as a result the Molochna River Basin became part of two different uezds. The land to the east of the Molochna River, holding the majority of Mennonites, sectarians, and Ukrainian Orthodox settlers, became Berdiansk uezd, while the land to the west of the river, holding most of the German settlers, became Melitopol uezd. This introduces serious statistical complications to the present study, particularly regarding Melitopol, because the change expanded the uezd's borders northward and westward to include a significant number of serfs and state peasants living on the shores of the Dnieper River, outside of the Molochna River Basin. This hampers comparisons with earlier periods and sometimes presents interpretative difficulties.

The most important published work on the demographic history of New Russia, V.M. Kabuzan's book *Zaselenie Novorossii*, does not cover Tavria guberniia.[11] A number of works, most notably Kabuzan's study *Narodonaselenie Rossii* and Druzhinina's four volumes on southern Ukraine, give guberniia-level population figures, but none give uezd-level figures.[12] A variety of primary sources give partial uezd-level population figures, but none are wholly adequate. The uezd-level records of the 1835 census do not survive in comprehensive and accessible form, but an 1842 document, apparently based on the 1835 census of the Russian Empire, gives the male population of the uezd. Other sources give the populations of specific groups for specific years.[13] It is often unclear whether such sources overlap or duplicate one another and consequently the population figures provided in appendix Table A.1 are tentative.

The data in Table A.1 points to the extremely rapid growth of the Molochna population between 1804 and 1861. Unfortunately, it is impossible to differentiate natural growth from migration, and consequently little can be said about birth and death rates, with the signal exception of Mennonites. Between 1806 and 1848 the Mennonite settlement achieved an astonishing average annual growth rate, excluding in-migration, of 2.93 per cent.[14] By comparison, Steven L. Hoch estimates the average growth rate of serfs in Petrovskoe, Tambov guberniia, in the same period at between 0.5 and 1.5 per cent, a figure consistent with population growth rates among peasants throughout Europe.[15]

The Limits of Planning: Central Policies and Regional Realities

Although the Russian state planned immigration to the Molochna region, once the settlers had arrived it had little control over their actions. Imperial Russia's inability to effectively administer its periphery is legendary. As historians Walter McKenzie Pinter and Don Karl Rowney

Figure 2.1   Patterns of administrative authority in Molochna

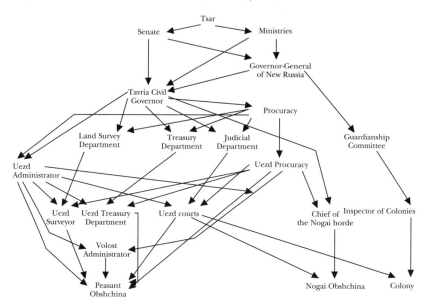

explain it, 'The most talented and best-trained men have served at the centre, but generally have had to depend on the least educated and least ambitious to execute their policies throughout the realm.'[16] The problem was magnified in regions like Molochna, where settlers were almost exclusively state peasants. Regional administrators were normally drawn from the nobility, but because there were few resident nobles to fill offices in Tavria and other frontier guberniias, civil governors had no option but the 'large-scale recruitment of nearly uneducated rural folk into the ranks of officialdom.'[17]

Even had local officials been competent, the complexities of the administrative system made effective administration impossible. The official system in Molochna is portrayed schematically in Figure 2.1. The bewildering web of overlapping jurisdictions and parallel, unintegrated channels of authority are expressed by arrows showing possible paths for the downward flow of orders. With authority so ill-defined it is little wonder that regional administration devolved into a gridlock of jurisdictional disputes and red tape.[18] Although regional officials collected statistical data about settlers in Molochna, there is little evidence that the state even tried to directly administer Orthodox or sectarian state peasants. The sole exception to this general rule was the administration of foreign settlers, which is dealt with in detail in Chapter 5. As for the Nogai Tatars, the state actively sought to change their agricultural practices, but its failure, detailed in Chapters 3 and 7, is the clearest evidence of the state's inability to effectively administer the Molochna region.

The lack of effective central control does not mean there were not significant, active local administrative organs in Molochna. Starting at the bottom, peasant contact with officialdom was mediated through the peasant obshchina. This body, composed of elected peasant elders (*starosti*), hundred-men (*sotskie*), fifty-men (*piatidesiatskie*), and ten-men (*desiatskie*), is often inaccurately described as a 'commune' owing to the redistributive function it sometimes filled.[19] In Molochna, where obshchina land redistribution did not begin until the 1840s, the obshchina nevertheless existed and served as the official representative of Nogai, Orthodox, and sectarian peasants to higher authorities. It was also the official conduit for disseminating orders from above to peasants. Foreign settlers had a parallel institution, the *Gemeinde*, with mayors (*Schultze*) and ten-men (*Zehnmänner*) serving similar functions.[20] There is little evidence regarding the obshchina's role in day-to-day peasant life in Molochna, but accounts of its function in other areas suggest it was a repository of 'unwritten customary law' and the 'ensurer of tranquillity' in the villages.[21]

The second rung in the administrative ladder was the volost, or for colonists, the Gebietsamt. Created by Tsar Paul I in 1797, the volost was an administrative unit intended to contain approximately 3,000 male souls.[22] In Molochna, volosts were always ethnically homogeneous. The volost administration consisted of a head-man (*volostnoi golova*), a scribe (*volostnoi pisar'*), a village representative (*sel'skii vybornyi*), and one *desiatskii* for each ten households in the volost.[23] The state charged these officials with publicizing new laws, encouraging church attendance, taking measures against epidemics and fire, ensuring maintenance of roads and bridges, and arbitrating minor disputes. It also gave them authority over agricultural practices and grain reserves.[24]

There was a large overlap between volost and obshchina authority, and the extent to which volost officials played an active role in local administration in Molochna is unclear. Unlike with the obshchina, there is almost no record of volost-level administrative activity in Molochna before the 1840s, although the Mennonite Gebietsamts were again a signal exception. The only significant examples of volost-level activities are harvest reports, and it is not clear whether these were actually assembled by volost officials or simply recorded as cumulative volost-level totals in reports. Bolotenko writes that the volost was artificial and ineffectual, and nothing in the Molochna case refutes this.[25] Certainly, volost administrative organs did not act as representatives of the peasants in the same way obshchinas did, for peasant petitions were almost always addressed by the obshchina directly to the tsar, the Senate, the governor general of New Russia, or the civil governor of the guberniia. By the same token, decrees from higher authorities to peasants bypassed volost authorities and directly addressed obshchinas.

At the uezd level there were, for the first time, sharp distinctions between the administration of Orthodox and sectarian state peasants, Nogai, and colonists. The regional administrator (*zemskii ispravnik*) was the most important regional official for Orthodox and sectarian state peasants. Nominated by the guberniia's civil governor and officially appointed by the Russian Senate, he had enormous discretionary powers in matters ranging from taxation to law enforcement to approval of obshchina officials.[26] Historian S. Frederick Starr describes *zemskie ispravniki*, with their four assistants (*zasedateli*), as a 'motley and ill-trained band' who were 'often the only representatives of the autocracy with whom most rural folk had any direct contact.'[27]

The *zemskii ispravnik's* authority did not extend to Nogai, who were instead administered by a 'chief' (*nachal'nik*) appointed by the governor general of New Russia but subject to the authority of the civil governor of Tavria. The civil governor arbitrated disputes, mainly pertaining to land, that arose periodically between the Melitopol *zemskii ispravnik* and the Nogai *nachal'nik*.

Colonists, too, were outside of the *zemskii ispravnik's* jurisdiction, answering instead to an inspector of colonies appointed by the Guardian-ship Committee for Foreign Settlers in New Russia (hereafter the Guardianship Committee), which operated under the auspices of the governor general of New Russia.[28] When disputes arose between the inspector of colonies and either the *zemskii ispravnik* or the Nogai *nachal'nik* they were theoretically subject to resolution by the governor general of New Russia, who was officially the superior of the civil governor of Tavria. In practice, however, the jurisdictions of the governor general and the civil governor were distinct, and interjurisdictional disputes sometimes had to be settled by the Senate in St Petersburg.[29]

In addition to the obshchina, volost, and uezd administrative organs, a variety of other regional administrative bodies effected life in

Molochna. Uezd-level courts, land survey offices, treasury offices, and procuracies all played a part in running the region. However, as will be shown in later chapters, the most important decisions in Molochna were made by the settlers themselves.

The state's policy towards the Molochna settlers was, first, one of paternal wardship, intended to ensure both their material and moral welfare. To this end it directed its most extensive administrative efforts at promoting agricultural self-sufficiency. The most substantial indication of state involvement in administration of the region comes from annual harvest reports collected at the village level and amalgamated into guberniia-wide reports for the Ministry of Internal Affairs in St Petersburg. These reveal that the state's principal yardstick for measuring the well-being of settlers was grain production. The state assumed that the minimum annual consumption requirement per male soul was two chetverts of grain. Where harvests fell below this, settlers were eligible for loans, either of grain or money to buy it. Where harvests rose above two chetverts, settlers had to contribute to grain reserves intended to alleviate shortages in future years.[30]

The state's first attempt to establish a systematic empire-wide grain reserve had come in 1767 when Catherine II ordered the construction in every village of a grain depot large enough to hold a one-year supply of grain for every member of the population.[31] The decree said nothing of how this might be done, or indeed of what constituted a one-year supply. Not surprisingly little came of the initiative. In 1794 there were still no grain depots in Tavria oblast. In that year Catherine ordered the construction of five grain depots: in Simferopol, Karasubazar, Feodosiia, Evpatoriia, and Perekop. At the same time she clarified the system of collecting grain, ordering each household to contribute one-eighth of a chetvert per year to a total of one and seven-eights chetverts.[32] In 1799 Paul I ordered the construction of a grain depot in every peasant village of more than fifty households and the collection of one-sixteenth chetvert per male soul per year to a total of three chetverts of rye and three-eights of a chetvert of wheat per male soul.[33] This shaped the basic outline of the grain reserve system for the empire until 1842 with the single exception that, by 1804, the reserve was decreased to two chetverts per male soul.[34]

After a nearly complete harvest failure in Tavria in 1821 the Senate, observing that earlier decrees had been ignored, reissued detailed instructions for the establishment of grain depots. It ordered the establishment of food-supply commissions in every guberniia and the construction of depots in every village. Alternatively, in poor agricultural regions it ordered the establishment of money reserves with which to buy grain when necessary. The Senate reiterated the requirement that peasants contribute one-sixteenth of a chetvert of grain per male soul per year to a total of two chetverts per male soul, or alternatively make a cash payment of twenty-five kopecks per male soul per year to a figure to be determined by prices in individual regions.[35]

These decrees were fundamentally flawed. At the rate of one-sixteenth of a chetvert per year the full reserve would have taken thirty-two years to accrue. Russia experienced significant harvest failures on eleven separate occasions between 1800 and 1850, an average of once every four and a half years, and the country never went more than eleven consecutive years without a failure.[36] Moreover, at least in Tavria guberniia, peasants never came close to constructing the required number of depots. As late as 1843 there were still only sixty-three grain depots in the entire guberniia, and most grain was still stored in pits in the ground. Grain reserves in 1843 amounted to about a half chetvert per male soul, barely a quarter the amount required by the 1822 decree, despite the fact that the required contributions had been tripled in 1842.[37]

Because local grain reserves were never adequate, when harvest failures occurred the state was forced either to lend peasants money to buy grain or to lend them grain from reserves in unaffected guberniias. In 1833 and 1834, when Russia experienced an empire-wide harvest failure, the state spent 8,475,172 paper rubles on grain for state peasants; 1,655,261 rubles of this went to Tavria guberniia alone.[38] Although such loans were supposed to be repaid, in practice they could go unpaid for a very long time indeed. In 1858 Tavria state peasants had still not fully repaid cash loans from 1833 and 1834, nor had they repaid loans of grain received in 1839.[39]

Still, in 1821, 1833, 1834, 1839, and 1848 the state showed an impressive ability to deal with crop failures, and although there were shortages and hardships, large-scale famines were avoided. But the cost of emergency efforts, and the failure of state peasants to adopt more efficient farming methods to improve yields and reduce the need for emergency measures, were constant sources of frustration to the state. Indeed, there was real suspicion in St Petersburg that the grain reserve program was a disincentive to increased peasant grain production. 'There is no doubt,' an adviser reported to Minister of State Domains Kiselev in 1840, 'that the ease with which the villages are issued loans, combined

Figure 2.2   Meat (per pud) and wheat meal (per chetvert) prices in
Molochna, 1819–1822

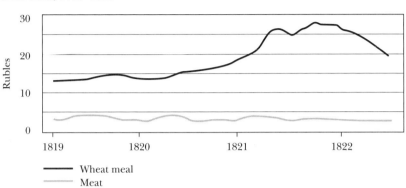

Source: GAKO, f. 27, op. 1, d. 1837–47, 1899–1999, 2127–38, 2266–76.

with the feebleness of supervision over the issuance of grain, is the
main reason for the inadequacy of personal reserves and the significant
increase in peasant arrears in paying grain [into the depots].'[40]

Such a claim must not be taken too seriously. State aid ensured
subsistence but hardly provided for ease, and it is doubtful whether the
peasantry as a whole relied on subsidies so heavily that it consciously
manipulated its grain production based on them. The claim may, however, have some credence for the Molochna region. It is striking that
the state took no notice of either livestock or gardens when it assessed
food reserves in Molochna. To be sure, during the 1821 harvest failure
the Molochna region did not receive aid because the uezd *nachal'nik*
took into account garden production, but this was the exception rather
than the rule. In eight of the twenty-three years for which detailed
grain production figures exist between 1803 and 1838 the state officially designated Molochna as a grain-deficit region and exempted it
from contributions to grain depots. The problem with this evaluation is
demonstrated in Figure 2.2, which shows meat and grain prices during
the 1821 harvest failure. Despite soaring grain prices, meat prices remained virtually unchanged, belying the existence of a subsistence crisis. Had there been a true crisis, surely meat prices would also have
risen. The state's inability to recognize such regional peculiarities in its
administrative policies meant there were large loopholes for Molochna
peasants to exploit. After all, why produce grain surpluses for public
reserves when meat and garden vegetables went untaxed?

Kiselev's advisers identified a second disincentive to state peasant grain production in the laws that hindered state peasants from exporting or selling grain outside their own uezds. These laws, intended to ensure that the state controlled how much grain remained in each uezd, were aimed specifically at preventing state peasant food shortages.[41] They were a clear example of the state's policy of wardship, for they promoted subsistence at the expense of commercial incentives. The transportation and sale of grain, like every commodity in the empire, was the monopoly of members of Russia's three merchant guilds. State peasants could sell grain at local markets, but only guild members could legally sell it in towns, and only members of the upper two guilds could transport it across uezd borders.[42]

In 1812 Alexander I issued two decrees that opened a legal avenue for state peasants to take part in trading activities by permitting them to purchase trading licences. To all intents and purposes these decrees granted state peasants equal status with guild members, although the legislation avoided the word 'guild,' referring instead to four different 'groups' (*rodi*) of peasant traders. The cost of licences, which had to be renewed annually, was very high, ranging from 2,500 rubles for a licence to trade internationally to 2 per cent of the value of the peasant's capital for a licence to trade within towns and uezds.[43] Members of the third merchant guild could not trade across uezd borders, and guberniia administrators naturally assumed similar restrictions would apply to the lower two categories of peasant licence-holders. Remarkably the Senate disagreed, ruling that peasants were not actually guild members, but rather holders of temporary permits. As long as licensed peasant traders obtained travel passes from uezd administrators through normal channels they could trade across uezd borders.[44]

Theoretically, then, it was possible for state peasants to trade in their own grain, but for most state peasants the cost of licences was prohibitive. This does not mean that state peasants did not trade in grain *illegally*. Laws, after all, are only as good as the state's ability to enforce them. Alexander himself acknowledged that it was 'well known that state peasants and serfs, sometimes in the name of merchants, and sometimes in the name of landlords, carry on various sorts of trade.'[45] He specifically intended the 1812 decrees to place controls on this practice. Still, for peasants in Molochna, who were isolated from markets anyway, such laws could only have been a further incentive to concentrate on subsistence agriculture and avoid the expenses related to either expanding their grain production or switching to commercial sheep-raising.

Different Peoples, Different Policies

Ultimately, the paternalistic Russian state saw all its peasants as wards. However, it had different policies towards different ethnocultural groups of Molochna settlers. These policies depended upon the state's percep- tion of the settlers' ability to be self-sufficient, their potential to contrib- ute to the state's welfare, and the threat they posed to the state's security. The state presumed that Orthodox state peasants required its wardship if they were to avoid starvation; the taxes peasants paid and the recruits they supplied to the tsar's armies were explicitly recognized as payment for such wardship. In contrast, the state expected foreign colonists to play a positive role in improving the region and consequently to assist the state in its wardship role. Thus, it gave colonists particularly gener- ous land grants, tax exemptions, and immunity from military conscrip- tion. The state perceived sectarians as a threat to its internal security, for they posed the danger of contaminating other settlers with their dissident religious beliefs. Consequently, it subjected them to special scrutiny and discrimination. Finally, the state perceived the Nogai as a threat to its external security, fearing that the one-time vassals of the Crimean Khanate might defect to the Ottoman Empire. Thus, the state also subjected the Nogai to special attention.

Orthodox State Peasants

Most Orthodox state peasant settlers came to the Molochna region from interior guberniias officially classified as land poor (*malozemel'naia*). The state's decision to relocate them to Molochna was motivated from the outset by wardship policies aimed at relieving demographic pres- sures in the guberniias that the settlers were leaving and ensuring that they were provided with sufficient land to feed themselves. The state had neither positive expectations about the role such settlers would play in Molochna, nor positive intentions to alter their agricultural practices. Indeed, the nuclear agricultural peasant villages typical of the interior guberniias that the settlers had come from were the state's model for 'civil' peasant society, and the state fully expected Orthodox settlers to recreate that society in the Molochna region.

The first Orthodox state peasant village in the Molochna River Basin was Bolshoi Tokmak, established in 1784.[46] In the following twenty years, three other villages sprang up, but the first major wave of Orthodox state peasant settlement began only in 1805. The 1805 settlers, from Smolensk guberniia, were 'economic peasants,' tenants of churches and monasteries prior to secularization in 1764, when they came under the administration of the College of the Economy.[47] In Smolensk in 1785 they had an average of just 3.7 desiatinas of land per male soul, and the state planned to move them to the land-rich Caucasus. However, in 1788 tensions between Russia and the Ottoman Empire interfered, and for the next fifteen years the future of the Smolensk peasants remained in limbo. In 1803 the state finally decided to relocate them to New Russia.[48]

That year Richelieu, who was governor general of New Russia, advised the internal affairs minister about administrative requirements for the move. Orthodox state peasants, Richelieu wrote, 'must be treated by the government with precisely the same care as are foreign immigrants.'[49] Richelieu recommended that they receive (1) assistance in relocating to their new land, (2) food supplies during the trip and until the first crops were harvested from their new land, (3) undisputed tenure of their new land, (4) exemption from the soul tax and all other exactions for five years, (5) loans from the state treasury subject to repayment beginning after five years and extending over a period of a further fifteen years, and (6) a land allotment of fifteen desiatinas per male soul. Richelieu further recommended that those peasants who wished to relocate to New Russia should send an advance party of trusted elders to select their land and choose a village site.[50]

In 1806 the state used Richelieu's program, initially formulated with specific reference to the Smolensk peasants, as a guideline for a broader program for all Orthodox state peasant resettlement to New Russia. The 1806 guideline contained a report from Samuel Contenius, chairman of the Guardianship Committee, proposing a budget of approximately 370 rubles per family for moving expenses and food.[51] The Ministry of Internal Affairs ultimately agreed to grant each Ukrainian family 100 rubles for relocation and construction expenses and for the purchase of agricultural implements, and to pay 'rather more' for Russian families, which would have to travel further.[52] The ministry hesitated to supply regular payments to settlers for food, fearing state peasants might become 'lazy and indifferent.' Instead, it chose to offer twenty to thirty rubles per family in cases of proven need.[53]

The guidelines formulated by Richelieu were a distinct departure from the plan of 1764, which had focused on foreign and military settlers.[54] In 1764 the focus had been on the positive development of the empire's newest territory. However, the Smolensk peasants and other Orthodox state peasants who followed them to New Russia from Poltava,

TABLE 2.1
Average village size in Melitopol uezd, 1821

	Villages	Population	Average
Orthodox state peasants	15	41,483	2,766
Serfs	10	6,494	649
Sectarians	8	2,514	314
Mennonites	30	4,983	166
German colonists	21	5,028	239
Nogai	?	?	?

Source: *GAKO, f.* 26, *op.* 1, *d.* 5394.

Chernigov, and other, primarily Ukrainian guberniias, were moved first and foremost as a matter of wardship to alleviate overcrowding in the guberniias they left, rather than to populate the guberniias that were their destination.[55] The change in attitude implicit in the new policy was spelled out explicitly in a 20 October 1805 decree which required authorities in regions from whence state peasants wished to emigrate to ensure that such peasants were 'truly in need' of relocation before granting them permission to leave.[56]

The state granted Orthodox state peasants in Molochna land allotments of fifteen desiatinas per male soul. In practice, average landholdings most of the time would have been lower than this, because the peasants received their allotment upon arrival in the region, and it was then increased after each subsequent census to account for natural population growth. Consequently, between censuses, as natural population growth drove the population higher, the average landholding fell lower.

The best land in the Molochna region, along the river flood plain, had already been designated for Nogai, colonist, and Doukhobor settlement, and as a result Orthodox peasants were assigned land on the upper reaches of the Molochna watershed on secondary streams. Such streams supplied year-round water in only a few places, and this placed a limit on possible settlement sites and led to the establishment of extraordinarily large villages at the tenable sites (see Table 2.1).[57]

The profusion of independent farmsteads (*khutors*) in New Russia is sometimes offered as evidence that a significant proportion of the total population was unaccounted for in the censuses and, indeed, that most immigrants came to the region illegally. Bolotenko goes so far as to say that khutors were the 'fundamental form of peasant landholding' in

New Russia.[58] However, this likely reverses the actual process of settlement. According to agronomist Wilhelm Bauman, who studied the village of Bolshoi Tokmak in 1844, khutors were summer agricultural encampments of peasants who maintained permanent winter homes in Bolshoi Tokmak. The khutors were located on Bolshoi Tokmak's allotment land, fully within the regulated settlement system.[59] Over time they could become de facto villages, and the state acknowledged this organic process by reviewing the size of khutors following each census and officially redesignating the largest as villages.[60] The resulting satellite villages often remained part of the original parent village's obshchina, thus creating multivillage obshchinas. The existence of multivillage obshchinas is sometimes used to argue that the obshchina institution was an arbitrary state imposition that undermined the traditional village as the natural first instance of peasant self-governance, but the Molochna case shows that such obshchinas could arise from organic processes.[61]

Nogai Tatars

After the Russian state brought the Orthodox state peasants to Molochna it seemed to lose interest in them, leaving them to fend for themselves from their arrival until the Great Drought of 1832–4 (see Chapter 4). In sharp contrast the state directed its strongest administrative efforts at Nogai, whom it actively sought to bring into conformity with other state peasants – an objective bluntly described by Johann Cornies as 'civilizing' the Nogai.[62] The state never precisely defined what it regarded as Nogai 'uncivility,' at least in positive terms, but official correspondence is full of allusions to what the Nogai were understood to be – nomads – and what they ought, in the eyes of Russian officials, to have become – sedentary peasant agriculturists.[63]

The Nogai splintered off the Golden Horde in the early fourteenth century, breaking into smaller groups that scattered across the steppe from the lower Trans-Volga to Bessarabia. In the 1770s and 1780s Catherine the Great resettled approximately 120,000 Nogai from Bessarabia and areas northeast of the Sea of Azov to the Kuban and the Caucasus.[64] In 1790 during the second Russo-Turkish war, Prince Gregory Potemkin again ordered the resettlement of some 1,000 Nogai families from the Caucasus, where he feared they might defect to the Turks, to the north shore of the Sea of Azov.[65] Arriving in 1792 this group was eventually joined by three others: a group from the Caucasus in 1796, one from Bessarabia in 1807, and another from the Caucasus in 1810.[66] This brought the total Nogai population in Melitopol uezd to about 30,000 persons. It would never grow much beyond that number, peaking at 35,149 in 1859.[67]

The land allotted to Nogai was bounded by the Sea of Azov to the south, the Iushanlee River to the north, the Molochna River to the west, and the Berda River to the east, encompassing 352,776 desiatinas. The state officially classified 285,000 desiatinas of this as 'useful' land and 67,776 desiatinas as 'not useful.' These vague terms reflected the vagueness of the Russian state's understanding of the region, for the Nogai land grant was on the Azov Lowlands and, with the exception of the shorelines of the Molochna and Iushanlee rivers and a few areas along the Obytochna River, the bulk of it was only suited to be used as rangeland. This was not a serious drawback from the Nogai perspective, for the Nogai were nomadic pastoralists, accustomed to eking out a living on the arid steppe.

Still, with just nineteen desiatinas of land per male soul, and this of the lowest quality, in 1810 Nogai landholdings were probably already insufficient for their pastoral economy. For the time being this was not a serious problem because much of the land to the north of their holdings along the upper reaches of the Kurushan and Tokmak rivers remained unoccupied. Consequently, Nogai could wander at will beyond the borders of their official allotment. However, as discussed below, the situation posed serious problems for the future.

The state made no attempt to apportion the Nogai land by household, instead leaving its distribution and use up to the Nogai themselves. This unusual exception to the normal practice of assigning fifteen desiatinas per male soul reflected the state's primary concern with security rather than wardship when the grant was first made, but it was also a tacit acknowledgment that the Nogai had distinct ethnocultural and economic traditions and were not amenable to conventional Russian peasant agricultural practices.

P.S. Pallas travelled through the Nogai lands in October 1794 and provides the earliest glimpse of the Melitopol Nogais. Pallas met with three Nogai clans: the Yedichkul Horde that ranged along the Berda River, the Dchambuiluk Horde that ranged along the Kaisak River, and the Yedissan Horde that ranged along the Molochna River. The first state-appointed *nachal'nik* of all Nogai in the region, Baiazet Bey, was drawn from the latter.[68]

The Nogai whom Pallas met lived in round wooden-framed felt-covered nomadic tents (*yurta*) typical of Central Asian nomads. Pallas describes how 'in the summer, these people, with their flocks, travel northward along the banks of the rivulets, where they sow wheat and millet in remote places, and neglect all further cultivation till the time of harvest. At the return of winter, they again approach the Sea of Azov.'[69] Nogai are a good example of what anthropologist A.M. Khazanov calls 'semi-nomadic pastoralism, characterised by extensive pastoralism and the periodic changing of pastures during the course of the entire, or the greater part of the year; but although pastoralism is the predominant activity, there is also agriculture in a secondary, supplementary capacity.'[70] Khazanov describes how Central Asian seminomadic pastoralists follow a seasonal migratory pattern, moving north in summer to take advantage of richer pastures in less arid regions, then returning south in winter where weather is warmer and snow cover not as deep or long-lasting.[71]

The Nogai whom Pallas saw had only recently arrived in the Molochna region, and it is not surprising that they retained seminomadic practices. Nevertheless, conditions in Molochna were not identical to those in the Caucasus, for the range of Nogai migration was limited by state peasant settlements to the immediate north on the Tokmak and Konskaia rivers. The first detailed map of the Molochna region, drawn in 1797 in the unrealized expectation of settling French peasants in the area, shows ten Nogai villages scattered along the banks of the Molochna and Iushanlee rivers.[72] There are grounds for believing that the villages were not simply temporary encampments; indeed, five of them, located north of the Iushanlee River beyond the borders of the Nogai land grant, were still in place in 1803 when the state ordered their occupants off the land to make way for Mennonites who had been ceded the area for colonization. In a petition to the civil governor of Tavria, Nogai *nachal'nik* Baiazet Bey asked: 'Who will pay for the houses they have built? ... Who will pay for the ... grain that stands in the fields of the places they have left?'[73] This is clearly not a description of temporary encampments. Still, Baiazet Bey describes the villages as 'winter homes' (*zimovniki*), suggesting that, while the Nogai had established permanent homes and fields, they still spent part of the year as migratory pastoralists.

In 1808 the state sharply changed its policy towards the Nogai, shifting its focus to wardship and away from the concern with security that had originally prompted relocation of the horde. It signalled the change by appointing Graf (Count) Demaison as Nogai *nachal'nik*. Demaison was a French nobleman of indeterminate background who had entered Russian service in 1802 as a state factory inspector.[74] After Baiazet Bey's death in 1805 the position of Nogai *nachal'nik* was filled by temporary appointees until Demaison took over in 1808; he would hold the position until 1825. Johann Cornies, who lived in the village of Ohrloff near the Nogai land grant, has left a glowing portrait of Demaison's tenure: 'Under the rule of that wise and unselfish *nachal'nik*, the Nogai made clear progress toward enlightenment and morality. Finding them dwelling in portable felt tents, which were highly deleterious to their health, he built them good izbas, ending their nomadic way of life, and arousing them to the work of agriculture with great zeal and profit. The philanthropic *graf* governed with fatherly patience and love, and only when all measures of indulgence proved ineffective did he turn to strong measures.'[75]

When the Duc de Richelieu, governor general of New Russia, appointed Demaison, he issued clear instructions to the count to move the Nogai from their tents to permanent settlements without delay.[76] A.I. Borozdin, civil governor of Tavria, in turn, ordered that sites be selected for permanent villages. However, as Demaison soon reported, the Nogai had a 'strong desire to settle their households in those buildings that they have already constructed for themselves,' and at his recommendation the district land surveyor simply approved the location of already-established villages.[77] Two years later Alexander I rewarded Demaison for this feat of legerdemain by making him a knight of the Order of the Apostle Prince Vladimir, fourth class.[78] The permanent settlement of the Nogai, then, apparently involved nothing more than designating as villages the permanent structures that they already occupied.

Although Cornies was effusive in his praise of Demaison, the count was less liked by the Nogai themselves. In 1815 they threatened a wholesale exodus from Molochna to Turkey. According to Cornies, the threat was prompted by 'one Sultan Moratkeres,' who 'arrived fleeing punishment for a crime committed in Constantinople. Claiming to have been sent by the Great Sultan, Moratkeres spread the story that the Molochna Nogai were to join their kinsmen in Turkey, and that the move only awaited orders from St Petersburg. Things went so far that many sold or bartered away their livestock and equipment ... Everyone once again looked to obtain a *yurt* and a two-wheeled wagon, and they were ready to depart when at last the groundlessness of the rumour became known.'[79] The unrest did not abate quickly. It was only in February 1817 that Demaison could report to Richelieu that things in the Nogai villages had 'returned to normal.'[80]

Cornies credited the threatened exodus to 'wicked rumours,' but for rumours to have had such an extreme effect there must have been widespread discontent among the Nogai. This discontent would rear its head again in 1820 when Nogai representatives petitioned the governor of Tavria, accusing Demaison of illegally selling salt from Nogai salt flats.[81] The terms of the Nogai land grant assigned proceeds of all salt trade to the Nogai public treasury, but according to the complaint, Demaison was ignoring the monopoly and selling salt rights to a Russian merchant. Allegedly the merchant, in turn, sold salt in coastal towns on the Sea of Azov at well below state-mandated monopoly prices. When a Nogai salt merchant named Sarsakaev protested, Demaison allegedly had him arrested in an effort to force him to recant. Sarsakaev refused and was released, but the complainants alleged that Demaison then sent four Cossacks to intimidate him. The Cossacks went to Sarsakaev's home and destroyed his salt supply, food, and clothing. Subsequent investigations proved that Nogai salt had indeed been illegally exported, but Demaison pleaded ignorance and suffered no repercussions.[82]

Before departing the Nogai lands for his retirement home in the Crimea, Demaison reflected on his accomplishments as Nogai *nachal'nik*, recounting his successes in settling the Nogai and forcing them to grow grain but acknowledging that there was still much to do. The problem, he wrote, was that the 'Nogai have, in every village, extra land amounting to more than fifteen desiatinas per soul, and this is to be lamented, for if they continue to be allowed to herd livestock like steppe nomads, then their transition to a sedentary status will remain in doubt.'[83] In other words, according to Demaison, the Nogai simply had too much land. The implied solution was to deprive them of the excess.

At the heart of Demaison's criticism was continued Nogai pastoralism. Nogai agricultural practices are examined more thoroughly in Chapter 3, but for the moment it must be noted that, while it is certainly true that arable husbandry played only a small role in the Nogai agricultural economy by 1825, it is also true that neighbouring Orthodox state peasants were no more inclined to produce crops than were the Nogai. Even setting aside the extraordinary (and questionable) harvest reports of 1816 to 1819, net Nogai harvests between 1808 and 1825 averaged 2.80 chetverts per male soul, marginally higher than the 2.78 chetverts per male soul in Orthodox state peasant villages (see Chapter 3).[84] Meanwhile, for all the rhetoric about excess Nogai lands, by 1825 the amount of good land per Nogai male soul had fallen to 17.47 desiatinas, only slightly higher than the fifteen desiatina Orthodox state peasant norm. Yet Orthodox state peasants did not attract the same criticism as the Nogai. At the root of this double standard was the Russian state's understanding of what constituted civil society. The Nogai, regardless

of their economic practices, did not conform in their social arrangements to the regulated, orderly agricultural villages that the state deemed
'civil.'

Doukhobor and Molokan Sectarians

Doukhobor and Molokan sectarians were the flip side of the Nogai
coin. While the state perceived the Nogai as a threat to Russia's external security and therefore moved them away from an unstable border,
it perceived sectarians, with their dissident religious beliefs, as a threat
to internal security and moved them to an unsettled frontier to quarantine them from Orthodox state peasants.

A pacifist Russian Christian sect, the Doukhobors are thought to have
come into existence in the mid-eighteenth century in the southern
regions of the Russian Empire. Competing theories link their beliefs to
the Bogomils, a tenth-century Bulgarian heretic group; the Cathars, a
thirteenth-century French heretic group; and, more plausibly, the teachings of the Ukrainian philosopher Georgii Skovoroda (1722–1794).[85]
Archbishop Amvrosii Serebrennikov of Ekaterinoslav apparently coined
the name Doukhobor – Spirit Wrestler – in 1785 as a derogatory epi-
thet, implying that Doukhobors wrestled *against* the Holy Ghost, but
the sectarians soon embraced the name, claiming to wrestle on *behalf* of
the Holy Ghost.[86] George Woodcock and Ivan Avakumovic describe the
main tenets of Doukhobor faith in their standard history:

> There is a central, constant element in Doukhobor Christianity from which
> the peculiar structure and behavior pattern of the sect naturally follow. It
> is the belief in the immanence of God, in the presence within each man of
> the Christ spirit, which not only renders priesthood unnecessary, since
> each man is his own priest in direct contact with the divine, but also makes
> the Bible obsolete, since every man can be guided, if he will only listen to
> it, by the voice within ... Since the direction of their behavior must come
> from within, they naturally deny the right of the state or other external
> authority to dictate their actions. And, since all men are vessels for the
> divine essence, they regard it as sinful to kill other men, even in war.[87]

By rejecting the authority of the state, the Russian Orthodox church,
and the Bible, the Doukhobors also rejected the principal sources of
education in Russia. They even rejected literacy, taking Paul's injunction to the Corinthians that 'the letter kills, but the spirit gives life' as a

religious tenet.[88] Consequently, Doukhobors have left few written documents. Because such defiance of authority invited state persecution, the Doukhobors became a highly secretive group, intentionally deceiving the state about the size and beliefs of the sect. This makes their history equally difficult to trace from official records. Finally, what records survive are often unreliable because accounts of state and church officials are frequently coloured by religious prejudice.

It is nonetheless possible to reconstruct the outlines of Doukhobor immigration to the Molochna region. They were permitted to immigrate by Tsar Alexander I's decree of January 1802, which Woodcock and Avakumovic characterize as a 'Charter of the Doukhobors.'[89] Earlier the Doukhobors, like all Russian sects, had been subject to official persecution, and over the last third of the eighteenth century the state dispersed many of them to peripheral regions of the empire.[90] On 17 March 1801, just one week after his ascension, Alexander decreed that such exiles could return to the south from places as far-flung as Finland and Siberia. In January 1802, reacting to reports of persecution of the newly returned sectarians, Alexander granted a request from New Russian Doukhobors that they be allowed to settle in Molochna.[91] Eventually approximately one-quarter of all Doukhobors did settle there.[92] This decree, a turn for the better in Doukhobor–state relations, demonstrated Alexander's religious tolerance and held out the hope that the wardship policies the tsar extended to his other peasants might be applied to the Doukhobors, too. Still, the decree must also be recognized as a cautious, security-conscious measure of an autocratic, Orthodox ruler. Although Alexander permitted the Doukhobors to group together as a community, he isolated them on the unsettled southern borderlands, far from Orthodox peasants whom he feared they might contaminate with their sectarian beliefs.[93]

The first Doukhobors arrived in Molochna in 1802. By 1811, 2,273 Doukhobor men, women, and children had settled in nine villages along the lower west bank of the river and the west bank of the Molochna estuary. Their numbers would grow to an estimated 4,100 by 1824. With Alexander's death and Nicholas I's ascension in 1825, increasing restrictions on Doukhobor migration slowed the influx, and a decree of October 1830 ended it.[94] On the eve of the Doukhobor exodus to the Caucasus in 1841 their population was about 5,000.[95]

Alexander originally chose Molochna for Doukhobor settlement because it was unsettled frontier while, as will be shown in Chapter 4, in the 1840s Nicholas exiled the Doukhobors in part to confiscate their disproportionately large landholdings. All of this makes understanding Doukhobor land allotment and tenure practices vitally important.

The economic success the Doukhobors achieved owed much to the exceptionally generous land grants the state allotted them. In the apparent expectation of far more Doukhobor immigrants than actually arrived, between 1802 and 1816 the state granted them 48,673 desiatinas of land, roughly thirty-four desiatinas per male soul based on the 1817 census.[96] It was a particularly rich land grant encompassing an extensive stretch of the fertile Molochna River flood plain.

In 1818 the size of Doukhobor land grants came under scrutiny when the state permitted the establishment of three new German villages on the west bank of the Molochna River.[97] There was still unoccupied land in the region, but east-bank land was largely reserved for Mennonite villages and because the west bank lacked the feeder streams that extended eastward from the Molochna and provided vital direct access to water, new settlements on the west bank could only be situated along the banks of the Molochna River itself. The Doukhobors controlled a disproportionately large share of this vital land.

Between 1817 and 1820 a series of contradictory reports between guberniia officials and their counterparts in St Petersburg argued that the Doukhobors needed *more* land for new immigration, or, alternatively, had too much land as a result of errors in assessments.[98] In 1820 Alexander I approved a Council of Ministers' decision that confirmed the land grant,[99] but in 1821 the land survey department reopened the question, finding 'no justification for granting [the Doukhobors] such a large amount,' and proposing a reduction of the allotment to the standard fifteen desiatinas per male soul.[100] The Doukhobors protested that their community had grown dramatically, their own count revealing an increase to 2,055 male souls.[101] Even if this figure had been accepted, the Doukhobors still faced a reduction of 17,848 desiatinas, and this was a best-case scenario.

In a remarkable 1824 petition the Doukhobors threatened to gather their belongings and flee if the state followed through with the land reduction.[102] Such defiance reflects a new-found unity among Doukhobors. Before coming to Molochna they had never constituted a single, united community. Although sharing common religious beliefs, they had dwelt in small communities across southern Russia and Ukraine. Now, gathered in the unfamiliar environment of Molochna, surrounded by Turkic-speaking Nogai Tatars and German-speaking colonists, the Doukhobors saw 'otherness' on all sides. Small wonder, then, that by

1824 they identified themselves as one, common community, committed to defending their beliefs even at the expense of defying the Russian state. The assembly of the Doukhobor faithful in Molochna had led to the growth of a 'Doukhobor Commonwealth' much like the assembly of the Mennonites in the same region had engendered a 'Mennonite Commonwealth.'[103] Doukhobors would require every bit of their new-found unity to face the challenges that loomed in the 1830s and 1840s.

In 1824 the Doukhobors reached a compromise with the state that reduced their land to the 21,795 desiatinas indicated by the 1817 census, but the state permitted them to lease the remaining 26,878 desiatinas 'in perpetuity' for twenty kopecks per desiatina per year.[104] At first this price was well above market rates – Cornies leased land for one kopeck per desiatina in the same period[105] – yet much of it was prime, river-front land, and by the time the Doukhobors left the region twenty years later the fixed lease payments were a real bargain; prime land in Molochna leased for as much as a ruble per desiatina in 1837.[106]

The 'perpetual' designation of the lease was figurative, for while the lease payment of twenty kopecks per desiatina was fixed, the arrangement called for new Doukhobor immigrants to be granted allotments from the leased area, so it would be gradually converted from leased to allotment land. The model for this arrangement was the colonist land grant system, which gave colonists reserve lands designated for settlement by future immigrants (see below).[107] The extension of the system to the Doukhobors is an important example of Alexander's continued liberal treatment of sectarians even late in his reign. Unfortunately for Doukhobors, when Nicholas I cut off Doukhobor immigration to the Molochna region in 1830 the justification for the surplus land was removed and the land became the focus of controversy (see Chapter 4).

If the early history of Doukhobors is vague, that of Molokans is all but non-existent. They seem to have originated in the eighteenth century in Tambov guberniia, probably as an off-shoot of Doukhobors. They were labelled Molokans or 'milk drinkers,' because they drank milk during Lent in defiance of Orthodox practice.[108] In most official Russian correspondence they were closely associated with Doukhobors, and indeed in 1837 P. Köppen found that a small splinter group of Molokans in the Molochna region called themselves 'Doukhobor Molokans.'[109] Although they shared the Doukhobors' pacifism and their rejection of worldly authority they broke sharply from the Doukhobors in their acceptance of the authority of the Bible.[110]

By the time Molokans arrived in Molochna the period of capricious land grants that had seen the Doukhobors acquire such huge tracts was over. Molokans received standard allotments of fifteen desiatinas per male soul on the east bank of the Molochna River, shoe-horned in among other settlers and with no provision for future expansion. Between 1822 and 1830 the state allotted the Molokans 12,705 desiatinas of land, a figure calculated using the 1817 census population of 847 male souls. However, by 1835 their number had grown to 1,352 male souls, reducing landholdings to less than ten desiatinas each.[111] Much of their land was of very poor quality, described by the Tavria office of the Ministry of State Domains as 'wild, dry and stony.'[112]

The settlement of Molokans in the Molochna region points to the state's continued perception of the region as frontier in the 1820s. Molochna provided a place for Alexander I to quarantine the Molokans just as he had the Doukhobors. However, if the destination was chosen for its supposed isolation, the reason for the departure of the Molokans from their previous homes was quite different from that of the Doukhobors. Like most Orthodox state peasant immigrants to Molochna, the Molokans were from land-poor interior guberniias where they had no longer held enough land to support themselves.[113] The state relocated them as a matter of wardship, as much for economic as religious reasons, and Molokans avoided much of the persecution the Doukhobors experienced. Administratively, Molokans were treated much like Orthodox state peasants.

German-Speaking Foreign Colonists

The state brought foreign colonists to the Molochna region with the expectation that they would play a positive role in economic development. This expectation was rooted in Catherine II's populationist policies and in the state's belief that the colonists were innately superior agriculturists to Orthodox state peasants and would serve as a model to their neighbours.[114] Their immigration to Molochna was governed by the 1764 'Plan concerning the distribution of state lands in the New Russian province for their settlement,' although Mennonites were subject to a special Charter of Privileges, granted in 1800, that modified the plan.[115] This charter specifically enjoined Mennonites to act as models to other settlers in New Russia, emphasizing the state's positive expectations for them. Russia actively recruited immigrants from Western Europe, offering inducements that included a ten-year tax exemption, freedom from military conscription, and financial subsidies to pay for the construction of homes and farm buildings and the purchase of livestock and agricultural implements.[116]

Foreign colonists are conventionally divided into two groups: German colonists – roughly one-quarter Lutherans and three-quarters Roman Catholics – and Mennonites. Mennonites came to Molochna from the Vistula–Nogat Delta, primarily from the regions of Danzig and Elbing. At the time of immigration about 38 per cent identified themselves as craftsmen, while nearly all came from rural areas where they had traditionally practised mixed farming with an emphasis on dairying.[117] German colonists came from all over the German states; an 1836 account lists immigrants from places as diverse as Württemburg, Nassau, Pomerania, Prussia, and Mecklenburg.[118] Only 10 per cent came from cities, while about 65 per cent identified themselves as craftsmen.[119]

Mennonites settled on the east bank of the Molochna River and its tributaries in villages of between sixteen and twenty-two households. Each family received a sixty-five desiatina land allotment. German colonist villages were larger, some containing as many as fifty households, each with a sixty desiatina allotment. Most German colonist villages were on the west bank, but a group of immigrants from Württemburg, arriving in 1819, settled in four villages to the east on the Berda River. They were not really in the Molochna River Basin at all, although they are grouped with the Molochna German colonists in state records. Included in all colonists' allotments were 1.5 desiatina home plots and a proportional share of the village's pasture, hay, and arable land. Families not intending to farm received only home plots, and one-sixth of each village's land was set aside for such families.[120]

Villages owned their land collectively, and individual allotments could not be subdivided, mortgaged, or sold outside the settlement. German colonists, abiding by the 1764 plan, practised ultimogeniture, the indivisible allotment passing to a single heir. Mennonite allotments, too, were indivisible, but their charter permitted Mennonites to follow their own inheritance customs. The heir who received the allotment bought it from the deceased's estate, the assets of which were liquidated and distributed equally to all heirs. If a man died without heirs or his heirs did not want to farm, the allotment could be sold to another settlement member, subject to approval by the village assembly and the state.[121]

To allow for natural population growth the state gave each village surplus land, equal to one-sixth its allotment land, for future distribution.[122] This gave village and district administrative organs in the colo-

TABLE 2.2
Mennonite land allocation in 1808

	Number	Desiatinas
Villages	18	
Households	351	
Allotment land[a]		22,815.0
Surplus land[b]		3,802.5
Total allocated land		26,617.5
Reserve land		96,622.5
Total Mennonite land grant		123,240.0

[a] 65 desiatinas per household.
[b] One-sixth of allocated land.
Source: Unruh, *Die niederländisch-niederdeutschen Hintergründe der mennonitischen Ostwanderungen im 16., 18. und 19. Jahrhundert*, 304–29.

nies an important area of autonomous authority, for it allowed them to respond to population growth by assigning new allotments, and it let them lease the unassigned portion of the surplus to village members. Orthodox peasants, by comparison, had to wait for the state to grant more land after the next census. This made voting rights in colonist villages, which were limited to the owners of land allotments, vitally important and lent far more prestige to office-holders in such villages than in Orthodox state peasant villages.

Colonists also had a large area of reserve land set aside for future settlement by new immigrants. As new colonists arrived, new villages were carved out of this reserve.[123] The state originally designated 123,240 desiatinas for Mennonite settlement and 73,433 desiatinas for German colonist settlement.[124] German colonist data are not available, but the initial allocation of Mennonite land was as shown in Table 2.2.

Mennonite communities were traditionally co-terminous with church congregations, and all members of a congregation were subject to its ethical rules. These were enforced by an elected Elder (*Ältester*), assisted by ministers (*Lehrer*) and deacons (*Diakonen*).[125] In Russia the state required Mennonites to conform to the administrative system that had been introduced in state peasant villages in 1797. Because the structure of the civil system closely resembled the traditional Mennonite congregational system, in the early years of settlement it provoked little controversy. Some later settlers even thought that it had been imported from Prussia by Mennonites.[126] The German colonists likewise were expected to conform to the Russian system.

The most important difference between the administration of foreign colonists and other Molochna settlers was the Guardianship Committee, a division of the Ministry of Internal Affairs until 1838 when it
passed to the jurisdiction of the Ministry of State Domains. The Guardianship Committee provided a remarkably progressive and efficient administrative organ that encouraged and financially supported agricultural innovation. Its activities are described in more detail in Chapters 3
and 5, but the person most important in its early administration, Samuel
Contenius, deserves special mention. Not only was Contenius an energetic proponent of agricultural innovation, but his wide contacts with
senior officials in St Petersburg allowed him to bypass much of the
bureaucratic red tape that hindered administration on the Russian periphery. His assistant, Alexander Fadeev, who supervised the Ekaterinoslav office of the Guardianship Committee from Contenius's retirement
in 1818 until 1836, was an equally gifted administrator. As a result of
the activities of the Guardianship Committee, state–colonist relations
were a rare exception to the general experience of other Molochna
settlers.[127]

Because the state expected foreign colonists to play a positive role in
the development of New Russia it placed many demands on them during their early years in the Molochna region. However, as often as not it
was the colonists themselves and not the state who seized the reins and
guided innovations in Molochna, and so a detailed examination of the
interplay between state and colonists will be left for Chapter 3.

Conclusion

The Russian state's official administrative system determined who could
immigrate to the Molochna region, provided the infrastructure that
permitted them to come, and determined where in the river basin they
would settle. To that point the state had fulfilled its self-assigned wardship duties admirably. However, the expectations of the state about
how the settlers would use the land they had been assigned were based
on a belief that environmental conditions were malleable and would
accommodate themselves to the wishes of the state. In reality the environment demanded adaptation, and if the state was not prepared to
adapt or to provide realistic guidance in this regard, settlers would have
no choice but to do so for themselves. The paths of adaptation they
would find and the ways these affected Molochna society as a whole are
the subject of Chapter 3.

CHAPTER THREE

Adaptation on the Land-Rich Steppe, 1783–1833

The principal adaptation by all settlers in the Molochna region in the early years consisted of variations on the single theme of animal husbandry. These variations grew out of the experiences of the settlers before their arrival in Molochna, and in particular out of their attitudes towards markets and commercial agriculture, as well as towards the ways the environment could be shaped to fit human needs. Nogai and Orthodox state peasants tended to understand the environment to have fixed, unalterable characteristics to which humans must adapt. These two groups of settlers followed the path of least resistance, quickly adopting agricultural practices that provided their subsistence. Because of this choice for subsistence, the Nogai and the Orthodox peasants were relatively unresponsive to interregional and international markets, which sought goods that were not easily produced in the Molochna. The foreign colonists and sectarians, however, understood the environment to have distinctive, but modifiable characteristics that could be managed to human specifications. These groups adapted slowly to life in the Molochna region because they expended considerable efforts to coerce the environment in the service of their commercial and cultural requirements; in the long term their adaptations laid the groundwork for their future prosperity.

Differing attitudes towards markets and the environment also found expression in self-administrative practices in Molochna. Nogai and Orthodox state peasants showed little inclination to manage their own society. For both of these groups the functional role of their traditional administrative system had been to manage scarce resources. In the first decades of settlement, however, land in the Molochna River Basin was plentiful, and this undermined the legitimacy of their traditional systems. The foreign colonists and sectarians brought with them their traditional religiously based self-administrative systems, which had previously been limited or suppressed by powerful central states. The isolation they found in Molochna provided an opportunity for their traditions to blossom, helping to create vibrant ethnocultural 'commonwealths.'

Carrying Capacity of Molochna Pasture Lands

Animal husbandry requires little labour, and it is thus a common agricultural adaptation to conditions of labour scarcity such as those in the Molochna region in the early nineteenth century.[1] Sheep breeding in particular was important because of the region's isolation from markets. The nearest ports were Mariupol, which was 170 kilometres to the east, and Feodosiia, 250 kilometres southwest. The costs involved in transporting agricultural products over such distances were an important strategic consideration for settlers. Wool had a high ratio of value to weight, while being relatively impervious to the rigours of slow travel over poor roads, making it a natural choice for commercially interested Molochna settlers.[2] Also, cattle and horses were important in Molochna. Oxen were the draft animal of choice for Orthodox and sectarian state peasants, while for Nogai ownership of cattle played a cultural role in defining social status. Horses were important both as draft animals and as status symbols, and Nogai in particular kept large horse herds.

The carrying capacity of range lands became a vital determinant of socioeconomic development in Molochna. What does carrying capacity of range land mean? Some sources report that pastoralists in New Russia kept as many as ten sheep per desiatina, which represents an enormously high ratio of livestock to pasture land.[3] Others suggest that even the richest hay lands in the irrigated flood plain, which constituted but a tiny proportion of the total pasture and hay land in the Molochna River Basin, could only produce enough hay to feed about five sheep per desiatina per year.[4] On the less arid range lands of Dneprovsk uezd, north and northwest of the Molochna River, owners of large private herds seldom achieved a ratio of more than two sheep per desiatina, while Mennonite colonists kept not more than 1.2 sheep per desiatina on their communal pastures (and this figure dropped temporarily to 0.48 sheep per desiatina after the severe winter of 1825).[5]

The discrepancies between such accounts make it necessary to look elsewhere for guidance. Modern agronomists conventionally measure carrying capacity of range land in animal unit months (AUMs), the number of months a given unit of land will support one 450 kilogram cow or horse or six sheep. This calculation is based on an average daily consumption of twelve kilograms of dry matter.[6] Cattle and horses in New Russia were small, averaging only about 200 kilograms each, although sheep achieved approximately the modern weight norm of about eighty kilograms.[7] Hence, for Molochna one nominal 450 kilogram animal unit (AU) was equal to about 2.25 cows or horses or six sheep.

Arid natural pasture lands like those in Molochna produce, at best, just over 1,200 kilograms of dry matter per desiatina.[8] This could be improved substantially by irrigating or growing specialized high-yield fodder crops. By 1835 only 1,385 desiatinas of hay land were under irrigation in the Molochna region, while specialized high-yield fodder crops were first introduced (on an experimental basis) only in the 1840s. Using a figure of 1,226 kilograms yield per desiatina, the AUM for one desiatina in Molochna was 3.35. This means that one desiatina of land could support one animal unit for 3.35 months and that about three and a half desiatinas were required per animal unit per year. Thus, in the Molochna region each desiatina of range land could support about two-thirds of a small local cow or horse or about one and three-quarter sheep.

Sometimes livestock populations temporarily surpass the carrying capacity of their pasture lands. Herds expand beyond the limit of carrying capacity, and die off from starvation and disease during droughts and epidemics. Among undernourished, livestock epidemics are all the more frequent. Eventually, populations stabilize again – at a lower level, determined in part by degeneration of pasture land caused by overgrazing and in part by human adaptation to agricultural systems that are less dependent on livestock.[9]

This process of animal population growth, decline, and levelling is known as an ungulate irruption. It often repeats itself in an irruptive oscillation, a cycle of livestock population growth and decline with a reciprocal decline and recovery of the pasture lands, albeit at a lower carrying capacity each time.[10] The severity of irruptive oscillations lessens as a balance is achieved. Typically, the entire levelling process takes thirty-five to forty years.[11]

Appendix Table A.2 shows total livestock in the Molochna region between 1805 and 1861 in real terms and in animal units. At their highest in 1846, the roughly 1.1 million head of livestock in Melitopol

Figure 3.1   Livestock in Molochna, 1843–1861

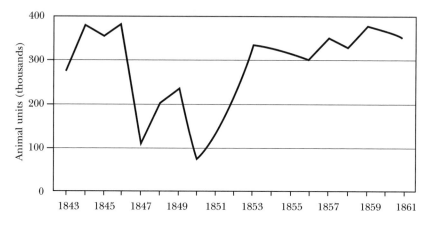

Sources: 'Otchety tavricheskikh gubernatorov,' 1841–61, *f.* 1281, *op.* 4–6.

and Berdiansk uezds would have required an estimated 1.33 million desiatinas of grazing land. According to the calculations of the Land Survey Department there was a total of just 1.49 million desiatinas of useful land in the entire Molochna region including arable land, village sites, and waste lands. Thus, total livestock must have been pushing close to the limits of the region's carrying capacity. As will be shown below, for some Molochna settlers the limit had already been exceeded.

The fluctuations in total livestock holdings after 1843 (the period for which there are adequate data) are portrayed graphically in Figure 3.1. This pattern is typical of an irruptive oscillation and tends to confirm that by the 1840s the pasture lands of the Molochna River Basin were used up and were probably experiencing ecological degradation from overgrazing.

Adapting to the Land: Nogai and Orthodox State Peasants

Nogai and Orthodox state peasants came to Molochna from utterly dissimilar environments. The adaptations required of them were likewise dissimilar. Orthodox peasants arrived from overcrowded interior guberniias where arable husbandry predominated. They found a landscape vastly different from the one they had left behind. The frontier was arid, treeless, and isolated from markets, and demanded a change to less intensive forms of agriculture than they had previously known. Nogai came to Molochna as seminomadic steppe pastoralists, fully accustomed to the environmental demands of their new location. For the Nogai adaptation meant a transformation to *more* intensive agricultural practices as the Molochna became more and more densely populated. Both groups found a common solution to their needs in the transition to sheep breeding, but as they adapted, the functional roles of their traditional administrative systems were undermined. The success of their adaptations would ultimately rest upon their ability to develop new administrative structures to replace the old.

Nogai Adaptation

There is little direct evidence about internal administration in the Nogai community in their first years in the Molochna region, but studies of Central Asian steppe nomads provide guidance. Nomadism placed limits on political authority, for nomads spent much of the year in small groups beyond the direct influence of political leaders.[12] Central Asian nomads lived in *auls*, which were mobile villages composed of as few as two and seldom more than ten households, each consisting of a man, his wife, and their unmarried children.[13] An aul was typically made up of households headed by close relatives and forming a primary kin group, which was led by the eldest male, who was advised and supported by the heads of other households.[14] Groups of auls often formed confederations known as hordes with common territorial rights.[15] All members of a horde traced their descent through the male line to one common ancestor, often Chingis Khan (Ghengis Khan), and such descent myths provided 'a theoretical foundation for social integration.'[16] The Nogai descent myth included Chingis Khan, but extended back to the biblical figure Ishmael, son of Abraham and Hagar.[17]

   The leader of a horde was the *bey*. His sons and close male relatives formed a hereditary nobility known as *murzas*, who led their own auls, which were often larger than the norm, containing as many as fifty households.[18] The murzas' control of the horde was based on their senior genealogical position, and it was 'frequently the aristocracy ... which [cultivated] knowledge of genealogies and [manipulated] them so as to give an ideological basis to their ruling positions.'[19] Beys and murzas were responsible for the allocation of key resources, the establishment and regulation of migration routes, the defence of the horde's territory, and other common interests.[20]

Beys, murzas, and leaders of auls gained economic advantages from their positions. They could arrogate to themselves the best grazing territory and exact labour services – particularly livestock supervision - from other clan members.[21] However, nomadism placed limits on economic differentiation, as well as on political authority. The most basic limitation was that the means of production, the pasturage, was held communally.[22] A second important constraint was that nomadic households required a minimum number of livestock to subsist. That placed a lower limit on the size of a viable household's herds, whereas the need for mobility and the environmental limitations of pasture lands placed maximum limits on herd sizes. Many of the trappings of wealth in sedentary society were simply impractical for nomads, who had to limit their personal belongings to what they could carry with them.[23] The stability of nomadic societies was ensured in part by the safety valve of surrounding sedentary societies, which provided an outlet for those whose herds grew too small to be viable, whether through misfortune or mismanagement, and for those who found the attraction of greater wealth irresistible.

As detailed in Chapter 2, the state's first administrative objective with Nogai was to end their nomadism and force them to abandon pastoralism in favour of arable husbandry. In 1825, when Cornies credited Demaison with arousing the Nogai 'to the work of agriculture with great zeal and profit,' it was Demaison's success in forcing Nogai to grow grain that he was referring to.[24] As Appendix Table A.3 shows, Nogai grain production increased sharply in 1816 and continued to show high yields for the following three years. Demaison achieved this by denying travel passes to Nogai men who did not first sow at least two chetverts of grain.[25] This restriction, implemented in 1816, was effective because many young Nogai men would travel to the Crimea each summer to work as herdsmen. Wages in the Crimea averaged twice those in Melitopol uezd, and a lead hand could earn as much as 600 rubles a year; thus, the travel passes were highly valued.[26]

Despite the apparent success of Demaison's scheme of grain for passes there are several reasons to treat the reported results with caution. To begin with, the accuracy of harvest reports is questionable. Between 1816 and 1819, when Nogai output-to-seed ratios reportedly averaged 6.09:1, Mennonite yields averaged just 5.89:1, and Orthodox state peasant yields just 4.6:1.[27] That Nogai pastoralists suddenly outstripped their more experienced neighbours in grain production is curious, to say the least. Indeed, harvest reports from at least one of the six Nogai volosts show clear evidence of falsification. For 1817 and 1818 they show that the Nogai volost of Ialanzachskaia had yields of over 10:1, about twice that of any other volost in the entire region! Such extraordinary success is more likely to be a reflection of creative record-keeping than of efficient farming. Even without Ialanzachskaia volost, Nogai yields in this period were better than they had been in earlier years or would be in later years, but the extent of the improvement is probably much exaggerated.

More significant is the fact that when, in 1821, Demaison retired from active participation in the administration of the Nogai, (he retained his title while an assistant did the work until he was officially replaced in 1825) grain production immediately returned to its earlier low levels.[28] In 1825 Cornies lamented that after Demaison's departure 'the economic and moral improvement of these people appears to almost be at a standstill. Worsened by last year's poor weather, their economic condition has deteriorated, and their laziness, quarrelsomeness, and thievery are on the increase.'[29] Apparently the grain-for-passes scheme had produced no lasting effect.

The clearest evidence that Demaison brought no fundamental change to the Nogai was their continued pastoralism. As Table A.2 shows, Nogai herds expanded enormously during Demaison's tenure. Pastoralism was a logical choice for Nogai from both an economic and environmental point of view, for as already noted, most Nogai land was unsuited to arable husbandry. However, it would be a mistake to conclude that Nogai pastoralism was based on either economic or environmental considerations, for as in most pastoral societies, livestock also played an important cultural role for Nogai.[30] If economics had decided the matter, Nogai would probably have raised sheep for wool. As Table 3.1 shows, over the course of Demaison's tenure the percentage of sheep in Nogai herds (expressed as AUs), almost tripled. This suggests that commercial concerns had begun to affect Nogai herding strategies. But in 1825 sheep still made up less than a third of Nogai livestock, and at the end of Demaison's tenure Nogai still concentrated primarily on cattle and horses. The Swiss missionary Daniel Schlatter, who made two lengthy visits to the Molochna region in the 1820s, even suggested that Nogai men valued their horses above their wives.[31]

From an environmental perspective, while the region was suited to pastoralism the enormous growth of Nogai herds during the time of Demaison was hardly desirable. In 1825 Cornies worried that Nogai were overgrazing their land, and he was probably right.[32] In 1819, when

TABLE 3.1
Sheep animal units (AUs) as a percentage of all AUs

Year	Percentage	Year	Percentage
1808	8.45	1816	17.35
1809	9.83	1817	19.02
1810	9.31	1818	19.72
1811	9.98	1819	19.95
1812	11.99	1823	20.99
1813	14.37	1825	23.64
1815	16.67		

Sources: 'Otchety Tavricheskikh Gubernatorov,' 1808–27, *RGIA*, f. 1281, *op.* 11, *d.* 131–3, Annual reports of Demaison to the governor of Tavria for 1817, 1818, and 1819, *GAKO*, f. 26, *op.* 1.

total livestock numbers peaked, Nogai were grazing 221,284 cattle and horses and 132,392 sheep. This is an enormous number of livestock for such arid land. Based on carrying capacity estimates, in 1819 Nogai herds would have needed some 387,000 desiatinas of grazing land – more than the total Nogai land allotment. Because Nogai pastures were strained to their limits, it is little wonder that the harsh winter of 1825 saw over 45,000 Nogai cattle and horses die and (expressed in AUs) an overall loss of more than 20 per cent of Nogai livestock. Figure 3.2 shows the total land requirements of Nogai livestock from 1807 to 1837. The pattern of expansion and contraction is highly characteristic of an ungulate irruption. By implication, the growth of Nogai herds had reached its upper limit by 1819, and probably by the mid-1820s over-stocking was leading to land degradation.

A critical element of the land problem facing Nogai by 1819 was the shrinking size of range lands available to them *outside* of their allotment. As noted in Chapter 2, by 1810, per capita Nogai landholdings were already too low to support a traditional pastoral economy, so the Nogai were dependent on grazing livestock on unoccupied range lands north of the Iushanlee River. Between 1819 and 1824 Mennonites established eighteen new villages on the upper reaches of the Iushanlee and Kurushan rivers, sharply reducing Nogai access to range land even as Nogai herds were expanding.[33] The consequences of this for Nogai society will be discussed below.

Although Demaison was not successful in transforming Nogai from pastoralists into agriculturists, the remarkable growth of their herds suggests that Nogai were undergoing a dramatic transformation all the

Figure 3.2   Nogai grazing land required and available, 1807–1837

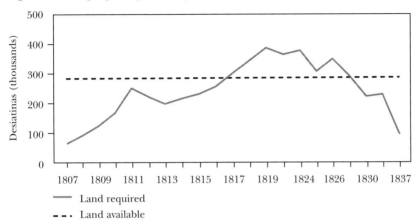

Sources: 'Otchetov Tavricheskikh Gubernatorov,' *RGIA, f.* 1281, *op.* 11: *d.* 131 (1808–10); *d.* 132 (1811–15), *d.* 133 part 1 (1816, 1822), *d.* 133 part 2 (1823–27); Annual reports of Demaison to the governor of Tavria: GAKO, *f.* 26, *op.* 1: *d.* 994 (1814), *d.* 2503 (1817), *d.* 3308 (1818), *d.* 4137 (1819), *d.* 5017 (1820), *d.* 5394 (1821); Sergeev, 'Nogaitsy na Molochnykh vodakh,' 61 (1828–31); Cornies, 'Landwirthschaftliche Notizen,' 1837, *PJBRMA*, file 992.

same. This transformation requires explanation. Livestock were the most important symbol of wealth and social status for Nogai. Schlatter reported that wealthy Nogai men could not be distinguished by the clothes they wore or the houses they lived in; the only true index of their wealth was the size of their herds of cattle and horses.[34] The rapid growth of herds was evidence of an enormous growth in wealth, but to what can this be attributed? In large part, no doubt, to the proximity of a growing population of peasant agriculturists. These agriculturists provided wages to Nogai, particularly during peak agricultural seasons.[35] They also provided a market for horses and cattle, tallow, hides, and meat. Nogai were converting their income from these sources into livestock.

Economic differentiation went hand in hand with the growth in Nogai herds. In the 1820s Schlatter saw poor Nogai begging for grain, and he frequently mentioned distinctions between poor and rich, although he was impressed by the equal access to land enjoyed by all Nogai and thought that all but the poorest had adequate incomes.[36] Living in a Nogai household, Schlatter said his host Ali was 'not rich, but all the same had thirty head of cattle and five horses.'[37] In 1824 the average Nogai household had nine horses, twenty-six head of cattle, and twenty-two sheep, so Ali was indeed poorer than the norm.[38] Notably, Ali owned no sheep, for Nogai were traditionally cattle herders and the transition to sheep raising by a small minority of Nogai was a sign of economic assimilation, a subject examined more fully below.

Schlatter also described the local Nogai administrative system, which differed sharply from the traditional nomadic model detailed above. Schlatter found the Nogai divided into typical Russian peasant villages with ten-, fifty-, and hundred-men, village elders, obshchinas, and volosts, all under the direction of the state-appointed *nachal'nik*.[39] The extent to which this formal substitution of Russian for Nogai institutions was reflected in practical administrative practices is unclear. As an outsider, Demaison could not have exercised his authority on the basis of lineage, as was the custom with traditional Nogai leaders. When necessary, Demaison even employed Cossack troops to enforce his orders, as the 1820 salt scandal described in Chapter 2 shows.

The Nogai threat of exodus in 1815 suggests that in that year traditional leadership structures still existed and were capable of opposing the new official structures. However, the extreme growth of Nogai herds shows that important regulatory functions of traditional leaders were eroding. With migration no longer a way of life, decisions about pasture allocation could no longer be made in traditional ways. The traditional checks on herd growth were being eliminated and the balance that nomads must achieve with the productive potentials of their environment was being lost. Yet the failure of Demaison's arrangement of grain for travel passes shows that the Russian system was not successfully replacing the failing traditional one. Instead, an administrative vacuum was developing.

Administration of the Nogai underwent an important change in 1825 when Johann Cornies began to take an active role. His first contact with Nogai had come in his father's home, where Johann Sr's reputation as a healer brought a wide range of people, including Nogai, to his door.[40] Perhaps motivated by this early contact, Cornies became a student of Nogai history and keen observer of contemporary Nogai life. In 1825 he first outlined his own program for their improvement: 'Cannot at least the principal town of Nogaisk itself be improved and enlarged and provided with a high school? Cannot a model colony be established in the region, for poor but industrious and willing Nogai, which could serve as a model for other Nogai villages? Cannot a flock of improved sheep be bought through the community treasury, to be paid for from the profits of the improved wool in the future?'[41] The Russian state never officially charged Cornies with improving the condition of the Nogai. Nevertheless, programs that he began to implement in 1825 and continued to supervise until his death in 1848 gained the state's full support.

Cornies's first major initiative was a project to improve the quality of Nogai sheep. This project was a clear departure from the efforts of Demaison, for emphasis had shifted from arable to animal husbandry. For several years prior to 1825 Cornies had already been placing sheep in the hands of Nogai and to a lesser degree Doukhobors, Molokans, and German colonists. But his new program signalled an important change. Prior to 1825 Cornies had paid a fixed rate per year per head of livestock, but now he moved from a simple business transaction to a program explicitly directed at benefiting the Nogai.[42] Conditions that Cornies incorporated into the project involved fundamental changes in the way Nogai supervised their herds. In effect, Cornies was trying to transform Nogai animal husbandry from pastoralist traditions with their emphasis on the cultural value of livestock to an organized, regulated, market-oriented system.

Starting in 1825 Cornies began lending merino sheep to Nogai, while encouraging Mennonites to follow suit.[43] This seems at odds with his concern about overgrazing Nogai land. Yet if, as Cornies intended, Nogai reduced the size of their cattle herds and concentrated on raising smaller numbers of more valuable merinos, pressure on their grazing land would be reduced at the same time as the value of their livestock increased.

The terms of Cornies's sheep loans were eventually formalized into a standardized contract. In the first extant example (from 1834), Cornies agreed to supply a Nogai named Kulman with forty-five ewes and five female lambs and pay half the cost of buying a ram for breeding.[44] Kulman was to pay for the other half of the ram, as well as all other costs during the four-year contract. He was to provide fodder in winter, ensure that the sheep drank only well water, prevent them from mixing with the native Nogai breed of sheep known as *kurdiuch* sheep (which might infect them with diseases), and refrain from slaughtering healthy sheep under any circumstances. In a concession to Nogai religious customs, which regarded allowing animals to die of disease as sinful, Kulman was permitted to slaughter diseased sheep, but only in the presence of two Nogai elders who would attest that the slaughtered sheep were truly

ill. Cornies and Kulman were to divide equally the annual wool production from the herd, and at the end of the four-year contract, after
Kulman returned to Cornies forty-five ewes and five female lambs to
match the original investment, the two would divide equally whatever
offspring remained. However, if the size of the herd shrank during the
four years, Kulman was to pay Cornies the full market value of lost
sheep, except those for which he could produce a hide and prove the
sheep had been diseased.

In essence this was a sharecropping – or more accurately share-pas-
turing – contract, albeit a very unusual one. In most sharecropping
contracts a landlord provides capital in the form of land and seed,
while the sharecropper provides only labour. But Cornies did not provide Kulman with land.[45] Indeed, Kulman's capital investment of land,
in effect, made him a partner with Cornies. Sharecropping is usually
described as exploitative, particularly by Marxian analysts for whom the
concentration of the means of production in the hands of landowners
is by definition exploitative.[46] Regardless of whether the Marxian definition is accepted, there are few historical examples of sharecropping
that have not been bad deals for the sharecroppers.[47] The contract
between Cornies and Kulman clearly was not exploitative. The clause
releasing Kulman from responsibility for sheep lost to disease protected
him from the most serious risk, and the contract was plainly structured
with the intention of leaving Kulman with his own flock of merino
sheep at its conclusion. Such sheep were worth five times as much as
the kurdiuch sheep kept by most Nogai.[48] This arrangement contrasts
sharply with the lot of most sharecroppers, who receive only the temporary use of land and never gain ownership of it.

Cornies's sharecropping contracts were generous. However, unlike
Demaison's earlier efforts they focused on a small economic elite. Because Nogai sharecroppers normally took charge of the sheep in late
October or November, at the end of the grazing season but well before
spring shearing, they had to supply fodder throughout the winter before receiving any income from wool. That was an expense that poor
Nogai could not meet. The requirement that sheep be watered only at
wells was also significant. Merino sheep were ill-adapted to conditions
in the Molochna region, and drinking the brackish local water was a
threat to their health.[49] However, groundwater was thirty to fifty-five
metres down, which made well-digging an expensive endeavour requiring specialized equipment and knowledge.[50] In 1840 the Ministry of
State Domains estimated that digging wells on the high steppe cost be-

tween 200 and 400 silver rubles per well.[51] Such wells also demanded constant maintenance. Thus, well-digging required an investment that would be fully repaid only over a period of several years. Again, poor Nogai could not afford wells. Consequently, most Nogai rejected the transition from cattle to sheep rearing, and the administrative strictures that went with it, and continued to practise traditional forms of husbandry.

Sharecropping contracts had important implications for traditional Nogai practices of land tenure. Nogai land had always been held communally. The sharecropping contracts, however, required that merino sheep be held apart from other livestock on the Nogai commons, and such contracts were made with individuals and not with the horde as a whole through its beys and murzas. When the contracts were initiated following the harsh winter of 1825 Nogai livestock numbers were very small, and the claims of Nogai sharecroppers to communal land did not conflict with the customary claims of other Nogai. As will be shown in Chapter 5, in the future, when demands on land changed, the sharecropping contracts would lead to conflict.

The contracts bypassed the role of the Nogai aristocracy in administering the allocation of pasture lands. Traditional administration of the pasture lands had its functional roots in a nomadic economy. However, the overgrazing of Nogai pasture lands in Molochna and the subsequent decimation of herds had already shown by 1825 that the traditional system was no longer effective under the new, sedentary conditions. Sharecropping, while contributing to undermining the old system, offered no replacement for that system because it benefited only a few individuals. Moreover, it placed the reins of administrative control in the hands of Cornies and other outsiders and not the Nogai. Sharecropping, with its lack of provisions for the poor, could not provide a basis for legitimizing wealth. The lack of cultural sanctions for economic differentiation did not bode well for Nogai development.

Between 1808 and 1833 the Russian state invested much well-intentioned effort into 'civilizing' the Nogai, but in the end there was little to show for it. The state's policies were based on a limited understanding of the horde as uncivilized nomads and an equally limited belief that if the outward manifestations of civilization – nuclear villages and commercial husbandry – could be imposed, civility would be achieved. The benefits of such civility were never explicitly spelled out. It was assumed that sedentarism and peasanthood were intrinsically superior to nomadism and pastoralism. To be sure, Cornies had an economic rationale for his sheep program – merinos were more valuable than traditional Nogai livestock – but Cornies linked economic prosperity to moral improvement, and morality was defined by orderly Mennonite practices.

The state's efforts to inculcate practices of arable husbandry among Nogai met with little success beyond the temporary increase in grain production during Demaison's grain-for-passes program. The majority of Nogai also ignored the transition from cattle rearing to sheep rearing that economic rationality demanded. Most Nogai continued to cling to their traditional pastoralist customs. Yet with the end of the economic viability of nomadism in the Molochna River Basin, the functional role of traditional Nogai administrative structures also ended. While failing to impose new economic and administrative structures, the state had successfully undermined the old, leaving only a vacuum.

Orthodox State Peasant Adaptation

In contrast to Nogai, Orthodox state peasants who came to the Molochna region were from land-poor regions of Russia where livestock holdings were extremely limited and arable agriculture dominated. Their understanding of the requirements of a viable agricultural village were clearly expressed by the advanced parties that came to New Russia to survey proposed village sites: they wanted good wells, hay meadows, forests, and fields for planting grain. As the peasants from Chernigov (quoted in Chapter 2), made clear in 1822, where the necessary environmental factors were not present they assumed that it would be impossible to establish successful villages.

The Chernigov peasants had a tradition of communal administration of land, and the advanced party represented the wishes of the community as a whole. It is impossible to know whether they had previously practised communal land repartition, but they were obviously familiar with the practice. Orthodox state peasant land in Molochna was officially allocated collectively to peasant obshchinas and not to individuals, but in practice obshchinas allotted arable and garden land to families in permanent hereditary tenure. This meant that after the initial allocation the obshchina retained no communal control. As for the commons, these were held communally, but the obshchinas placed no conditions on their use. Given the abundance of land in the Molochna region during the early years of settlement this arrangement is not surprising, but it is notable that it resulted in the Orthodox state peasants being the only group in Molochna without any collective administrative control over land allocation.

With the obshchina having so little influence over the most important element in the economy, there could be little attraction or benefit to participating in obshchina administration. This helps account for the failure of Orthodox peasants to follow the path of sectarians and foreign colonists and develop a strong sense of corporate identity in the Molochna region. After the advanced parties approved the land grants, the obshchina as a representative of peasant interests disappeared almost completely from official records until the 1830s. It should also be noted that, given the obshchina's role as the first instance of state control over peasants, its lack of status in Molochna was potentially a problem for the state too.

Despite Orthodox peasants' preconceptions about what constituted a viable environment for settlement, they showed a remarkable ability to adapt to a region where there was little good water, no forests, and no market for the products of arable husbandry. They almost immediately converted to animal husbandry as their primary agricultural activity. One of the most distinctive features of Orthodox settlement in Molochna was the disregard that settlers showed for crop production. Travellers to the region were inevitably dismayed by the poor condition of the Orthodox group's fields. Manuring was almost unheard of. Instead, manure was being dried and burned as fuel. An anonymous observer wrote that many peasants did not even bother to replough their spring fields before sowing them with winter crops: 'Some find it sufficient to throw the seed on the unploughed field and drive over it with oxen or a plough, and that concludes the working of the winter fields.'[52] As late as 1842 Baron von Haxthausen observed that some peasants did not even return to tend their fields between sowing and harvest.[53]

Land allotments to the Orthodox state peasants were not atomized into the small interstripped holdings that were typical of state peasant villages in central guberniias. In 1834 Witte observed that field rotations were 'very distinctive' because they were 'not subject to common regulation, but absolutely [depended] on the arbitrary decision of each householder.'[54] It would have been impossible to maintain such an unregulated system where interstripping prevailed. The peasants employed a long fallow system, sowing one area of the arable land for several consecutive years, then allowing it to lie fallow for several more. Based on zemstvo data collected in the 1880s, V.E. Postnikov described peasants using fields for six to nine years, then leaving them fallow for two to three.[55] However, according to A. Shmidt, in the early years of settlement in Kherson guberniia, west of Molochna, peasants sowed

TABLE 3.2
Net grain harvests per Orthodox male soul, 1808–1833

Year	Chetverts per soul	Year	Chetverts per soul
1808	4.35	1821	0.65
1809	3.66	1822	3.59
1810	2.04	1823	0.30
1811	4.89	1824	0.54
1812	1.77	1825	2.13
1813	0.19	1826	3.13
1814	2.03	1827	2.68
1815	1.30	1828	–
1816	3.74	1829	4.72
1817	3.39	1830	1.45
1818	4.42	1831	3.84
1819	3.44	1832	–
		1833	0.00
Average			2.43

Sources: *RGIA*, *f*. 1281, *op*. 11, *d*. 131–3; *GAKO*, *f*. 26, *op*. 1, *d*. 994, 2503, 3308, 4137, 501, 5394; *GAOO*, *f*. 1, *op*. 190, *d*. 12, 29, 62; 'Svedenie ...', 1833, *PJBRMA*, file 610, 19.

their fields for four or five years, then left them fallow for ten. This pattern also can be inferred from Witte's description of the Molochna region in the 1830s.[56] The shorter cropping period and longer fallow was possible because of the abundance of land in the early period.

As explained in Chapter 2, the state regarded two chetverts of grain per male soul per year to be a subsistence minimum. As Table 3.2 shows, on average Orthodox peasants in Molochna produced very little more.[57] Annual per capita grain production averaged about 1.2 chetverts (roughly 140 kilograms), enough to meet about two-thirds of the *minimum* subsistence needs of an average person.[58] Peasants typically consume all food production up to 350 kilograms in grain equivalents per capita, while it is only when production exceeds 500 kilograms per capita per year that the use of draft animals in agriculture becomes worthwhile.[59] The Molochna average was far below this, and in poor years it could not have left anything at all for the market. This low level of production was obviously intentional. Whenever net harvests exceeded four chetverts per male soul – about 232 kilograms per capita – Orthodox peasants reacted by planting *less* grain in the following year, giving

Figure 3.3   Rye and wheat prices (per chetvert) in Melitopol uezd and Tavria guberniia, 1817–1821

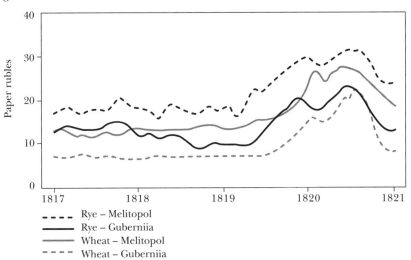

        Rye – Melitopol
        Rye – Guberniia
        Wheat – Melitopol
        Wheat – Guberniia

Sources: GAKO, f. 27, op. 1, d. 1675–82, 1769–79, 1837–47, 1989–99, 2127–38, 2266–76, n.p.

a distinct indication that they saw little purpose in producing grain surpluses. On average between 1808 and 1833 Orthodox state peasants planted just 1.05 chetverts of grain per male soul per year, an amount that would have required just 1.05 desiatinas of land following existing sowing conventions in the region.[60]

This disregard for arable husbandry was not solely a reaction to the lack of markets in the region. Figure 3.3 shows the relationship between prices for wheat and rye in Melitopol compared with the rest of the guberniia. Prices were markedly lower in Melitopol uezd, reflecting isolation and the cost of transporting grain to major markets. Nevertheless, the figures imply a linkage between prices in the uezd and the guberniia. To be sure, given shared climatic conditions some similarity in price fluctuations must be expected regardless of whether there were shared markets. However, Table 3.3 demonstrates that the similarity had to do with more than the weather. It shows the results of a regression analysis of fluctuations in the price of rye and wheat, with the price in the guberniia as independent variable and the price in Melitopol uezd as dependent variable. The result for rye prices ($r^2 = 0.37$) indi-

TABLE 3.3
Regression analysis of monthly changes in the price of rye flour and wheat meal in
Tavria guberniia (independent variable) and Melitopol uezd, 1817–1822

	Rye	Wheat
Constant	6.35	−3.98
SE Y Est	2.93	1.95
R^2	0.32	0.87
Observations (n)	72.00	72.00
DOF	70.00	70.00
X Coefficient(s)	0.29	0.95
SE of Coef.	0.05	0.04

Sources: *GAKO*, *f.* 27, *op.* 1, *d.* 1675–82, 1769–99, 1837–47, 1989–99, 2127–38, 2266–76.

cates that there was no significant correlation between changes in rye prices in Melitopol uezd and the rest of Tavria guberniia. Thus, the similarities reflected in Figure 3.3 may well be nothing more than a reflection of common climatic conditions. However, the relationship between wheat price fluctuations in the guberniia and the uezd ($r^2 = 0.87$) is strong evidence that changes in wheat prices in Melitopol were closely linked to price changes in the rest of the guberniia. This would indicate that there was a larger regional market that wheat producers in Melitopol were reacting to. The result for wheat is all the more convincing in light of the result for rye, and the difference between the two belies a simple climatic explanation, which would have affected rye and wheat identically.

Wheat surpluses were probably viewed as a windfall in the Molochna River Basin. Peasants planted enough to meet their subsistence needs, and in good years they sold their surplus. Good years could be very good indeed, for their land was on the fertile Azov Uplands. This accounts for the region's interaction with the larger guberniia market. Bad years, however, could be disastrous, and settlers necessarily had to concern themselves with worst-case scenarios. The worst case came in various forms in 1812, 1815, 1821, 1825, and 1833, when drought, cold, locusts, or hail obliterated grain crops and reduced harvests to dangerously low levels.

Peasants in Melitopol uezd could anticipate at least a partial crop failure one out of about every five years. This could halt the transportation of grain altogether because the oxen that pulled carts across the steppe consumed grass and water, two things in desperately short supply during a drought.[61] As a result peasants could not base agricultural strategies on potential profits from exporting wheat, for they knew that in the years when crops failed they would be left without food from their own fields, and at the same time it would be impossible for the state to import food to where they lived. Without a local port to permit the import of grain in years of harvest failure, the peasants' first priority had to be self-sufficiency.

Gardening was the second major element of Orthodox state peasant arable husbandry in the Molochna region, which is the clearest evidence of this subsistence priority. These peasants devoted relatively little, ill-tended land to growing grain. However, they devoted extraordinarily large areas of prime river flood plain to gardens. No detailed records survive from the pre-1833 period, but figures for 1848 from Orekhov volost, the northern-most volost of Melitopol uezd, offer an indication of how much land was involved. The villages in Orekhov devoted on average a full desiatina per household to gardens.[62] Garden sizes may have been shrinking by 1848, as total land holdings per capita shrank, but the amount of garden per male soul was still impressive. If Orthodox peasants worked their arable land poorly, they gardened well. In 1847 the civil governor of Tavria even described state peasants in the villages of Bolshaia and Malaia Znamenka in Dneprovsk uezd as 'exceptional gardeners,' and in good years, as the governor reported in 1837, state peasants living near towns or colonist villages throughout the guberniia sold 'significant quantities' of their produce.[63]

The contribution of the gardens to village food production is impossible to define. In the late nineteenth and early twentieth centuries Russian peasants obtained about 12 per cent of their consumption needs from gardens. However, this has little application to the first half of the nineteenth century before the tax demands of the growing state and pressures exerted by the international grain market shrank the amount of land peasants could afford to reserve for their own use.[64] Indications are clear that gardens in the Molochna region played an essential role in the early years of settlement. The most explicit appear in reports from the nachal'niks of Melitopol and Dneprovsk uezds. When torrential rains and locusts combined in 1821 to destroy crops and lead to near-famine conditions, the state scrambled to find grain to feed peasants in the Crimea.[65] However, Melitopol and Dneprovsk peasants, who experienced an equally poor harvest, did not receive grain from the state because, as the Melitopol nachal'nik reported, they would 'be able to fare for themselves adequately from their household plots ... and from their own livestock.'[66] Gardening was labour intensive and would have detracted from time in the fields, but unlike grain fields, gardens, as long as they were located close to rivers, could be watered and would yield up their crops even in years of drought.

Turning to animal husbandry, as appendix Table A.2 shows, between 1808 and 1827 (the period for which records exist) Orthodox peasant livestock holdings grew rapidly. By 1827 the average Orthodox family had six cows and thirteen sheep; there were two horses for every three families. Herds were slowly filling available pasture lands, but by 1827 they had not yet overflowed them. In that year pasture land require-ments were about eight desiatinas per male soul, or just over half of the allotment norm. With both livestock and human populations continu-ing to grow the potential for future problems was looming, but the lack of post-1827 livestock figures makes it impossible to say exactly when the critical point was reached.

Although holdings of all types of livestock grew between 1814 and 1827, sheep holdings grew at a faster rate. Following the harsh winter of 1825 horse and cattle holdings declined, while sheep holdings contin-ued to grow (see Figure 3.4). By implication, Orthodox state peasants, unlike Nogai, were interested in the commercial potential of sheep relative to other livestock.

There is no indication that Orthodox state peasants shifted from raising kurdiuch sheep to the more-valuable merinos. The Nogai transi-tion to merinos came during the decimation of their herds that had begun in 1825 and continued into the 1830s, when Nogai herds had already exceeded the carrying capacity of their land grant. Merinos gave more value per unit of land, but required more labour. This repre-sented a substitution of more labour-intensive, higher-yielding husbandry for an existing system – under which, however, income per land unit had already been maximized. The Orthodox settlers had not yet reached this point in 1827, and as long as they experienced economic growth under the existing system there was little motivation to take on the increased labour and capital costs of the transition to merinos. This was particularly true considering that the Orthodox group was not offered the same generous sharecropping contracts that Nogai received from Cornies to subsidize such a transition. A second, equally important consideration was the relative durability of kurdiuch sheep. They were hardy and well adapted to the steppe, requiring little care and less water than merinos. Kurdiuch sheep were also less susceptible to dis-

Figure 3.4   Livestock holdings, 1814–1827

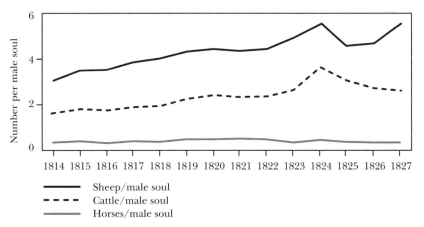

Sources: 'Otchety Tavricheskikh Gubernatorov,' 1808–16, 1822–7, *RGIA,*
f. 1281, *op.* 11.

ease and bred more rapidly.[67] Isolated from export and import markets,
the first priority of Molochna peasants was the food, tallow, clothing,
shoes, and manure they could obtain from the sheep for their own
uses. The market value of wool came a distant second. Thus from a
subsistence perspective kurdiuch sheep made more sense than merinos.

   The agricultural adaptations described so far are graphically summarized on Map 4. Based on an 1848 map, Map 4 retains the characteristic
features of Orthodox villages in the early years of settlement in the
Molochna River Basin. The village proper (as opposed to the commons
and arable land) was extraordinarily long and narrow, stretching along
the banks of the river and up the two creeks that fed it to ensure that
each household had its piece of the invaluable flood plain. One
Molochna village, Bolshoi Tokmak, stretched along more than six
kilometres by the mid-1840s, demonstrating just how elongated such
villages could become.[68]

   The most unusual characteristic of Orthodox villages was the arrangement of the commons and arable land, which reversed the typical land
allocation pattern in most of Russia and Western Europe.[69] As I.U.
Witte described it in 1834, 'The fields lie far from the villages, and
sometimes several dozen *versts.* Immediately beside the villages, where

in other countries the very best, or, so-to-say, primary fields ... are located, the pasture is located in [New Russia].'[70] The standard practice of placing arable land close to the village and pasture further away derives from the fact that cattle and sheep can be tended by relatively few people and can quickly transport themselves to and from distant pastures, while agricultural implements and crops are heavy and cumbersome and large numbers of people travel to and from grain fields during the peak work seasons. The reversal of the normal arrangement in Molochna vividly illustrates the low priority given to grain production by Orthodox peasants.

The arrangement also emphasizes how, in the Molochna region, grain competed unsuccessfully with livestock and kitchen gardens for water. Grain fields were relegated to the high steppe where groundwater lay at unreachable depths of thirty or more metres, whereas the rich flood plains were reserved for gardens. Grain production from such fields was utterly dependent on Molochna's unreliable precipitation. In this light it may be useful to reconceptualize state peasant 'kitchen gardens' as infields in an infield–outfield agricultural system, making the point that state peasants in Molochna were really not living far from their land allotments at all.[71] Indeed, the most valuable part of their land was right at their doorsteps.

Yet the state assessed the self-sufficiency of its peasants in terms of grain production, and by this standard Orthodox settlers in Molochna were notable failures. In 1837, when Köppen surveyed the Molochna region, he expressed the state's frustration with its intractable wards: 'What has been done in the colonies can be done by the state peasants also. It is well known in what comfort, and even prosperity, the colonists live, but their Russian and Little Russian neighbours adopt nothing from them. [The Orthodox state peasants] know very well and recount at great length how the Germans conduct their farming, but to the question, why do they themselves not imitate these practices, each and every one gives the same reply: "Our fathers didn't do it like that."'[72]

Surely the most important lesson to be learned from studying the Orthodox state peasants in Molochna is that Köppen's assessment was not true. These peasants, who had come from land-poor guberniias, arrived on the virtually unpopulated steppe and immediately and successfully adapted to their new conditions. They settled into a way of life diametrically opposed to that of their fathers. Within just a few short years they abandoned the intensive three-field agriculture they had known in Russia's interior guberniias and turned instead primarily to pastoralism, then gardening, and finally long-fallow agriculture. What defined Orthodox peasants in Molochna was not their inability to adapt, but their stubborn insistence on a subsistence adaptation.

In a sense this was all the state really expected of them. After all the state structured its administration of the Orthodox state peasants around a policy of ensuring them a subsistence food ration. The state's exasperation with Melitopol peasants was the result of policies based on peasant agricultural practices and subsistence requirements in interior guberniias. Land survey departments conducted thousands of surveys and drew thousands of maps of New Russia, but the state never learned – at least not before 1833 – that all land is not equal. It never addressed access to water or access to markets, and it assessed peasant conditions using grain harvest figures that were based on the food consumption patterns of peasants from interior guberniias. These had no relation whatsoever to consumption patterns on the steppe, where peasants had large livestock holdings and, in the Molochna region at least, bountiful gardens.

Underpinning the state's frustration with Orthodox peasants was the implicit acknowledgment that it had little control over their actions. The Orthodox community held their land in permanent hereditary tenure, and the state had no effective administrative organs at local levels to force them to accept central guidance. Indeed, it seems evident that there were not even local self-administrative organs guiding peasant agricultural activities.

Probably the peasants understood that the state could not be relied on to treat them as anything other than an undifferentiated part of the state peasant whole. Peasants knew better than to abandon agricultural practices that left their chances of survival in their own hands instead of in the hands of a state that plainly did not understand how or where they lived. It must also be remembered that the peasants were, in their own fashion, doing well enough – the growing size of their herds attests to this. By 1827 there was no sign in Orthodox society of the problems of poverty and economic differentiation that were already apparent in Nogai society. To be sure, the situation that had created problems for Nogai was looming for Orthodox peasants, as well. Their extensive land allocation practices were based on the assumption that there were no limits on the availability of land and that, as their population grew, the state would just grant them more land.[73] As long as land remained available, the Orthodox community did not have to face the problem of how to deal with the poor; consequently, there was also no need to justify the wealth that some peasants were accumulating. The state's failure to understand the unique conditions presented by the steppe could also work to the peasants' benefit. The peasants must have known that the state assessed their condition by the size of their grain harvests and not by the livestock in their fields and the vegetables in their gardens. It is altogether possible that, while Nikolai Gogol's Akaky Akakieviches of St Petersburg shuffled hungrily home to their wretched rooms, the peasants in Molochna were smugly slurping their cabbage soup – and most assuredly *with* meat!

Changing the Land: Sectarians and Foreign Colonists

For Nogai and Orthodox societies, immigration to the Molochna region undermined traditional corporate structures. For Mennonites and Doukhobors, it permitted a flourishing of traditional corporate identities that were rooted in religious belief and practice. The evidence is too scarce to permit a close reading of developments among other German colonists and the Molokan sectarians, but it is fair to conjecture that the processes were similar. The ethnoreligious minorities, faced with the alien physical and ethnocultural landscape of Molochna, turned inward to their fellow believers and developed strongly united communities able to adjust to markets and bend the environment to their needs.

Like Orthodox state peasants, sectarians received little input from the state regarding agricultural practices. Unlike Orthodox peasants, the sectarians proved to be highly conscious of market demands. Indeed, observers singled out sectarians along with foreign colonists as extraordinarily prosperous settlers. The Molokan case is particularly interesting because, while Doukhobors and foreign colonists had particularly generous land allotments, Molokans prospered on the poorest land grant in the region. Arguably, then, the success of all three groups had less to do with generous land grants than it did with social organization and particularly with the maintenance of a degree of public control over land. The ability to meet the challenges of the frontier as large cohesive groups rather than as discrete individuals gave colonists, Doukhobors, and Molokans significant advantages over their Orthodox and Nogai neighbours.

Sectarians

When Savelii Kapustin, leader of the Doukhobors from 1790 to 1820, arrived in the Molochna region in 1805, he established a system of communal tenure.[74] However, Englishman Robert Pinkerton, who visited the Doukhobors in 1816, reported that 'every family has its own private property, cattle, fields, etc.' Pinkerton also noted that Doukhobors had 'fields of corn, gardens and flocks which belong to the whole community, and the revenues of which are applied for the common benefit of the society.'[75] Some element of communalism survived to 1837, when Melitopol District Administrator (*zemskii ispravnik*) Kolosov described how 'Kapustin, seeing the inconvenience of the communal system that was already provoking grumbling, ordered the division of everything that had been held collectively into two parts, half of which was divided up equally among the villagers, and half of which remained in common and was administered under Kapustin's authority by his adherents, the so-called Apostles, as well as other privileged persons.'[76]

The Doukhobors were officially state peasants, and the state kept no economic records of them separate from their Orthodox neighbours. This makes knowledge of their agricultural practices as distinct from other peasants difficult to obtain. Anecdotal evidence suggests that they were superior farmers, sober (in both a literal and figurative sense), and industrious. In 1832 a report by M.S. Vorontsov, governor general of New Russia, described them as 'among the best of the Government's colonies,'[77] and in 1838, as consensus was building to exile them, Russian regional historian A.A. Skal'kovskii described them as 'a rather useful people who have established many orderly villages.'[78]

Like everyone else in the region, the Doukhobors concentrated their agricultural efforts on animal husbandry.[79] Vorontsov wrote in 1832 that the Doukhobors were involved in an 'enormous cattle-raising enterprise and improved sheep breeding,' and other eyewitnesses also mention the impressively large Doukhobor herds. Some Doukhobors even followed the Mennonite lead and leased merino sheep to neighbouring Nogai for a half-share of the resulting wool and lambs.[80] In 1840 a Doukhobor named Lukian Verigan was owner of one of the largest herds of merino sheep in Molochna with 1,500 head, while after their exile to the Caucasus in the 1840s the sectarians enjoyed enormous economic success based on the merino sheep-raising practices that they had perfected in Molochna.[81] The Doukhobors, like the Nogai, at first concentrated on raising cattle, but by the 1820s they increasingly turned to raising the commercially lucrative merino sheep.

Disputes in the Canadian Doukhobor community in the twentieth century often centred around the issue of communalism, so Kolosov's description of Doukhobor 'grumbling' over the same issue in the early nineteenth century is not surprising.[82] Reports of serious disputes in the Doukhobor community in the 1830s are usually ascribed to the unfair privileges Kapustin granted to his Apostles.[83] These disputes will be considered in detail in Chapter 4, but for the moment their economic significance must be noted. One of the curiosities of the Doukhobor faith is that in spite of their implicitly egalitarian belief in the in-dwelling spirit of God in every person, the Doukhobors credited their leaders with a larger than normal share of God's spirit, entitling them to lead by divine right.[84] Savelii Kapustin and his heirs ruled all aspects of Doukhobor society, issuing orders and resolving disputes from a building known as the Orphans' Home in the village of Terpenie. They exercised their authority with the help of the Apostles, who in 1816 numbered twenty-five.[85] The Apostles, in turn, benefited from their positions by receiving particularly large land allotments, which permitted some of them to own as many as 1,000 head of livestock.[86]

If this arrangement provoked 'grumbling,' it was not apparent before 1830. Indeed, the unity expressed by the Doukhobors in 1824 during their land dispute with the state (see Chapter 2) suggests that they were a strongly united community. Arguably, the existence of an internal unofficial administrative system based on religious principles played an important role in the economic prosperity of that united community. The expense of the transition to raising merino sheep has already been discussed in reference to Orthodox peasants and Nogai. Orthodox peasants faced the larger world as individuals, or at best as members of village obshchinas that possessed little independent authority, and so they were unlikely to have sufficient personal wealth to invest in the transition to merino sheep. Some wealthy Nogai made this transition, but they accomplished it only through subsidies from Cornies and other Mennonites. The majority of Nogai were left out of this process. Doukhobors, with a system that provided for community-wide economic cooperation and investment, managed the transition on their own.

The Apostles represented a community-sanctioned form of economic differentiation that provided an engine to drive Doukhobor economic progress within a system that also protected the welfare of the broader community through communally held and distributed property. The legitimacy of the Doukhobor leader and his appointed Apostles was formally based on religious doctrine, and the ability of the system to achieve economic success must be considered an important element in its strength. In the administrative vacuum of the Molochna region, the Doukhobors were building for themselves a commonwealth based on economic success, as well as faith.

Unfortunately, there is no record of how Molokans administered their land and little record of their agricultural practices. However, their status as latecomers to Molochna, and their resultant lack of good land, set them sharply apart from other groups of settlers. Two isolated accounts from 1847 suggest that Molokans found distinctive solutions to the problems this created for them. The first comes from the civil governor of Tavria, who noted that Molokans were the best gardeners in the region and grew so much produce that they sold the excess in neighbouring communities.[87] Gardening as intensive agriculture has already been discussed. For Molokans, with their small, poor land holdings, gardening was a way of getting the most from what little good land they had. The second account comes from the agronomist Wilhelm Bauman, who wrote that Molokans bred the best horses in the Molochna region and that colonists had an expressed preference for such horses, paying as much as 300 rubles per head.[88] Apparently Molokans, who had insufficient land to raise large numbers of livestock, had elected to concentrate, instead, on raising smaller numbers of high-quality livestock, serving a niche market in Molochna.

The success of both Doukhobors and Molokans in adapting to conditions in Molochna deserves attention. Doukhobors were unusually well endowed with land, and this gave them an advantage over Orthodox state peasants. Nogai, too, had a large land grant; however, they did not enjoy comparable success. Arguably, the internal administrative arrangements in the Doukhobor community, based on their religious organization, made it possible for Doukhobors to react as a community to the challenges posed by the frontier. The success of Molokans is particularly interesting in this light, because they received the poorest land allotment of all settler groups in the region and could not base their success on sheep breeding, as could most others. There is little evidence about the internal organization in Molokan villages, but if they shared the well-developed internal religious administrative structures of the Doukhobors, this may go far to explaining their successful, unique adaptation based on market gardening and horse breeding.

Foreign Colonists

The success that foreign colonists enjoyed in New Russia is commonly attributed to the large size of their land allotments and to land tenure regulations that prevented subdivision of allotments and ensured that they remained of economically viable size.[89] The benefit of these provisions to colonists is undeniable, but the provisions also had the potential to be divisive, as developments in Mennonite society would show.

In 1806 Governor General Richelieu said, 'The Mennonites are astonishing, the Bulgarians incomparable, and the Germans intolerable.' This statement is often repeated as a general indictment of German colonists. However, if the 1813 account of Inspector of Colonies Zieber is accepted, German colonists in Molochna were far from 'intolerable.'[90] Zieber found that 315 of 417 German colonist families ran excellent farms, seventy-four had problems because of deaths or illnesses, and just twenty-four were failing because of 'insufficient love of work.'[91] There is much less data on German colonists than Mennonites, but there are no obvious reasons for treating the economic development of the two groups in the Molochna region separately.

Data on foreign colonist agricultural production show that, on average, Mennonites were the most prosperous colonists, but German colonists followed a similar pattern of development and were prosperous in their own right. The first generation of colonists produced grain. Quantities were small and were probably only intended to satisfy consumption needs (see Table 3.4). As with Orthodox state peasants, commercial grain production in the colonies was likely an incidental result of years with particularly good weather conditions. For colonists, as for other Molochna settlers, the most important innovation in the first years of settlement was the transition to sheep breeding. As appendix Table A.2 shows, the number of sheep in the colonies rose dramatically beginning in the 1820s.

This transition was initiated and supported by the state. Samuel Contenius, head of the Guardianship Committee, began distributing fine-woolled merino sheep to Mennonites in the Khortitsa settlement in 1803. Governor General Richelieu extended this practice to Molochna in 1808.[92] The focus of Contenius's effort was interbreeding merino sheep with the local kurdiuch breed to engender the hardiness of the native sheep and the fine wool of the imports. In 1828 wool from the resultant mixed breeds sold for twenty-seven rubles per *pud*, about 80 per cent of the value of pure-bred merino wool and seven times the

TABLE 3.4
Net grain harvests (in chetverts) per capita in colonist villages, 1805–1832

	Mennonites	German colonists
1805	0.73	0.58
1817	2.78	
1818	1.57	
1819	0.99	
1820	1.02	
1821	0.62	
1825	2.15	
1826	3.54	
1828	2.55	1.45
1829	6.37	5.55
1830	2.32	2.27
1831	7.55	7.91
1832	3.33	3.07

Sources: *GADO, f.* 134, *op.* 1, *d.* 246, 310, 786; *GAKO, f.* 26, *op.* 1, *d.* 2503, 3308, 4137, 5017, 5394, 2503; *GAOO, f.* 6, *op.* 1, *d.* 1236; 'Tabellen: über den Zustand der Molotschner Kolonisten,' 1848, *PJBRMA*, file 1138, 1ob-37ob; 'S otchetami mestnykh kolonistskim nachal'stvo so sostoianii kolonii za 1828,' *RGIA f.* 383, *op.* 29, *d.* 627–31.

value of coarse kurdiuch wool.[93] Contenius had his inspectors keep close track of sheep breeding in the colonies and compile detailed monthly reports. In 1824 General I.N. Inzov, who in 1818 had succeeded Contenius as head of the Guardianship Committee, created the 'Organization for the Improvement of Sheep Breeding' headed by Cornies.[94] Although the organization had no authority to dictate sheep-breeding practices, its correspondence implied that it expected cooperation from colonists, and the rapid growth of merino flocks implies that it received it.[95]

Besides sheep breeding the state placed heavy emphasis on growing trees. Managed forestry was an increasing concern throughout Europe in the first half of the nineteenth century and, inspired by the German development of 'forest mathematics,' Alexander I appointed a *Forstmeister* in every Russian guberniia.[96] The basic assumption of forestry policies was that where the environment did not conform to human needs it could be transformed. This was an assumption the colonists shared. Mennonites, in particular, were familiar with western forestry practices, being renowned for their use of trees to stabilize the banks of rivers in swampy regions of the Vistula–Nogat Delta. Encouraged by the state

Mennonites quickly established tree plantations in Molochna. In 1815 there were 9,400 mature mulberry trees (grown for an ill-fated attempt to establish a silk industry), 2,268 mature fruit trees, 608 mature forest trees, and 71,235 saplings in the colonies.[97] In 1825 there were over 233,000 mature trees, and by 1834 Mennonites alone had 254,058 trees, and the German colonists had 121,021.[98]

Following the pattern established with sheep, in 1830, on Contenius's advice, the Guardianship Committee created a 'Society for the effective propagation of afforestation, horticulture, sericulture, and viticulture' (hereafter the Forestry Society), with Cornies as its chairman-for-life.[99] This was the forerunner of the controversial 'Society for the improvement of agriculture and trade' (hereafter the Agricultural Society), established in 1836. It is vital to emphasize that the Forestry Society did not have the broad authority and jurisdiction of the Agricultural Society, concerning itself almost exclusively with planting and care for trees.[100] Like the 'Organization for the Improvement of Sheep Breeding,' the function of the Forestry Society was intended to be advisory rather than regulatory.

Historians traditionally have divided controversies in the Molochna Mennonite settlement into religious disputes born of conflicts between religious and civil authorities in the 1830s and 1840s, and economic disputes born of landlessness in the 1850s and 1860s. Arguably, the two shared a common origin in land allocation practices established at the foundation of the settlement. Turmoil in the 1840s centred on secular infringements on the traditional jurisdiction of Mennonite religious institutions; this is described in Chapter 5. The relationship between secular and religious authority in earlier decades demands close attention, for many future disputes grew out of land allocation practices established in the first years of settlement.

As described in Chapter 2, the Russian state established a secular administrative system to parallel the traditional congregational one in Mennonite communities.[101] It was only when secular Mennonite institutions gained the authority to overturn the decisions of congregational institutions in the 1840s that significant conflicts arose between the two systems. Cornies, by the 1840s the foremost representative of secular authority in the Mennonite settlement, was the focal point of unrest (see Chapter 5). To a significant degree, however, the problems of the 1840s were a natural consequence of geographic isolation and an administrative system that put Mennonites in control of their community land.

The Russian state encouraged foreigners to immigrate because it expected them to positively influence agriculture in New Russia, and it provided plenty of land to ensure that every colonist that wished to could farm. Yet, surprisingly, in Mennonite villages, where an egalitarian ethic of mutual support might have been expected to prevail, economic differentiation arose at an early date. Mennonites were not an economically homogeneous group when they arrived in the Molochna region. Of the first 293 immigrant families, 178 had combined assets of 269,923 rubles when they entered Russia; the remaining 115 families had assets of just 35,253 rubles.[102] As Figure 3.5 shows, by 1808 the livestock holdings of the wealthiest fifth of the Mennonite population were three times greater than those of the poorest fifth.[103] In itself this is not surprising, for it was not wealth but poverty that Mennonites opposed. As long as an individual was prepared to employ his wealth to allay the poverty of other members of his congregation when necessary, wealth in itself was not discouraged.[104] What Mennonites did oppose was social differentiation. It was to prevent the social manifestation of economic differentiation – the sin of pride – that Mennonite congregations imposed on their members conformity in dwellings, clothing, and other areas that carried the potential for the outward expression of wealth.

Extant records of landlessness in Mennonite villages are summarized in Table 3.5. The earliest record is from 1813 when, just a decade after the establishment of the settlement, 12 per cent of the Mennonite population was landless.[105] By 1839 this figure had climbed to 47 per cent.[106] In theory surplus land should have forestalled such landlessness, but in practice it did not.[107] The problem was that although the surplus land was supposed to constitute one-sixth of all types of land including pasture, arable land, meadows, and waste, the original settlers could ill-afford to leave any part of their village's best land – the river flood plain – unused in the first years of settlement.

In those early years Molochna was far from the 'oasis' that later observers would see. The treeless, arid steppe was unlike the land of the Vistula–Nogat Delta that the Mennonite settlers had left behind, and the virgin steppe with its thickly matted sod was enormously difficult to plough. As late as 1813 the Inspector of Colonies reported that many settlers had still not ploughed any land on the high steppe, concentrating instead on planting the flood plain.[108] Unlike Orthodox peasants, Mennonite colonists did not focus all their attention on animal hus-

Figure 3.5   Differentiation in Mennonite villages (from poorest quintile to richest), 1808

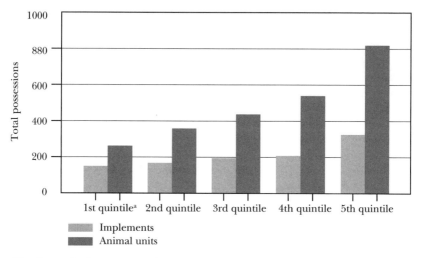

[a]The first quintile comprises 71 families; the other four each have 70 families.
Source: Unruh, *Die niederländisch-niederdeutschen Hintergründe der mennonitischen Ostwanderungen im 16., 19. und 18 Jahrhundert*, 304–29.

bandry in the first years of settlement. Instead, they devoted extensive amounts of labour and resources to arable husbandry and tree planting. These efforts to change the environment to more closely resemble the one that they had left behind were quite different from the Orthodox state peasant and Nogai example of adapting their practices to the new environment. Although this would benefit the colonists in the future, in the short term it meant that they frequently faced shortages and had to turn to the state for subsidies.[109] Under such circumstances the first colonists naturally allotted to themselves all of the best land. This helped them to survive those first hard years, but left them with little good land for future generations. All that remained of the surplus was the high steppe, suitable only as pasture land.[110] Unlike Orthodox peasants, who received new land after each census, Mennonite colonists could not turn to the state for new land as their population grew. From the state's point of view the surplus land already provided Mennonites with more than enough.

Despite the increase in families in the Mennonite settlement from 351 in 1808 to 569 in 1818, just thirty-one new land allotments were

TABLE 3.5
Landlessness among foreign colonists in Molochna, 1813–1839

	Mennonites		Other colonists	
	Landless families as % of all families	Landless population as % of all population	Landless families as % of all families	Landless population as % of all population
1813	17.16	11.89	8.89	8.26
1815	19.74	14.84	15.43	13.83
1816	22.57	16.31	19.60	16.23
1817	24.70	19.39	19.72	17.43
1818	32.86	29.20	20.88	17.34
1820	44.19	–	–	–
1826	32.92	25.37	–	–
1830	41.14	32.25	–	–
1834	47.27	36.42	18.69	13.37
1839	56.99	46.83	21.02	15.97

Sources: *GAOO, f. 6, op.* 1, *d.* 773, 973, 1024, 1236; 'Verzeichnis: der Mennonisten Kolonien an der Molotschna, über die Familien und Seelenzahl in derselben Vieh Bestand und Acker Geräte,' 1818, *PJBRMA*, file 17, 6–19; 'Haupt Listen: der Molotschner Mennonisten Collonie [sic], wie gross in derselben die Seelenzahl, Viehe Gestand, Acker und handwerke Geräte,' 1818, *PJBRMA*, file 19, 33ob-35; *GADO, f.* 134, *op.* 1. *d.* 786, 893, 981.

awarded, including sixteen to newly arrived colonists who founded the village of Rueckenau in 1811. In the early 1820s landlessness momentarily declined as the Mennonite settlement used reserve land to found new villages for new immigrants, but the trend reversed and landlessness again grew sharply in the 1830s. Although a degree of landlessness was anticipated at the settlement's foundation – some people were expected to prefer employment in crafts or commerce – the failure of so many families to acquire allotments obviously reflects the growth of a poor segment in Mennonite society.

An important factor mitigating the impoverishment of the landless was the Mennonite inheritance system. On the death of a landowner all of his or her property was liquidated, and the proceeds were distributed equally among the surviving sons and daughters. This system provided for redistribution of wealth to landless families, promoting capital investment by the landless and contributing to the economic growth and diversification of the Mennonite community.[111] Yet land was the key source of wealth in predominantly agricultural Molochna, and the best that most of the landless could hope for was to lease land from the crown or from neighbouring estates. This practice was widespread. However, because leased land was more expensive than village allotment land, and because it was often of lower quality, differentiation still grew.

In Prussia congregations had governed public life, but Mennonites there did not hold property communally; the acquisition and use of land lay outside of the authority of the congregation. Allotment holders in Molochna controlled their own land. However, they also controlled their village's surplus land, and this gave them influence over the economic opportunities of their fellow Mennonites quite unlike anything they had known in Prussia. Allotment holders used their authority to impose strict limitations on access to land and insisted that recipients of the few available new allotments have sufficient capital to purchase implements and livestock. This effectively excluded the poor from owning land.[112]

Such official sanctioning of economic differentiation was rooted in the need to protect the welfare of the whole community by ensuring that all viable land was farmed efficiently. Still, community authority over land allocation was a distinct departure from the traditional jurisdiction of the Mennonite congregation.

Owning land had always been an essential attribute for full membership in Mennonite society. Consequently, Mennonites had no traditional social sanction for economic differentiation. By 1833 it had become clear that not everyone in Molochna would be able to own land. The challenge facing the Mennonite community was to find a way to provide for its poor, while legitimizing the rich. In the long run this problem would pose fundamental challenges to congregational unity. It also had positive implications: the self-administration of land in the Mennonite settlement, as in the Doukhobor community, gave self-administrative structures an important functional role that was not present in Orthodox communities. The landed had a vested interest in resolving the problem and, as with the Doukhobors, this stimulus to active involvement in public life encouraged the development of a Mennonite commonwealth. This subject is taken up more fully in Chapter 5.

The growth of landlessness was paralleled by the closely related phenomenon of rapid growth of livestock populations in the Mennonite settlement. As Table 3.6 shows, by 1830 Mennonites no longer had enough allotment land to feed their livestock, making it necessary for them to lease land. A significant source of leased land was their own

TABLE 3.6
Pasture requirements (in desiatinas) of the Molochna Mennonite settlement,
1825–1835

	1825	1830	1835
Total allotted land	53,840	58,851	64,833
Household plots	1,833	2,366	2,984
Arable (estimated)[a]	6,582	14,483	19,913
Allotted land available as pasture	43,592	39,696	38,952
Surplus land (estimated)[b]	8,873	9,642	10,552
Mennonite-controlled pasture	52,465	49,338	49,504
Pasture required	37,139	62,339	120,773
Pasture surplus or deficit	15,326	(13,001)	(71,209)
Reserve land	60,527	57,855	54,747
Pasture surplus or deficit including reserve	75,853	41,746	(13,414)

[a] Based on data from 1824, 1827, and 1834, showing that Mennonites planted
approximately 0.60 chetverts per desiatina (see *GADO, f.* 134, *op.* 1, *d.* 786, 837,
981).
[b] One-sixth of total land allotted to landed families.

Sources: *GADO, f.* 134, *op.* 1, *d.* 786, 893, n.p.; 'Historische Übersicht der am rechten
Ufer des Molotschna Flusses angesiedelten deutschen Kolonisten und dessen
Zustand,' 1836, *PJBRMA*, file 375, 1–14.

reserve lands which were administered by the Guardianship Committee
and leased to Mennonites on the same basis as other unsettled crown
land.[113] As Cornies noted in 1831, such leased land had 'the disagree-
able aspect that it involves the fulfilment of conditions difficult for the
poor, [although] for the rich and the moderately [prosperous], who
possess the means to fulfil [the conditions], they are not so difficult.'[114]
Even including this reserve land, by 1835 Mennonites in the Molochna
River Basin did not have enough pasture land for their livestock.

Mennonites had several options to fill the gap between the forage
their land provided and the food their livestock required. They could
improve the quality of grazing land through irrigation, plant high-yield
pasture grasses, or grow fodder crops; they could harvest hay on the
high steppe; or they could lease land to expand their grazing area. The
cost of irrigation or of introducing non-native grasses was prohibitively
high, and the first such experiments were only begun in the late 1830s.[115]
Mennonites grew significant quantities of oats (about one chetvert for
every horse in the colony in the 1830s) primarily as a fodder crop, and

haying on the high steppe, although labour-intensive, began as early as the mid-1820s. However, shortages of labour meant that during haying season workers could demand high wages.[116]

Hay and oats reduced the gap between land and livestock, but did not close it altogether, making land leasing necessary. This had its price, but here at least landowners could control some of their costs. By 1834 Mennonites were leasing 10,637 desiatinas of surplus land from their villages along with unknown amounts from the state and neighbouring settlers.[117] Because landowners controlled the disposition of the surplus land, they could and did grant themselves very cheap leases. The state granted them cheap leases on reserve land, as well, to encourage sheep breeding.[118]

Cornies and other leaders in the transition to sheep breeding acquired large areas of cheap leased land in the 1820s, when it was still plentiful and rented for as little as a kopeck per desiatina per year. By the early 1830s, however, when latecomers joined the sheep bonanza, leased land had become expensive.[119] Land requests of Molokans and Orthodox state peasants (detailed in Chapter 4) show that non-Mennonite sources of rental land were drying up, while isolated data from Cornies' estates at Iushanlee and Tashchenak document the rapid increase in rental costs, although their interpretation raises difficulties.

Instead of renting land, Cornies paid neighbouring Nogai and, to a lesser degree, Orthodox state peasants, Doukhobors, Molokans, and even German colonists to pasture and care for sheep for fixed periods. The amount Cornies paid to different contractors varied by as much as 100 per cent in any given year, and the rate for sheep was anywhere from one-seventh to one-fifteenth the rate for cattle and horses, a reflection of the higher land requirements and supervisory costs of the latter. Because Cornies was paying for labour as well as land these data cannot be compared directly with land rental rates from other sources, but the rate of increase is illuminating. Between 1824 and 1834 Cornies's land and herding costs rose by 250 per cent for cows and horses and by 286 per cent for sheep.[120] The same sources show that Cornies paid the Mennonite Gebietsamt 623 rubles to lease surplus land in 1829 and 1,221 rubles in 1833. The amount of land Cornies leased is not recorded, but the rate could have been no more than the open-market price of sixty kopecks per desiatina in 1837, and it was almost certainly much less. In other words, Cornies alone was leasing no less than 2,035 desiatinas of the Mennonite settlement's 10,637 desiatinas of surplus land in 1833, or 20 per cent of the settlement's entire supply of surplus land.

Although the surplus land was range land and could not have been used to provide allotments to the landless, the fact that it went to a handful of rich landowners at artificially low rates must have seemed unjust to the landless. In effect, by 1830 the landless found themselves competing for land with the sheep of the landed. They did not compete as equals. The situation precisely parallels that of the 1860s, when some few Mennonite landowners used their influence in village administrative organs to grant themselves inexpensive leases on surplus lands. The landless had no vote in the assemblies and could not defend their own interests.

There is no evidence of protest by the landless. This must be credited to the efforts of Mennonite leaders to find economic alternatives for them. These efforts are detailed in Chapter 5, so only the early development of labour markets will be sketched here. The main options for the landless were to take up a craft or work as labourers. Mennonites in Prussia had been extensively involved in trade and handicrafts, and some 38 per cent were trained in a craft when they arrived in the Molochna.[121] However, Prussia was different from Molochna. Danzig and Elbing were important port cities, while the surrounding regions were heavily populated, providing a ready market for Mennonite craft production.[122] In the Molochna region there was no nearby port, and neighbouring settlers produced most of their own requirements. In 1808 craftsmen were among the wealthiest Mennonites in Molochna, but demand for their products was limited, and by the 1830s few could boast a large enough trade to keep a permanent stock or own wagons and horses to deliver their goods.[123] By 1834 'poor but industrious' landless Molochna Mennonite families were a noticeable feature to travellers,[124] and Mennonite memoirists recall such families working long, gruelling days producing handicrafts.[125]

By the 1840s landowners would have twice the income of craftsmen and as much as ten times the income of labourers.[126] This enormous gap between incomes suggests an oversupply of labourers, raising questions about the natural labour absorption rate in Molochna. One way to estimate this rate is to look at German colonists, who had similar Western European backgrounds, similar land tenure arrangements, but far less landlessness. Table 3.7 shows the growth of landlessness in both groups. It does not tell the whole story, however, for about a third of the German landless lived in one village, Molotschna (later renamed Prishib), which was apparently designated as a market town from the time of its establishment.[127]

TABLE 3.7
Occupation of Mennonite landless population, 1826–1834

	Total landless population (n)	Working-age (n)	Craftsmen (n)	Labourers (n)
1826	1,631	916	402	514
1830	2,505	1,426	440	986
1834	3,202	1,828	485	1,343

Sources: *GADO, f.* 134, *op.* 1, *d.* 786, 893, 981, n.p.

Other German villages had an average of just six landless families each in 1839, a sharp difference from Mennonite villages where over half the families (but 47 per cent of the population) were landless. The German colonists kept landlessness low partly by distributing their surplus land, rather than leasing it out. They also avoided the problem by maintaining large, multigenerational households, a practice that hid underemployment in the German villages.[128] Still, with fewer restrictions on landowning, a greater proportion of Germans could farm, so arguably the rate of landlessness more closely approximated the natural rate of labour absorption. In 1839 only 16 per cent of German colonists were landless compared with 47 per cent of Mennonites. If the German level was natural, by implication forty-seven landless persons competed for every sixteen jobs in the Mennonite settlement. Some landless householders from both groups leased land, so this overstates the extent of competition for labour. Nevertheless, the difference between the two groups still implies a significant level of underemployment in the Mennonite settlement. Little wonder that wages were low.

Some types of craft work could be lucrative, and some landless Mennonites chose it in preference to farming. As Table 3.7 shows, however, between 1826 and 1834 the number of craftsmen in the settlement grew very slowly, by just 2.4 per cent per annum, whereas the number of labourers grew by 12.75 per cent per annum, far outstripping the 4 per cent per annum growth rate of the Mennonite settlement as a whole.

In Prussia landless Mennonites competed for jobs in a proto-industrialized region where their industriousness and skill made them valuable employees. The surrounding non-Mennonite economy provided landless Mennonites with employment and a market for the products of cottage industry. In Russia Mennonites were virtually the only signifi-

cant employers, owning the few agricultural estates, mills, textile manufactures, and brick works that offered the landless jobs. Demand for
manufactured goods was minimal, for the Molochna region was isolated from export markets, and neighbouring villagers had a largely
self-sufficient subsistence economy. The result, of necessity, was the creation of an employer–employee relationship that parallelled the landed–
landless relationship. The isolation imposed by the move to Molochna
had taken away the economic options available to landless Mennonites
in Prussia and created distinct new divisions in Mennonite society.

The connection between this economic differentiation and the religious disputes that dogged Molochna Mennonites can only be inferred.
Mennonites traditionally styled themselves the 'quiet in the land,' allud-
ing to their religious ideal of withdrawal from secular entanglements.
They possessed a foundation myth of agricultural life as the ideal expression of their withdrawal from 'the world.'[129] In Prussia, Holland,
the United States, and elsewhere, Mennonite communities experienced
a constant erosion as ambitious entrepreneurial Mennonites moved to
town to pursue their fortunes in the world, while poor landless Mennonites moved to town to find work to survive. It is worth noting that this
process closely parallels the way that rich and poor elements in nomadic societies drift away to sedentary communities. With Mennonites,
as with nomads, the process made a necessary contribution to the survival of traditional, landed Mennonite society by removing potentially
disquieting elements – the entrepreneurial and the poor – from Mennonite communities. Not coincidentally, many eighteenth-century Prussian Mennonite religious conflicts manifested themselves as disputes
between conservative rural and progressive urban congregations.[130]

Immigration to the Molochna region brought a physical withdrawal
from the world to match the Mennonite ideal of spiritual withdrawal.
However, it was also a withdrawal from the economic safety valves of the
industrializing West. Ambitious entrepreneurial Mennonites remained
in the settlement, for the land they were allotted or that they leased
cheaply provided their only avenue to wealth. Poor Mennonites, lacking access to towns and markets and not even speaking the same language as the surrounding population that formed the bulk of any in-
cipient regional market, were also forced to remain in the settlement
and work for wealthy Mennonites.

In this pressurized situation two significant conservative congregations sprang up: the Kleine Gemeinde (in 1812) and the Large Flemish
Congregation (in 1824).[131] Historian Delbert Plett speculates about the

socioeconomic make-up of the Kleine Gemeinde, based on an 1808 census, concluding that members 'were of no particular socio-economic status'; however, the list of Kleine Gemeinde families that Plett provides is, by his own admission, fragmentary, while the census data on which his calculations rest was compiled four years prior to the formation of the congregation.[132] Without more complete information, no useful socioeconomic portrait can be attempted. As for the Large Flemish Congregation, there is neither a comprehensive list of its members nor a census from which to evaluate their socioeconomic condition, so here again, no quantitative analysis is possible.

All the same, there is much in the recorded religious beliefs of both conservative congregations to support the contention that these beliefs reflected fundamental economic divisions. In 1833 Heinrich Balzer, the most erudite member of the Kleine Gemeinde, launched a passionate attack on the growing extravagance of the wealthy in Molochna Mennonite society. Denouncing 'pride, ostentation, vanity, greed for money and lust for wealth, avarice, drunkenness, luxury, vicious life, masquerades, obscene songs, gambling, and above all the miserable smoking of tobacco,' Balzer called on Mennonites to strive only for 'the lowest state, that of husbandman' as that 'most conducive ... for the preservation of genuine simplicity in God.'[133] This contrast between wealthy worldliness and simple husbandry is a clear indictment of rising economic differentiation, although the equation of rectitude with husbandry must have been cold comfort to the landless poor. The date of Balzer's sermon must be stressed. By 1833 pastures were overcrowded and landlessness was rising rapidly. This was also the middle of the Great Drought (see Chapter 4), when some accounts claim no rain fell for twenty consecutive months and the Molochna Estuary itself dried up.[134] That winter families used thatch from their roofs to feed their livestock.[135] Drought, overcrowding, landlessness, and religious discord – the connections seem compelling.

Conclusion

By 1833 the first stage of adaptation in the Molochna region was over. The river basin was crowded with sheep, the flood plain was crowded with villages, and the settlers were about to face the new challenge of how to adapt the economy that they had built on the basis of inexhaustible availability of land to a landscape that was becoming increasingly exhausted.

Nogai were the least prepared for the looming challenge. Only a small economic elite had participated in the transition to sheep breeding and this group, which owed its prosperity to Mennonite subsidies, possessed no claim to the leadership of the Nogai majority. Indeed, their success, based as it was on the use of public land for private gain, at once undermined traditional Nogai administrative structures and threatened the economic welfare of the entire Nogai community. By 1833 there was no sign of the organic development of a new self-administrative system to legitimize economic differentiation and ensure subsistence for the poor.

If Orthodox state peasants were in better shape than the Nogai, it was not by dint of good planning. They too had expanded the size of their herds as fast as they could, and although the growth rate was slower than that of Nogai, this was likely only because Nogai had the advantage of greater experience with pastoralism. Like the majority of Nogai the Orthodox peasants had shown little interest in commercial husbandry, ignoring the transition to merino sheep that markets demanded. With the full occupation of all viable crown land looming on the horizon, Orthodox peasants would soon also face the problems of land shortages and economic differentiation. They too lacked a tradition that legitimized economic differentiation, and any attempt to reinstate their traditional system of obshchina authority over land was bound to face opposition from wealthy landowners.

Sectarians faced the new challenges from a position of strength. Molokans, who held the poorest land allotment in the Molochna region, had never had the luxury of relying on extensive agriculture, and they were already shrewdly employing their limited resources to prosper as market gardeners and speciality horse breeders. Doukhobors controlled disproportionately large tracts of the Molochna flood plain and had shown their good commercial sense by investing early in the transition to merino sheep. They had never abandoned communal control of property and consequently had well-established provisions for the general welfare of their community, while the appearance of a wealthy minority, which provided a ratchet to the economic development of the whole community, was legitimized by a religiously based internal administrative system. What could go wrong?

Foreign colonists, whether German broadly speaking or Mennonite, also seemed well prepared for the new challenges. Their land was held in indivisible allotments, so demographic growth posed no threat to the viability of their agricultural economy. However, the indivisibility of allotments also meant that, unlike other settlers who were guaranteed a portion of land either by the state or by their community, the colonists were faced with growing numbers of landless people. In 1833 this problem had been partially avoided in the German settlement by distributing surplus land, but at some point in the not too distant future it would have to be faced. In the Mennonite settlement landlessness was already a serious problem. Unlike the Doukhobors, Mennonites had no traditional system to sanction economic differentiation and protect the welfare of the landless, and the congregational system had little flexibility to adapt to new demands. The conflicts that loomed for Mennonites posed a fundamental challenge to their beliefs, but at least it was a challenge that progressive Mennonites were conscious of and prepared to address head-on.

CHAPTER FOUR

The Great Drought of 1832–1834

On Saturday, 1 September 1832, a light rain spattered the dusty fields of the Molochna River Basin, then quickly blew away west. It would hardly be an event worth noting were it not that no precipitation fell again for seven long months, and it was twenty months before the spring rains of 1834 released Molochna settlers from the grips of drought and hunger.[1] Following hard on the heels of the cholera epidemic of 1830 and 1831, the Great Drought of 1832–4 left a permanent mark on Molochna society, pressing home the need for more efficient agriculture and more efficient administration.

The Great Drought was not confined to the Molochna region. Twelve guberniias in the south and west of the Russian Empire experienced total harvest failures in 1833, and many also had desperately poor harvests in 1834.[2] The need for broadly based reform at the national level was driven home to the state by famine relief expenses that climbed to over eight million rubles. In the following years Russia sharply altered its approach to state peasant administration, turning away from wardship policies and towards new goals of efficiency and standardization, signalled most notably by the creation of the Ministry of State Domains in 1838.

In the long run both Molochna settlers and the state would see that the only solution to their common problem was to use land more efficiently. In the short run, however, both looked to solve the problem by finding more land to exploit in the old, extensive ways. The urgency for reform among Molochna settlers was heightened by the misperceptions of central officials; the state still thought that Molochna was underpopulated and, consequently, looked to it as a place to resettle peasants from overcrowded interior guberniias. But the drought had forced the people who already lived there to realize that their supply of land was on the verge of exhaustion. With the state looking for land for peasants from the interior and Molochna settlers looking for land for themselves, conflicts between regional and central administrators were looming. The ability of settlers to face down central administrators and defend their rights to land became vitally important.

This chapter describes the administrative changes that grew out of the Great Drought and the cholera epidemic. It employs the story of the exile of the Doukhobors as a case study of the interaction of land shortages, policies of standardization, and the lack of effective central administrative control. All of this provides a backdrop to the evolution of social and economic institutions that will be described in Chapters 5 and 6.

The Cholera Epidemic of 1830–1831

Asiatic cholera first appeared in India in 1817 and reached pandemic proportions across Europe in 1830 and 1831.[3] In Russia the official death toll from cholera was 234,604 persons, and there were countless additional unrecorded deaths.[4] At first the state reacted with little urgency, imposing poorly enforced quarantines on regional outbreaks and leaving medical treatment to local officials. But as the disease spread up the Volga, westward to Ukraine, and finally, in the autumn of 1830, to Moscow and St Petersburg, panic set in, and the state imposed draconian quarantine measures, cutting off infected regions and bringing interregional trade to a standstill throughout much of the empire. By the summer of 1831 riots and rebellions swept infected regions, leading to conditions that historian Roderick E. McGrew characterizes as 'a state of civil war.'[5] In 1832 the cholera epidemic finally receded and the state restored order.

Cholera first appeared in the Molochna region in the Nogai village of Kakbas in September or early October 1830.[6] Fearing a quarantine, at first the Nogai concealed the outbreak, but it was soon too severe to hide. By mid-December cholera raged throughout the Nogai district, and although no exact count is available, deaths were thought to be in the hundreds.[7] Johann Cornies was dismayed at Nogai preventative measures, which consisted of sacrificing a black cow, then dragging the hide around the infected village. After a representative of the Central Cholera Committee visited Cornies on 16 and 17 December, the state imposed a strict quarantine on the Nogai district.[8] This measure was apparently effective. By early January the outbreak, which had never spread beyond the Nogai villages, died out.[9] A second outbreak appeared on 14 July 1832, this time in the Orthodox village of Bolshoi Tokmak. Within two weeks deaths were reported in Orthodox and Nogai villages throughout the Molochna region, but this time there is no record of its severity or persistence. The German and Mennonite villages were again spared.[10]

If the cholera epidemic directly affected life in Molochna, there is no obvious record of it. Certainly, there were no riots or rebellions, for Cornies would undoubtedly have recorded such events. However, the epidemic had a catalytic effect on social tensions throughout Russia and Europe, and it is fair to assume that Molochna settlers were not immune to the fears and passions that arose elsewhere. Among the outlets for such tensions, identified in McGrew's standard history of the epidemic, are 'religious fervour, [and] outbursts against popular scapegoats.' This has particular resonance with the story of the Doukhobor exile from Molochna (related below). But before the exile, and hard on the heels of the cholera epidemic, came the Great Drought, and it is impossible to disentangle the effects of the first catastrophe from the second.

The Great Drought

Dry spells were not uncommon in the Molochna River Basin, and the rainless autumn of 1832 aroused little concern. By the following March, though, Johann Cornies wrote to his friend Daniel Schlatter: 'Not even the oldest people here can remember such weather. The ground is like a dry rock, without any moisture.'[11] By mid-June Orthodox and Nogai villages were reporting deaths from starvation.[12] Mennonites and Germans fared better, but their livestock faced the same fate as that of all settlers – Molochna pasture lands were barren, and only a few days of heavy rain in early July permitted livestock to survive that summer.[13] The July rains were too little and too late for grain crops, and Mennonites established a community fund to buy grain and fodder, sending representatives to surrounding districts to purchase whatever provisions they could find.[14] Both Mennonites and Germans sold off a quarter of their horses at minimal prices, keeping only those they absolutely needed for field work in the coming year.[15] During the winter of 1833–4 those who could afford to moved their livestock to regions less severely affected, paying as much as five rubles per sheep to rent pasture; poorer

settlers could only wait and watch as their livestock died. By January the
only fodder available to most Molochna settlers was a local weed called
kurrei, which sometimes caused fatal diarrhoea in sheep.[16] By February
even the kurrei was gone, and settlers fed their livestock thatch from
the roofs of their homes.[17] Some desperate Nogai, facing starvation,
raided Mennonite and German cattle herds, and colonists began post-
ing guards in response.[18] Disease swept through weakened livestock and
thousands of head, already weakened by hunger, died.[19] Only the state's
emergency efforts at famine relief prevented similar massive fatalities in
the human population before rain and warm weather finally returned
in April 1834.[20]

The Aftermath: Demographic Pressures and Reform Measures

The exact toll of human and livestock deaths during the Great Drought
remains unknown. Normal record-keeping procedures fell by the way-
side, and the state even delayed its planned 1833 national census until
1835. Combined Orthodox state peasant and Nogai populations in
Melitopol uezd declined by 7.85 per cent between December 1831 and
December 1835; however, the role of out-migration in this decline is
impossible to estimate.[21] Mennonites, the only group for whom death
rates are available, showed no sign of increased mortality during the
drought. The combined German and Mennonite population actually
rose by 13 per cent between 1831 and 1835, but a significant though
indefinable part of this growth came from new immigration.[22] Total
livestock numbers in foreign colonist villages at the end of 1834 were
30 per cent lower than they had been two years earlier (expressed in
AUs), while cattle numbers were 47 per cent lower – and, according to
Cornies, colonists had fared far better than most of their neighbours.[23]

Demographic losses during the cholera epidemic and famine were by
no means severe enough to relieve the overcrowding that was increasingly a problem in the Molochna region. The eighth Russian census,
completed in 1835, found 97,450 Orthodox, sectarian, and Nogai state
peasant male souls living on crown land in the two mainland uezds of
Tavria guberniia.[24] Total crown land in the two uezds was 1,494,363
desiatinas, meaning that if all available land had been distributed there
would still have been only 15.32 desiatinas per male soul.[25] In fact,
245,390 desiatinas remained unassigned; thus, the average allotment
was just 12.81 desiatinas per male soul.[26] The unassigned land, scattered
in the remotest parts of the two uezds, could not be conveniently assigned to peasants living in the most crowded areas, and this meant that

for most state peasants the time when 'land was free and you tilled where you wished' was gone.

Overcrowding had been creeping up on Molochna settlers for many years, and the fact that the critical point hit at almost exactly the same time as cholera and drought is sheerest coincidence. However, the ways people reacted to land shortages were heavily influenced by experiences of epidemics and hunger.

The first indication of serious overcrowding in Molochna came in 1832, when Molokan villagers appealed to the state for more land.[27] Within a year the Orthodox villages of Berestova, Nikolaevka, and Popovka would also ask the state for assistance, requesting that the Ministry of Internal Affairs step in and repartition their land.[28] In its typical foot-dragging fashion the state did not address the matter seriously until the late 1830s, and the broader issue of repartition will be left for Chapter 6. Nevertheless, information that the state assembled about the villages, based on the 1835 census, shows how crowded things had become in some areas in Melitopol uezd. The three villages were populated by 8,042 male souls and had 56,882 desiatinas of good land – just 7.07 desiatinas per male soul. The state's first thought was to assign more land. After all, wasn't Tavria guberniia 'land rich'? It soon became apparent, however, that there was simply no land left to assign. In 1835 there were just 92,940 unassigned desiatinas in all of Melitopol, and these, located on the high steppe, were of questionable value.[29] For the peasants in Berestova, Nikolaevka, and Popovka, the six cows, thirteen sheep, and 0.66 horses that the average Orthodox household had owned in 1827 were already too many for their land. Something had to give.

The state was already in the process of devising a national policy to deal with land shortages among state peasants. Over and over again, dating back into the previous century, plans for reforming the administration of the peasantry had been considered and rejected, and the early years of Tsar Nicholas's reign saw a number of serious proposals.[30] In February 1836 Nicholas made P.D. Kiselev head of the Fifth Department of the tsar's personal chancery, calling him 'my chief of staff for peasant affairs.'[31] Kiselev's mandate was to define the peasant problem and devise a solution. In January 1838, the tsar ordered Kiselev to take charge of the newly created Ministry of State Domains, vesting him with the authority to implement his solutions.[32]

Kiselev's objective was to improve peasant conditions and his preferred method was standardization. This was not good news for Molochna residents. Peasants in interior guberniias were in far worse condition than those on the periphery, and Kiselev hoped to move peasants from the overcrowded interior to what he perceived to be unoccupied land in the Molochna region.[33] When local protests made it clear that Molochna peasants had no land to spare, the Ministry of State Domains tried to free up land. In March 1841 Kiselev declared the guberniia to be 'land poor' and ordered the reduction of all allotments to eight desiatinas per male soul.[34] With a stroke of the pen this decision produced 695,149 'free' desiatinas, room enough for 87,000 new male souls to immigrate.

It is easier to order unpopular changes than to enact them, and this would prove the case in Molochna. The Orthodox state peasants responded with protest petitions declaring, 'On eight desiatinas of poor land one may hardly obtain enough grain to feed oneself.'[35] Regional authorities entered the fray on the side of the peasants, for the first time displaying a consciousness of the region's unique environmental conditions. Baron von Rosen, who headed the guberniia office of the Ministry of State Domains in Simferopol, wrote to Kiselev pointing out that eight desiatinas of land was 'too little, because the land in this region is for the most part without water, and in places, saline.'[36] Admiral M.S. Mordvinov, newly appointed governor general of New Russia, joined in the protests, noting that much of the land in question was 'unsuited to crop-raising. Therefore, [the peasants] employ themselves for the most part in livestock raising, which demands large pastures.'[37]

These protests did not go unnoticed. As George L. Yaney observes, Kiselev relied upon peasant consent to enact reforms and would 'call off his reform programs on the state lands whenever they aroused determined opposition.'[38] Although there is no evidence that the state ever officially reversed its decision to reduce land allotments, there is equally no evidence that it implemented this decision. Still, the decision to reclassify the guberniia as 'land poor' was not without consequences. Prior to 1841 the state's policy was to maintain allotments of fifteen desiatinas per male soul by allotting new land as the population increased. After 1841 this was no longer the case. The state assigned whatever unoccupied land was available to peasants from other guberniias, and when large tracts of new land became available after the exile of Doukhobor and Molokan sectarians, much of this, too, was distributed to new immigrants. Consequently, landholdings shrank, slowly placing pressure on peasants to alter their land use practices to more intensive agricultural methods.

Immediate Consequences: The Doukhobor Exile

Before examining the transition to new agricultural methods (in Chapters 5 and 6), the immediate social consequences of the crises of the 1830s demand attention. These are most vividly illustrated in the story of the Doukhobor exile, which, not coincidentally, had its direct antecedents in the land requests made by Molokans in 1832.

In many ways Molochna Doukhobors occupy a unique place in the history of Orthodox Russia's relationship with its religious dissenters. The bulk of that history is one of repression, but for a brief time Doukhobors experienced the benefit of Tsar Alexander I's most liberal impulses and not only overcame official discrimination, but found themselves among the most privileged settlers in the Molochna region. Doukhobors seized the moment, coalescing religiously and economically into a remarkably cohesive community – a 'Doukhobor commonwealth' – that stood firm in the face of persecution and exile after Nicholas I became tsar in 1825.[39] The unity of this commonwealth is a key factor in the Doukhobors' fame, and indeed, in their notoriety. Rather than renouncing their beliefs, they suffered exile from Molochna to the Caucasus in the 1840s, from the Caucasus to Canada in 1895, and discrimination and vilification in Canada as recently as the 1970s.

The Molokan land requests that sparked the Doukhobor exile at first fell on deaf ears, and it was only after a group of Molokans asked permission to leave Molochna and emigrate to the Caucasus that the Ministry of Internal Affairs conducted a close investigation of their concerns.[40] The Molokan population had grown to 1,352 male souls, leaving them with less than ten desiatinas per male soul.[41] In 1834 the state proposed resolving the problem by pooling together all 'sectarian land,' Molokan and Doukhobor alike, and redistributing it at the rate of fifteen desiatinas per male soul.[42] However, Doukhobors did not hold their excess land as allotment land, which was subject to redistribution by fiat based on population size. Instead, they held land under a perpetual lease granted by imperial decree and exempt from arbitrary manipulations by local officials. Local officials questioned the Doukhobors' right to the 'privilege' of such a large and rich land grant, pointing out that much of the land had been given to the Doukhobors under the now invalid assumption that more Doukhobors would immigrate to the region. Officials could not break the Doukhobor lease on these grounds. However, the investigation of the sectarians that grew out of such renewed state attention marks the starting point of the chain of events leading to the exile of the Doukhobors in the 1840s.

Allegations against the Doukhobors in the 1830s drew upon suspicions and prejudices dating from earlier investigations. In 1815 former members of the sect accused Doukhobor leaders of various crimes, prompting an inquiry by an Orthodox priest, Father Nalimskii, and the arrest of Doukhobor leader Savelii Kapustin together with sixteen of his Apostles.[43] Labelling Kapustin the 'leading false teacher' of the Doukhobors, Nalimskii accused him and his followers of vaguely defined 'illegal and evil acts,' dangerous 'not only to the Christian religion, but to the state.'[44] L.A. Langeron, vice-governor of New Russia and a harsh critic of Doukhobors, reacted by proposing that the Doukhobor community be broken up and dispersed, but Alexander I, demonstrating his liberal attitudes towards sectarians, intervened, dismissing the charges and ordering the release of Kapustin and his followers.[45]

Any understanding of the change in Doukhobor fortunes must begin with the shift in state religious policy after the death of Alexander I in 1825. Almost immediately after his accession, Nicholas I introduced sharply reactionary policies towards sectarians. An important objective of his 'official nationality,' with its tenets of 'Orthodoxy, autocracy, and nationality,' was to reaffirm the commonality of goals of church and state.[46] This rather amorphous principle could have had little focused expression at regional levels, for the inefficiency of tsarist administration in peripheral regions is legendary. Still, the general tenor of Nicholas's policies must have made Doukhobors an obvious target for regional officials, for the sectarians could no longer expect support from St Petersburg. On 20 October 1830, Nicholas issued a decree directed at 'Doukhobors, Ikonobors, Molokans, Judaizers, and others recognized as particularly pernicious heresies.'[47] The first clause of the decree reflects a sharp turn in Doukhobor affairs, ordering that 'all dissenters ... accused of spreading their heresies and attracting others to them, [and] also [accused of] temptation, unruliness, and insolence against the church and the clergy of the Orthodox faith are to be handed over to the courts.' The exile of the Doukhobors must be seen within the context of such policies.

Although Nicholas's reactionary policies worked against the Doukhobors, oddly enough it was his efforts at peasant reforms that harmed them most. The decision to reduce land allotments in the Molochna region to eight desiatinas per male soul served as a crucial impetus to renewed persecution of Doukhobors in the 1830s, for under such circumstances the particularly large Doukhobor allotments were bound to attract the attention of the central administration.

This renewed attention began with the arrival of P. Köppen in Molochna in 1837. Known as the 'father of Russian statistics,' Köppen was one of the most trusted and influential men in Russia. He came to Molochna during his survey of Tavria guberniia for the Fifth Department of the Tsar's chancery, forerunner of the Ministry of State Domains and the body responsible for reviewing the condition of the state peasantry.[48] In his reports, Köppen had little to say about the material well-being of Doukhobors, but he repeated accounts of crimes in the villages provided to him by Melitopol District Administrator Kolosov.

Kolosov, from 1827 to 1830 chair of the district court in Melitopol, sat on a commission of inquiry that investigated Doukhobor crimes in 1835–6.[49] Hostile to Doukhobors, Kolosov told Köppen that the death of Doukhobor leader Vasilii Kalmykov and inheritance of leadership by his son Ilarion in 1832 was followed by 'unusual peril amongst the Doukhobors; many murders occurred for various reasons, and many military deserters and bandits hid among them.'[50] Doukhobors, Kolosov claimed, had committed twenty-four murders, seven 'tyrannical acts of torture,' eleven robberies, and had hidden eight army deserters.[51]

This was a strategically pivotal report that became the key justification for exiling the Doukhobors. It detailed four murders, including a lurid description of the burial alive of a mute, crippled Doukhobor girl named Elisaveta Voronova, and concluded that if the sect leaders could be exiled to 'some place else' the remaining Doukhobors would easily convert to Orthodoxy.[52] Köppen appended Kolosov's report to his own, repeated Kolosov's recommendation, and concluded that the 'greater part of [the Doukhobors] are discontented with the abuses of the principal sectarians, and can be ... returned to Orthodoxy.'[53] This observation found ready acceptance in St Petersburg.

In February 1838 Kiselev, newly appointed minister of state domains, forwarded a copy of Köppen's report to D.N. Bludov, the minister of internal affairs. In an accompanying letter, Kiselev wrote: 'His Highness the Emperor, upon reviewing the report, has expressed his Imperial pleasure that I come to an agreement with Your Excellency and the Lord Over-Procurator of the Holy State Synod on measures for the conversion of the majority of the dissenters to Orthodoxy.'[54] Bludov responded that most Doukhobors could 'easily be converted to Orthodoxy, as soon as the state will take actions to exile the principal sectarians.'[55] He forwarded this proposal to M.S. Vorontsov, governor general of New Russia,[56] who at first defended the Doukhobors on the grounds that they 'raise cattle and sheep, and grow outstanding crops ... [and] can be an extremely useful community and even serve as model agriculturists.'[57] However, in August, bowing to the wishes of the Ministry of Internal Affairs, Vorontsov sent Bludov a detailed plan for forcing Doukhobors to convert by exiling to the Caucasus those who refused.[58] Nicholas signed the fateful decree ordering the Doukhobors into exile on 17 February 1839.[59] In most particulars, it followed Vorontsov's recommendations.

Ultimately, the state ordered 773 Doukhobors into exile in the summer of 1841 'without option' (*bez zhrebiia*).[60] The remaining Doukhobors, exiled in groups during the following four summers, had the option to convert to Orthodoxy and remain in Molochna.[61] Ministry reactions to Köppen's original report and the reports of officials supervising the exile indicate that the state expected most Doukhobors to convert. At the highest levels of the administration, then, the point was not punishment, but conversion. This is clear evidence of the shift in policy that had accompanied Alexander's death and Nicholas's ascension to the Russian throne. For Nicholas, no group, no matter how small and isolated, would be permitted to stray from the state's official Orthodox ideology.

This conversion strategy of divide and conquer could only work, of course, if the allegations of disruptions in the community were true. In the event, only 248 Doukhobors converted to Orthodoxy, while 4,992 affirmed their faith and took the long trek to the Caucasus. This demonstration of solidarity refutes the claim that the Doukhobor commonwealth was disrupted and consequently raises serious doubts about the truth of the principal evidence of disruption, the murder accusations.[62]

Some of the accusations are detailed in an 'extract from the ongoing investigation of various crimes carried out in the Doukhobor and Molokan settlements of Melitopol *uezd*.'[63] In the absence of extant official records from the investigation, this document is of potential importance, but it is also problematic, for it is undated, and there is no indication of its provenance.[64] Its most recent testimony dates from 4 March 1836, the year in which, according to Kolosov, the investigation ended.[65] It does, however, describe just nineteen murders, not twenty-four as mentioned by Kolosov or twenty-one as appear, uncredited, in the influential study by nineteenth-century Russian historian Orest Novitskii.[66] Nevertheless, the nineteen include all four that Kolosov specifically mentioned in his report. Whether or not the extract is complete, it sheds significant light on the charges against the Doukhobors. As a closer examination reveals, many of those charges can only be described as unfounded rumour.

To begin with, it must be emphasized that some of the alleged murders almost certainly did occur. In two cases the murderers confessed, and one of these, the 1825 murder of seventeen-year-old Elisaveta Voronova, was the most notorious of all the crimes ascribed to Doukhobors.[67] The extract recounts the confession of Ivan Voronov, Elisaveta's brother: 'He told how, finding the maintenance of Elisaveta, a mute and a cripple, a burden on his shoulders, he first intended to bury her in his garden and put a haystack over the grave, but because his wife Marina refused to go away and stay in the cabin [where she could not have witnessed the murder] because she thought he wanted to sneak away to meet with another woman, he was forced to dig the grave on the steppe instead.' Ivan described how he buried his sister alive, then confessed to his mother and the village elders. The unfortunate Elisaveta's body was reportedly moved to an unmarked grave in the village cemetery which was made 'invisible by sending cattle to trample over it.'

The accusation that Doukhobors buried people alive surfaces again and again in subsequent accounts. Vorontsov abandoned his defence of Doukhobors in part, he wrote, because they 'bury the living in the ground.'[68] He drew his information from Kolosov's report, and it thus appears that the example of the single, admittedly gruesome murder of Voronova was exaggerated into a common Doukhobor practice. In the most famous description of the crimes, Baron August Freiherr von Haxthausen, author of the enormously influential nineteenth-century study entitled *The Russian Empire*, wrote that 'bodies were found buried alive,' although he offered no proof of the claim; both Orest Novitskii and George Woodcock and Ivan Avakumovic echoed Haxthausen.[69]

The second confessed murder was that of Evdokim Lukianov.[70] One day in 1827, Lukianov, a convert from the Doukhobor faith to Orthodoxy, reportedly set out for the Doukhobor village of Bogdanovka to borrow some money from his father. Walking along the road he met three other Doukhobors, Onisim Botkin and the brothers Semon and Stepan Voikin, who offered him a lift in their wagon. He discovered that they were illegally transporting vodka, demanded some, and threatened to turn them in if they refused. In the ensuing brawl, Lukianov was killed.

Two other alleged murders, although unproved, also have an air of authenticity. In 1803, in a dispute over an unpaid debt, Semen Negreev was allegedly stabbed to death by his brother Pavl and another man.[71] In 1820, during a dispute over a cow, a certain Karp Susoev was allegedly beaten and later died.[72] These three cases, if true, reveal a degree of violence in Doukhobor society, but hardly a profound crisis. Rather, they suggest that Doukhobor society shared in the violent characteristics common to all peasant societies.

Apart from these four murders there is little in the extract that bears up under close scrutiny. Several cases were less mundane, but also less believable because of their reliance on extremely questionable witnesses. The state's star witnesses were Iosif Gankin, a one-time Doukhobor village elder, and his son Fomin. They testified in six cases involving thirteen accused murderers and seven victims. Earlier they had testified in five of these cases during a district court trial (in 1828), but at that time the charges had been dismissed and Iosif and Fomin had been imprisoned for giving false evidence. The two escaped and ran off to Ekaterinoslav, where they converted to Orthodoxy 'for protection,' and returned with a letter from the bishop who had converted them asking for leniency. This did not impress District Court Judge Sokolovskii who threw them back in jail. They again escaped, this time to Simferopol, where they appealed to Langeron, by now retired from his vice-gubernatorial position but still influential. Armed with a letter from Langeron, they returned again, and the still-unimpressed Judge Sokolovskii jailed them again, concluding that Langeron's letter 'protected their heads but not their bodies.' This time the apparently much-improved penal system managed to hold onto Iosif, but Fomin slipped away again, back to Langeron in Simferopol, who finally contrived to have the charges dismissed. Vindicated, the two returned to the stand to repeat their testimony during the later investigation.[73]

The most interesting case in which the Gankins testified was the alleged 1821 murder of Petr Plaksin and a friend, identified only as 'Sergei.'[74] Later anecdotal accounts of Doukhobor crimes often mention the exhumation of bodies during the investigation, but the Plaksin case is the only example of exhumation to appear in the extract.[75] According to the Gankins, Petr and Sergei were Doukhobors who had been raised in Molochna and returned there in 1820 as army deserters. They were supposedly soon heard making drunken threats to burn down the houses of the elders who had singled them out for conscription. Village officials arrested them, intending to turn them over to the authorities, but the two threatened to reveal the names of other deserters in the Doukhobor villages. The Gankins claimed that Vasilii

Kalmykov, leader of the Doukhobors, ordered the two murdered to prevent them testifying, and his orders were carried out by five Apostles who disposed of the bodies in a dry well. Doukhobor witnesses, however, disputed the Gankins's testimony, claiming the two men had simply disappeared and were thought to have fled to the town of Azov. During the investigation the commission had the well dug up and found it filled with horse bones, and among them 'one bone, broken in two, that resembled a human arm, and also two more bones that resembled human bones.' This the commission accepted as verification of the Gankins's story.

The principal witness in six of the other cases was a Molokan woman, Agafiia Nemanikhina, who had no personal knowledge of the murders and simply relayed rumours heard by her husband Grigorii, who could not testify himself because he was 'crazy in the brain' (*pomeshatel'stvo v ume*).[76] One of the six cases was that of Elisaveta Voronova, described above, but the others were more dubious. The least convincing is short enough to quote in full: 'The Fifth [Case]: Concerning two unknown merchants from the city of Feodosiia who came to purchase wool in an unknown year. The Molokan woman Agafiia Nemanikhina reports the rumour that of two merchants who came to the village of Terpenie to buy wool, one was drowned by Doukhobors in the Molochna River, and the other has disappeared; concerning these people nothing further is known.'[77]

Several aspects of the accusations demand comment. The nineteen murders alleged in the extract were not part of a savage mid-1830s spree, but occurred over a period of twenty-six years, from 1802 to 1828. This is in sharp contrast to published accounts, which rely heavily on Haxthausen. Travelling through Molochna in 1843, ten years after the murders had allegedly occured, Haxthausen discussed the Doukhobors with Johann Cornies, visiting a Doukhobor village in Cornies's company. According to Haxthausen, Ilarion Kalmykov, who inherited the leadership of the Doukhobors in 1832, was an ineffectual leader who spent his time in drunken orgies, while the real administration of the community fell to a Council of Elders. The Orphans' Home, the Doukhobor seat of administration, soon became a 'den of crime,' while the Council of Elders 'constituted itself a terrible inquisitional tribunal. The principle, "Whoso denies his God shall perish by the sword," was interpreted according to their caprice; the house of justice was called *Rai i muka*, paradise and torture; the place of execution was on the island at the mouth of the Molochna. A mere suspicion of treachery, or of an intention to go over to the Russian Church, was punished with torture and death.'[78]

In the English version, Haxthausen claims the council had two hundred people murdered, while the German and French versions give the number as four hundred.[79] Novitskii cites the French version, but qualifies it, saying, 'If one does not believe the rumours about the number of Doukhobor murders, one must in any case accept the results of the investigative commission. It, through all of its persistent and skillful unearthing of secret crimes, revealed twenty-one murders.'[80] Novitskii then questions his own conclusions, admitting, 'Unfortunately, the documents addressing this matter, the most interesting and important in the history of the Melitopol Doukhobors during the reign of [Nicholas I], have still not come to light.'[81] Even the most judicious study, by Woodcock and Avakumovic, quotes Haxthausen at length. It rejects his claims regarding the number of deaths, but accepts Novitskii's reduced figure of twenty-one.[82] The new evidence cited here finally gives firm grounds for dismissing Haxthausen's exaggerated claims.

Even the nineteen alleged murders described in the extract were based on the most tenuous of evidence. In only two cases did the accused murderers confess their crimes. In nine the bodies of the alleged victims were never found. Thirteen of the fourteen cases that had previously been investigated had not led to a conviction. One had originally been ruled death by illness, one a suicide, and one a drowning. Eleven relied heavily on rumours related by Doukhobor converts to Orthodoxy, and none of these converts had first-hand knowledge of the events they testified to. Six of the cases had as their primary witness the Molokan Nemanikhina, who relied exclusively on rumours, while another six relied on Iosif and Fomin Gankin, who had previously been jailed for giving false testimony. These reports are no more credible than the accusations of ritual murder levelled so often against Jews. They provide no basis for concluding that the Doukhobor community was deeply troubled in the 1830s.

A second report of Doukhobor crimes makes the claims of a split in the community even more doubtful. A December 1840 report by Melitopol uezd Procurator (*Striapchik*) Andreevskii provides a summary of the 'crimes committed by Doukhobors in Melitopol uezd' in the period 1831 to 1840.[83] Andreevskii lists fifty-three significant incidents: eleven cases of arson, eleven of robbery, two of desecrating holy icons, two of concealing runaways, one each of illegally freeing a prisoner, possessing counterfeit money, insolence to a village administrator, and abuse of office, one of carrying out a death penalty on a condemned man without obtaining the proper authorization of the authorities, twelve premature deaths from illness, four premature deaths from excessive consumption of alcohol, one suicide, one attempted suicide, and finally, one – just one – murder. The report specifically excluded crimes 'presently [under] consideration by the Senate,' partly because their disposition had not yet been decided, and partly because they included 'cases that occurred prior to the [specified] ten years.' Presumably, the excluded murders were precisely those for which the Doukhobors were about to be exiled. In other words, at the time of Andreevskii's report – a full twenty-two months after Nicholas had ordered the exile – the Senate had still not ruled on the alleged Doukhobor crimes.

Andreevskii's reports of arson must raise the eyebrows of anyone familiar with the history of Doukhobors in Canada, but because of the dearth of surviving court records regarding crime in neighbouring communities it is impossible to know if this represents an unusual pattern or incidence of crime.[84] Desecrating icons was certain to attract the attention of the Orthodox state, but two incidents in ten years could hardly have warranted a wholesale exile. Harbouring runaways was the most common complaint against Doukhobors, but again Andreevskii reports only two instances. Altogether, the total number of incidents – an average of just 5.3 per year – is not indicative of severe disturbances in the community, and eleven of these 'incidents' were deaths by illness, hardly evidence of a community torn apart by internal dissension. By comparison, Steven L. Hoch documents an average of 256 disciplinary actions *per year* in the 3,500-person serf estate of Petrovskoe in Tambov guberniia in the same era.[85] Barring the discovery of the full records of the investigative commission, the accusations of mass murder must be treated as groundless. Most of the murders probably never happened.

Unfortunately, the state believed they did, and this requires an explanation. The state based its decision on Köppen's report, and by extension on District Administrator Kolosov's description of the crimes. Kolosov implied that the murders were proved beyond a shadow of doubt, but as shown above this was clearly not so. What explains this harsh attack on Doukhobors?

Religious prejudice, officially endorsed by Nicholas I's official nationality policy, must be given a prominent place in any explanation for the exile of the Doukhobors. Still, it is not by itself a sufficient explanation. After all, there is no evidence that the Molokans were subjected to similar pressures, despite the common perception that they were all but identical to the Doukhobors. Kolosov's report, so openly hostile to the Doukhobors, says only that the Molokans were 'distinct' from their sectarian neighbours. Köppen gives a fuller description, concluding that 'a significant portion of the Molokans, while not renouncing the general tenets of that sect and their mistaken attitudes towards Orthodoxy and the performance of their duties, show in their written addresses the feelings of devotion to the throne of faithful subjects, and are prepared to affirm their obligations.'[86]

An important reason for this differing attitude towards the two sectarian groups was the influence of Mennonite Johann Cornies. He held Molokans, who were people of the Book, in much higher esteem than Doukhobors. Cornies endorsed the charges against Doukhobors, and this carried weight. As chairman for life of the Molochna region's Agricultural Society, and a frequent correspondent of Minister of State Domains Kiselev and other top officials, Cornies was the most powerful, trusted, and influential man in Molochna.[87] In the 1830s he was unhappy over what he saw as the Doukhobors' unscrupulous sharecropping agreements with the Nogai Tatars. In an 1836 letter to his friend Aleksandr Fadeev, head of the Guardianship Committee which supervised colonists in New Russia, Cornies expressed revulsion at the crimes described in the investigative commission's report, writing, 'I have come to an end with the Doukhobors, crime upon crime, it makes your skin crawl.'[88] Köppen, in his report to Kiselev, named Cornies as a primary informant on Doukhobor religious practices, implying that Cornies supported his conclusions. This endorsement must have reassured Kiselev and helped create support in the capital for Köppen's recommendations.

Cornies's part in determining the Doukhobors' fate points to a vital characteristic of the entire affair: regional interests played a dominant role. The Great Drought of 1832–4 had given other Molochna residents practical reasons to support the Doukhobor exile. Under such circumstances, the Doukhobors' large landholdings must have prompted jealousy among neighbours. Jews in Russia and elsewhere often found themselves singled out as scapegoats in times of economic crises, and Doukhobors, as a prominent religious minority, may have suffered from a similar pattern of discrimination.[89]

The crisis of 1833–4 was only the worst manifestation of the larger problem of overcrowding that loomed over Molochna. The Doukhobors' exceptionally large holdings had already attracted the attention of their neighbours. Indeed, it was their landholdings that brought them back under state scrutiny in 1832, in reaction to Molokan requests for land.

The investigations of the 1830s, and the subsequent exile, broke the Doukhobors' perpetual lease and freed their land for reallotment. The Doukhobors themselves claimed that their exile was motivated solely by the desire of local officials to profit from this process. In 1841, in a petition appealing their exile, they specifically identified District Administrator Kolosov as the true source of their troubles, accusing him of 'enriching himself in various oppressive ways with our money and estates.'[90] A group of Doukhobor exiles en route to the Caucasus in 1843 told German zoologist Moritz Wagner that their money 'filled many an official pocket,'[91] while in 1903 Joseph Elkinton reported a Doukhobor tradition that their exile was sparked by false accusations of a single, unidentified official angered by their refusal to meet his blackmail demands.[92]

The Doukhobors' reference in their 1841 petition to their 'estates' is particularly important, for the only Doukhobor land that figured in Kolosov's denunciation, which weighed so heavily in the ultimate decision to order the exile, was the 26,878 desiatinas of leased land. Kolosov objected to the advantage that Doukhobors gained over neighbouring 'land poor' Orthodox state peasants by renting the large tract and also to their paying only an 'insignificant price' for it.[93] His concerns were echoed by Köppen, who observed that similar land brought lease payments of as much as sixty kopecks per desiatina.[94] In 1838 the confiscation of this 'excess land' figured prominently in recommendations made by the Ministry of Internal Affairs for dealing with the Doukhobors.[95] In 1842, in rejecting a Doukhobor plea to maintain control of the land, an official in the Ministry of State Domains concluded, 'In as much as the land is extremely good and contains everything needed for new settlers, and considering that the treasury can realize from it an incomparably greater return, while it now receives only a token payment of twenty kopecks per desiatina ... I recommend that it be returned to the treasury, particularly in view of the fact that the Doukhobors have in no way earned such kindness from the state.'[96]

This attention to Doukhobor landholdings reveals a three-sided interaction among the ideological prescripts of Nicholas's official nationality policies and the more practical concerns that regional and central officials faced with providing land for Russia's rapidly growing peasant population. Local Molochna officials, motivated generally by local land shortages and particularly by the 1832–4 drought, and quite possibly also motivated by the opportunity to profit personally from the exercise, used dubious charges to free up Doukhobor land. Central officials, concerned with the empire-wide shortage of land for state peasants, accepted the dubious charges and ordered the Doukhobor exile. Yet, whatever the practical concerns, the exile was officially justified as an attempt to convert the sectarians to Orthodoxy.[97]

Unfortunately for the Doukhobors, the state accepted the accusations made against them. The 26 January 1841 proclamation of exile reads: 'All your crimes have been discovered, and the innocent blood which you have shed calls down upon your heads the rigours of the law. By your actions you have rendered yourselves unworthy of the indulgence and pardon which were granted to you by his Majesty, and you have exhausted the patience of the authorities, who are in the end convinced that you should be transferred into distant regions where you will no longer be injurious to your fellow men.'[98]

The Doukhobors did not go without complaint. In March 1841 they petitioned the state, describing their fate in pathetic terms: 'We unfortunate 4,000 souls, torn from our homes and the land which we, over dozens of years and with great difficulty obtained, and spilling tears in comprehension of our fate, must set out on a journey, a long journey, and settle in a barren climate on infertile land, impoverished, brought almost to the sacrifice of our lives, comforted only by the knowledge that we are guiltless.'[99]

In the petition they asked permission to stay in Molochna, but reasserted the unity of the Doukhobor commonwealth by adamantly refusing to abandon their religious convictions. A second petition, from the group designated for exile without appeal, asked only that the exile be delayed by a year so they could obtain fair prices for the belongings that they could not take with them.[100] A third petition, turning to the question of property, asked that Doukhobors be allowed to retain control of their leased land, presumably by subletting it.[101] All of these petitions were refused.

As for the final benefactors in the reallotment process, most Doukhobor land went to land-short Orthodox peasants. The Molokans, whose need for land had initiated the investigation, also benefited; in 1842 they were granted enough Doukhobor land to bring their total holdings to fifteen desiatinas per male soul.[102] This did not completely satisfy the Molokans; 678 of them asked for and received permission to join the Doukhobor trek to the Caucasus. Such permission was given only grudgingly, for there were suspicions in some quarters that

Molokans were simply trying to avoid tax arrears that had built up during the crop failures of 1839.[103] Those Molokans who remained in Molochna after 1845 no longer held the state's attention. For the most part, the governor of Tavria guberniia contented himself with one or two sentences in annual reports to St Petersburg, reassuring the capital that the local sectarians were an exemplary lot, farming their fields, tending their gardens, and keeping their religious views to themselves.[104]

The single largest benefactors of the Doukhobor exile were Johann Cornies and his brother David. In 1845, 4,039 desiatinas of the land taken from the Doukhobors passed into their hands. The lease price was the same low original twenty kopecks per desiatina per year.[105] Although there is no explicit evidence in this regard, one may well wonder whether Johann Cornies's own well-known thirst for land had influenced the assessment of the Doukhobors that he gave to Köppen in 1837.[106] There is no small irony that the Cornies brothers received land that was taken away from Doukhobors in part because of religion, in part because it exceeded the standard state peasant allotment, and in part because the lease payment of twenty kopecks per desiatina was only 'token.' After all, Johann and David were also not Orthodox, and were themselves state peasants. But the Cornies brothers were peasants in name only. Johann, the most powerful man in Molochna, had hosted both Alexander I and Nicholas I in his home, and as chairman for life of the region's Agricultural Society he acted as the main local representative of the Ministry of State Domains. No doubt he had 'earned such kindness' from the state.[107]

Conclusion

The Doukhobor experience in the Molochna region is of interest on many levels. Most basically, it disputes the accuracy of published accounts of the sectarians by refuting the charges of mass murder that have been levelled against them and the concomitant assumptions about instability, strife, and disruptions in their community. Even Woodcock and Avakumovic, who are at once judicious and sympathetic towards the Doukhobors, are constrained to conclude, 'It is not impossible that at one moment in their history the Doukhobors, isolated at [the Molochna River] like the Anabaptists in Münster, should have found the sense of their divine mission becoming so demanding that destruction did not seem too bad a fate for the heretical.'[108] The violence of the alleged crimes has always stood at odds with the Doukhobors' self-proclaimed belief in the in-dwelling spirit of God, and consequently in pacifism, and thus it has raised doubts about the consistency of those beliefs. With evidence of the murders debunked, what remains are accounts of a prosperous and uncommonly cohesive religious community, victimized by religious persecution, not the victimizer.

The Doukhobor story also reflects the complex interplay of region and centre, religious ideology, and practical administrative concerns. In terms of central policy towards religious dissent, Alexander I's well-known religious tolerance and Nicholas's equally well-known intolerance are clearly demonstrated by their treatment of Doukhobors. Most interestingly, the story evidences the impact of Nicholas's policies on administrative practices. Whatever the religious prejudices of administrators, they had no legal means to seize the Doukhobors' excess land holdings. As late as 1834, when Nicholas's official nationality ideology was already clearly enunciated, Doukhobors were able to resist the state's attempts to redistribute their leased land to land-poor Molokans. Regional and central administrators broke the Doukhobors' hold on the land by playing upon official religious prejudices. The accusations levelled against Doukhobors were accepted in spite of the dubious quality of the evidence because they offered an avenue around inconvenient legal barriers.

There is nothing surprising in the final outcome of the Doukhobor sojourn in the Molochna region. Had the religious beliefs of a small group of dissenting peasants won out over the ideological imperatives of an Orthodox tsar, or had the economic well-being of peasants in a regional backwater won out over the rationalizing programs of the central administrative apparatus, this would have been news indeed. The cohesiveness that the Doukhobors showed in the face of persecution is arguably itself a consequence of their time in Molochna. The isolation they experienced in the first years of settlement, when their only neighbours were Turkic-speaking Tatars and German-speaking foreign colonists, served to emphasize their own distinct identity. Under Nicholas I, their faith was tempered in the furnace of religious persecution, forging them into a Doukhobor commonwealth.

By the 1830s all Molochna settlers faced the need to renegotiate their relationship with the central state. Doukhobors, confronted by both religious prejudice and jealousy because of their large land holdings, could not defend themselves against the abuse of power and consequently were exiled. How other settlers answered the need to defend their landholdings against both central and regional demands is taken up more fully in Chapters 5 and 6.

CHAPTER FIVE

Johann Cornies and the Birth
of a New Mennonite World View

By the 1860s Mennonites would become the best-known minority in all
of Russia. Their economic success in both agriculture and industry
made them a shining example of what could be accomplished in the
empire; it also made them a target for growing Russian xenophobia.
Early in the nineteenth century the tsar and his administrators publi-
cized the Mennonite example widely, and Mennonites were urged to
share their methods with other state peasants both locally and, through
articles in newspapers and various government journals, nationally, as
well. Mennonites became both the prime movers of economic development in the Molochna River Basin and poster children for Russian
imperial economic planning. Their story demands careful assessment.

The dominant figure in Russian Mennonite society in the first half of
the nineteenth century was Johann Cornies. His influence spread far
beyond the Molochna region, extending to the halls of the Ministry of
State Domains in St Petersburg and even to the tsar. Denounced as the
'tree devil' by outraged conservative Mennonite contemporaries, grouped
with Menno Simons himself by Mennonite historian P.M. Friesen in
1911, and labelled the 'prophet of progress' by anthropologist James
Urry in 1989, Cornies and his legacy of modernization, secularization,
and religious discord remains controversial to this day.[1]

Cornies's actions guided Mennonite society along a path to great
prosperity, broke down the barriers insulating Mennonites from secular
authority, and led to serious religious dissension. About this there can
be no dispute. However, the dominant image that has survived is of
Cornies as a secular figure acting outside of and in opposition to traditional Mennonite society. This interpretation obscures one fundamental point: Johann Cornies was a devout Mennonite who owed his initial

prominence in Mennonite society as much to his position as a leading congregational figure as to his role in secular administrative organs. Indeed, Cornies was the leader, not of a secular movement, but of a religious one. This is what made his actions so politically divisive in a Mennonite world that was politically dominated by congregations.

The vision of civil society that Cornies began to develop in the 1820s, and had shaped into an articulate and all-encompassing model by the 1840s, was a *moral* vision. Cornies's vision was born at once of his sophisticated understanding of the challenges facing Mennonites and of his equally sophisticated assessment of the options available to them – if they wished to survive *as Mennonites*. Cornies changed the face of the Russian Mennonite religious world, but only to ensure its survival in a changing secular world. Along the way, he helped to transform the entire Molochna economy.

The Mennonite Congregational World

Mennonite relations with secular authority had always been both complex and contradictory. The Mennonite religious ideal was to live apart from the secular world in self-sufficient agricultural communities, self-administered in accordance with religious principles. Nevertheless, most Mennonites lived within the European states system, with the civic, fiscal, and administrative demands that this necessarily entailed. The compromise that Mennonites reached was to pay taxes and accept secular laws insofar as those laws did not violate their fundamental religious principles – most controversially, the principle of pacifism. This compromise was acceptable to the European states that welcomed Mennonites because Mennonites had something to offer: they were among the most progressive and productive agriculturists in Europe.[2]

Traditions of insularity and pacifism meant that, before coming to Russia, Mennonites themselves had not taken up secular administrative positions. The requirement to abide by secular laws and pay secular taxes, however, meant that the internal Mennonite congregational administrative system had to cooperate at some level with the secular system. Congregational authorities thus walked a tightrope between secular and religious worlds, the smallest slip often plunging them into controversy.

The first Mennonite immigrants to Russia came from Prussia. The communities that they left were by then divided between two congregations, the Flemish and Frisian. The Flemish congregation was more insular, conservative, and strict in its application of congregational discipline than the Frisian congregation, which, for example, was more willing to accept outsiders and sanction intercongregational marriages.[3] The first Mennonite settlers in the Molochna region were almost exclusively drawn from the Flemish congregation.

In Danzig in 1808 the two congregations united. In the following years the new, united congregation became increasingly open to ideas drawn from non-Mennonite, particularly pietistic Christian, groups.[4] When in 1818 the Russian state authorized a new immigration of several thousand Mennonites from Prussia, it opened the door to religious controversy by bringing into the conservative Molochna community a large group of Danzig Mennonites, who were regarded by Flemish congregationalists in Molochna as Frisians.[5]

The newcomers, most of whom settled in villages on the upper Iushanlee River, were led by elder Franz Görz and minister Heinrich Balzer. Elder Jacob Fast, leader of the Molochna Flemish congregation, and Bernhard Fast who succeeded him as elder in 1820, tried to establish good relations with the newcomers. In 1820 Bernhard Fast broke with tradition – and angered many members of his congregation – by being ordained by Görz rather than by the senior Flemish clergyman from Khortitsa, as was customary.[6] That same year Fast supported the creation of the Christian School Association, which in 1822 accomplished its aim of opening a secondary school in Ohrloff.[7] Mennonite villages already had primary schools to provide basic literacy and numeracy. However, while all Mennonites needed to be able to read the Bible, conservatives feared that any further education would encourage children to question traditional beliefs, which could only lead to unwanted innovations. Moreover, religious education was the prerogative of ministers, and the creation of a Christian school seemed to challenge this prerogative. To make matters worse, the Christian School Association imported from Prussia Tobias Voth, who was known to hold controversial pietistic religious views, as the Ohrloff school-master.[8]

In 1821, when representatives of the Russian Bible Association visited the Molochna region, Fast and Flemish elder Peter Wedel joined Görz in forming a Molochna chapter of the association, dedicated to the distribution of Bibles among Mennonites and in the surrounding communities. This again angered conservative Flemish congregationalists, who disapproved of any affiliation with non-Mennonite Christian organizations. They particularly distrusted the administrative system of the Bible association because it was not under congregational control and had officers with unfamiliar, and to a conservative way of thinking, militaristic titles such as president, director, and secretary.[9]

The final straw for the Flemish congregationalists came in 1822 when, against all tradition, Fast permitted a visiting non-Mennonite missionary, Johann Moritz, to address a prayer meeting and take communion in Ohrloff. Although Fast quickly acknowledged his mistake and apologized, conservative leaders could not be placated. In 1824 they formed a new congregation, the Large Flemish congregation, under the leadership of Altona minister Jacob Warkentin. Roughly three-quarters of the original Flemish congregation joined them.[10] There were now three official Mennonite congregations in the Molochna, the Frisian, the Flemish (which now became known as the Old Flemish), and the Large Flemish, along with the conservative Small Congregation (*Kleine Gemeinde*) that had no official status.

Building a Civil Society in Molochna

Johann Cornies first came to prominence in the Mennonite congregational world in 1817 when he was put in charge of the settlement committee that supervised the arrival of new Mennonite settlers.[11] It is unclear whether a formal administrative title accompanied this position. In correspondence of the Guardianship Committee Cornies is sometimes addressed as district mayor (*Oberschulz*), but this title properly belonged to the head of the Mennonite district, a post Cornies never held.[12] Cornies's biographer, David H. Epp, says rather vaguely that the congregation gave Cornies 'power of attorney.'[13] Whatever his correct title, Cornies was twenty-eight years of age when the Flemish congregation appointed him to this responsible position, a sign of the respect that his energy and talent had already garnered among Molochna Mennonites. Cornies was not only energetic and talented. He was also strong willed and opinionated, and it would not take long for him to become embroiled in religious controversy.

Because he supervised the founding of the new villages, and the newcomers were considered to be Frisians, many Flemish congregationalists associated Cornies with the views of Frisians. Always a strong believer in the value of education, Cornies was also a founding member of the controversial Christian School Association in 1820, and in 1822 he accepted the role of supervisor of the Bible association's distribution depot. As a result of his involvement in these endeavours, Cornies was at the heart of the religious disputes that troubled the Molochna settlement in the 1820s.

Contrary to conservative Flemish assumptions that Cornies was politically aligned with Görz and the Frisians, in truth he was a religious moderate and remained a member of the original Old Flemish congregation led by Bernhard Fast. Cornies had little patience with the pietistic beliefs of the Frisian leaders, referring to them dismissively in his private correspondence as the troublesome folk 'up there on the Iushanlee.'[14] He was particularly unhappy with Voth, the Ohrloff schoolmaster. At first Cornies strongly supported Voth, but he eventually concluded that the schoolmaster's involvement in religious affairs was interfering with the practical demands of teaching.[15] In 1829, under pressure from Cornies and the school association, Voth resigned, and he was replaced by the more moderate Old Flemish congregationalist Heinrich Heese. But Voth was influential among the Frisians, and the dispute between Voth and Cornies brought Cornies into conflict with the new villages, a number of which withdrew their support from the Bible association in reaction to Voth's departure from the school.[16] Thus, by 1829 Cornies was at odds with both the conservative Large Flemish congregation and the liberal Frisian congregation.

Most accounts of Cornies's life focus on his secular (and secularizing) activities, and there is little attempt in the historical literature to define his religious world view. Yet Cornies's correspondence is filled with obviously genuine Christian sentiments, as shown in this excerpt from a letter to a Prussian Mennonite acquaintance, where Cornies is bemoaning fatalistic Nogai attitudes towards the cholera epidemic of 1831:

[The Nogai] say [cholera] is a spirit with 3 heads and 500 assistants which was sent by God to remove the vicious people from this earth, and for this reason it is very sinful to apply methods against this divine judgement and whoever among them uses [such methods] dies as a Christian and has no part in the joy of the Muslim heaven ... I have had conversations with the priests themselves in an attempt to convince them that they should permit the lay people to use at least some medicines, but ... the Tatars whom I had taught as doctors to deal with those ill with cholera had to give up on the matter and could speak no further word about it, much less give medicine ...

Now they feel sorry for me that I have so little faith in God's help ... I do not see any doctor as God and no medicine as the Saviour, but I believe firmly that if God does not give his blessing to our daily bread, it will not nourish us, and [if he does not bless] the medicine, it will not heal anything.[17]

Here, however imprecisely, is the religious justification of most of Cornies's actions. Cornies believed in free will, assuming that God's approval of his actions is confirmed by their success. He balanced this confidence with an acceptance of even the most severe personal setbacks as reflective of God's will. After the great blizzard of 1825 Cornies wrote, 'There was great external damage due to snowstorms but the benefit for eternity [was] definitely much greater. My loss, not less than 30 thousand rubles[!], was, I believe and feel, permitted by the Lord for my salvation and therefore I praise and glorify His goodness which he shows to His children.'[18] This was not mere fatalism. Cornies invariably learned from such events and based his future plans on the practical lessons they offered.

Cornies's own understanding of what constituted a civil society probably began to develop from the time he took charge of settling new Mennonite immigrants in 1817. This task brought him into close association with Samuel Contenius, who was the head of the Guardianship Committee, and Contenius's cameralist administrative philosophy had a fundamental formative influence on Cornies. In 1820 the Guardianship Committee appointed Cornies to supervise the settlement on the Berda River of new immigrants arriving from Württemberg. The development of his administrative world view continued, and by the time he took a close interest in Nogai in 1825 he was already formulating his own blueprint for society.

Cornies's efforts to improve Nogai sheep have already been discussed in Chapter 3. However, the prize exhibit in his program to 'civilize' the Nogai was the model village of Akkerman. Cornies first mentioned the idea of creating a model village in 1825, and by 1832 the project had developed into a full-scale plan.[19] Built in 1835 on the Iushanlee River near Cornies's estate, Akkerman represented Cornies's vision of an ideal community. His instructions comprised thirty-five articles defining every aspect of the village's construction and administration. Houses were to be 'precisely' aligned along both sides of a single street, 'exactly' aligned with the house on the opposite side of the street, 'exactly' four *sazhens* (about 8.5 metres) from neighbouring houses, with a surrounding ditch 'exactly' two *arshins* (about 1.4 metres) wide and 1.5 arshins deep. Each yard was to be divided into corrals, gardens, threshing yards, and courtyards by ditches 'exactly' 1.75 arshins wide and 1.25 arshins deep, each with a single gate 'exactly' centred on the property. Each house was to have a front porch, and doors, shutters, and gables painted with oil paints. Each house was to be of 'good and solid but simple and inexpensive construction,' and so on.[20] Rules of conduct ranged from procedures for filing a complaint with the village elder to the injunction: 'It is strictly forbidden for anyone to enter or exit the yard from the street by stepping over the ditches, and everyone must enter and exit in the proper manner, through the gates, and children must not go into the ditches, so that the ditches will not become filled in.'[21]

Akkerman was an extension of the state's earlier policies towards Nogai, for it upheld the regulated, organized peasant village as a symbol of civility. It must be emphasized that the model village was not solely Cornies's project; it was strongly supported by the state. The cameralist policies that defined Russia's ambitions for its state peasants had been clearly laid out in 1797 in the laws governing their administration.[22] What distinguished Cornies was his success in applying such cameralist policies at the local level. Yet Cornies took them further. Cornies took the prescripts of cameralism, incorporated the practical lessons he learned in building Akkerman, combined them with his religious beliefs, and conceived a model for society that went well beyond the aspirations of the state. Akkerman was to replicate a Mennonite village, and taken to its furthest extreme, it also became Cornies's model for the future of Mennonite society.

The nuclear villages in New Russia were themselves a recent innovation in Mennonite society. When the Mennonites first arrived in New Russia in 1789 they intended to settle on dispersed farmsteads, but the threat of marauding Cossacks and Tatars forced them to build compact nuclear villages instead.[23] The uniformity of these villages was a reflection of Mennonite traditions, following 'logically from the community-minded tenets of Mennonite theology, from a mixture of bitter and prideful memories of a common martyr past, dating back to the Reformation, and from the obvious need for solidarity if the community was to survive as a small ethnic and religious minority in Russia.'[24]

The attempt to impose an ideal version of this outer, physical manifestation of Mennonite religious beliefs on Islamic Nogai provides a fascinating glimpse into Cornies's philosophy. Mennonite commitment to peaceful withdrawal from the secular world effectively precluded proselytization.[25] There are no records of Mennonite attempts to convert Nogai. Indeed, Cornies's regulations for Akkerman emphasized obedience to Islamic law. The implicit assumption governing planning of the model village, however, was that strict physical adherence to this outward manifestation of Cornies's idealized version of Mennonite society was the key to what Cornies elsewhere called the 'external prosperity' of the Nogai.[26] Nor can there be any doubt that, for Cornies, improving the economic condition of the Nogai was tantamount to improving their *moral* condition.

The Akkerman project can be interpreted as evidence that Cornies understood the Mennonite system of social organization as nothing more than an efficient vehicle for economic advancement, equally applicable to Islamic Nogai and Christian Mennonites. However, an examination of Cornies's other activities suggests that he more likely viewed the project as a reaffirmation of his belief in Mennonite society and even, perhaps, as an act of proselytization.

The Forestry Society

Akkerman was not Cornies's most far-reaching attempt at social engineering. The Guardianship Committee for Foreign Colonists's main vehicles for improving agriculture were its various husbandry societies, beginning with the Sheep Society, established in 1824, and followed by the Forestry Society (1830) and the Agricultural Society (1836). It was through the latter two organizations that Cornies would apply the lessons learned from his experiments on Nogai society to Mennonites.

The Forestry Society was a state agency, not a Mennonite one. Cornies was appointed its chairman for life by the Guardianship Committee, without any consultation with Mennonite district and village administrations. The Guardianship Committee justified the establishment of a distinct body (the Forestry Society) to do work that ought to have been supervised by existing Mennonite administrative bodies on the grounds that 'the extent of [the Molochna and Khortitsa settlements], which are still increasing regularly and currently encompass fifty-seven [villages], constantly keeps the district officials busy with affairs in respect to administration, settlement, collection of taxes, keeping of accounts, etc., and even with their best intentions, it becomes impossible for them to conduct the exact supervision that is required for success.'[27]

The creation of this new administrative body would lead to future discord, but at first Cornies's position was not cause for Mennonite discontent. The Forestry Society is often inaccurately conflated with its successor, the Agricultural Society. However, the Forestry Society's jurisdiction was much narrower than the later agricultural organization.[28] It was intended 'to impart advice and instruction to settlers inexperienced in the cultivation [of trees],' and its instructions placed special emphasis on giving 'these directions in a clear and well-meaning manner.'[29] Nevertheless, the instructions included the ominous injunction that farm owners 'were to be warned in advance, that those among them who are disobedient, and pay no attention to these suggestions, will eventually lose their farmsteads, which are then to be given over to other dependable young householders, who must commit themselves to fulfil what the government demands of them for their own advantage.'[30]

The Guardianship Committee gave the Forestry Society no independent means to enforce its orders, instead leaving it to issue directions itself to village assemblies which were then responsible for carrying them out. Because the village elders were de facto congregational appointees, in practice the Forestry Society was constrained to appealing to congregations to impose congregational discipline on those who ignored its recommendations. Consequently, Cornies's position did not impinge directly upon Mennonite traditions that forbade Mennonites from wielding secular authority over fellow Mennonites.

The Forestry Society was supposed to bring about the systematic cultivation of trees in the Molochna River Basin. Trees were understood by the Russian state – and indeed by all nineteenth-century European states – to be an essential element of an agricultural economy. Trees provided fuel for heating and cooking, construction materials for homes, outbuildings, implements, and furniture, windbreaks to prevent soil erosion, fruit, and, in the case of mulberry bushes, a basic element for silk production.[31]

The creation of the Forestry Society shows the unique outlook of the Guardianship Committee, which was distinguished from most Russian administrative organs by its flexibility and willingness to accept advice from local experts. In 1831 the committee sent a draft set of the Forestry Society Regulations to Cornies and asked for advice from him and the other members of the Molochna Forestry Society on its final formulation.[32] In the end, the regulations observed that each region had its own unique soils and climates, and the committee enjoined the Molochna Forestry Society to research broadly in afforestation literature, establish a library of relevant books, and develop programs appropriate to local conditions. This attention to regional conditions was an important element of the Guardianship Committee's success in administering Mennonite and other German colonists. Because the committee was regionally based, its members were aware of local conditions and able to take them into account. The administration of Orthodox state peasants was centralized in St Petersburg.

It is difficult to know whether the signal success of the Molochna Forestry Society should be credited to this remarkably enlightened Guardianship Committee policy or to Cornies's willingness to seize the reins when they were offered and place his own stamp firmly on the society's activities. Within a few years the society's library included a broad collection of books and periodicals on forestry in German and Russian,[33] and by 1847 circulars from the Ministry of State Domains in St Petersburg were referring to Cornies (a self-acknowledged neophyte at forestry in 1831) as an expert who had 'mastered steppe forestry through experimentation.'[34]

Cornies's Nogai projects had already shown that he possessed a clear vision of an orderly civil society. Echoing the approach to the Nogai that he first elucidated in 1825, Cornies established a model tree plantation at his Iushanlee estate in 1831. There he experimented with various species of trees and developed and refined specialized implements. The estate also served as his headquarters for overseeing the inspection of existing tree stocks in the Molochna region.[35] By the end of 1832 Cornies had developed a systematic and rigorous program for tree planting. This program combined the basic principles defined in society regulations with knowledge that Cornies had collected through reading and experimentation, along with his own preconceptions about the importance of order and uniformity.

The original society regulations specified that each village establish a tree plantation of a size equal to one-half desiatina per village household and that 'every householder is assigned the duty of laying out an orchard behind his house of such size as the local situation and the means of the householder permit.'[36] The Molochna Forestry Society confirmed the requirement that villages establish tree plantations and added the specification that each householder set aside one desiatina of his or her home plot for an orchard, and plant between ten and forty trees per year until the orchard area was completely planted.[37] The society supplied seeds and saplings and issued detailed instructions on topics such as soil preparation, appropriate distances between saplings, and care for the saplings.

There was nothing implicitly controversial in these instructions. Afforestation was among the obligations imposed on Mennonites by the charter they were issued in 1800, and Molochna Mennonites had enthusiastically supported the state's afforestation programs since first arriving in Russia. Their accomplishments in forestry were a source of community pride. Indeed, in their address to Alexander I when he passed through the settlement in 1825 they had even promised to redouble their efforts.[38] Although the creation of the Forestry Society marked more rigorous control over tree planting, its demands were not unusual or excessive. Uniformity in tree planting was fully in keeping with uniformity in housing and the layout of farmsteads, and with all the other community norms accepted by Mennonites. Consider, for example, the 1824 precedent of the Sheep Society. The state had supplied merino sheep, and rigorously defined a program for interbreeding them with native sheep. In 1823, describing the purpose of the proposed Sheep Society, Contenius produced detailed directions on interbreeding through five generations and instructed that 'local authorities must pay attention, not just to the entire herd, but to each and every individual generation of sheep.'[39] The sheep program, administered in the Molochna region by Cornies, met with no opposition and was quickly implemented. With the Sheep Society as precedent there was little reason to expect opposition to the Forestry Society. This was particularly true in view of the fact that by 1830 the religious disputes of the 1820s seemed to have died down, giving Cornies hope that an accommodation had been reached among Molochna Mennonite congregations.[40]

Unfortunately, just as Forestry Society activities were passing from planning to implementation the Great Drought of 1832–4 struck. Families frantically feeding their thatch roofs to starving livestock, understandably, had little time for orders to plant trees, and policies that need not have been controversial under normal circumstances soon provoked bitter disputes. As usual, for Mennonites the congregational system provided the medium for political debate.

The first indications of opposition to Cornies appeared immediately on the heels of the Great Drought. Some landowners ignored instructions from the Forestry Society, and to Cornies this smacked of 'a secret incitement to rebellion against [tree] planting.'[41] In one of the most serious examples of resistance, in January 1835 the mayor and deputy mayor of Blumstein experienced so much opposition to their attempts to enforce Forestry Society orders that they resigned.[42] Cornies's reaction to such opposition is instructive. Because the Forestry Society had no direct authority, he appealed to congregational officials for support. In an effort to win the cooperation of district chairman Johann Regier, Cornies invited him to attend the Forestry Society's meetings,[43] and in an 1836 letter to congregational officials Cornies wrote: 'If the unhappy dissension which has existed between the spiritual and worldly leaders from our first settlement here on the Molochna until now is to be set aside and ended, so that the community can be placed on an orderly, solid footing of order and morality and to provide a basis for its general well-being at present and for its most distant descendants, then it is necessary that every elder admonish and encourage his congregation, particularly in accordance with the basis of its confession of faith, so that the congregation in general and every member strive especially and sincerely to fulfil punctually all orders and regulations of the administration.'[44] Obviously, in 1836 congregational authority remained intact in the Molochna, for Cornies required congregational support to implement his programs. But equally obviously, Cornies was conscious of the conflict between congregational and civil authority and was increasingly insistent that civil authority prevail.

The Agricultural Society

The Great Drought was a turning point in the development of Cornies's world view. It forced him to reassess the Molochna Mennonite economy and brought him face to face with the fact that, given prevailing agricultural techniques and land allocation practices, Mennonites could not support themselves through a prolonged crisis. In the autumn of 1833 Cornies wrote to Aleksandr Fadeev, Chairman of the Guardianship Committee: 'This is a year of testing in many respects. Even though the total crop failure this year will set the settlers back for several years, we will also reconsider many things, deal with them and carry them out better, in order to prevent similar disasters in the future.'[45]

The next summer Fadeev proposed extending the authority of the Forestry Society to the entire Molochna economy. Cornies, confronted with both the knowledge of the previous year's economic disaster and the resulting strong resistance within the Mennonite community to the Forestry Society, advised against this.[46] Two years later, however, in February 1836, Cornies reminded Fadeev of his proposal, suggesting that the timing was now 'expedient' for such reorganization.[47] He assured Fadeev, somewhat disingenuously given ongoing opposition to the Forestry Society, that 'until now, the society has been able to take pleasure in the punctual compliance to its orders by the members of the community and hopes that the same will also occur in the future.' Nevertheless, Cornies went on to recommend: 'It would be very much to the purpose if His Excellency, the Chief Guardian [i.e., Inzov] were to be so kind as to release a communication to the combined local church conference, in which all ministers were emphatically admonished that, as possessors of 65 desiatinas of land, they must act as an example to the members of the community through their orderly industry in the plantations and are obligated to support the society in cases that occur by admonishing the community members to obey and follow the orders of the society punctually.'[48]

Cornies's growing impatience with resistance to reforms was rapidly leading him to break with the traditional division between secular and congregational authority in Mennonite society. In future years he would turn more and more to the state for support in his attempts to oblige Mennonites to deal systematically and effectively with the economic problems they faced.

The Guardianship Committee created the Agricultural Society in 1836. Its proper name, the Society for the Improvement of Agriculture and Trade, indicates the breadth of responsibilities it was expected to take on, while Cornies's appeal to Fadeev for support (quoted above) suggests the weight of authority he wanted it to carry. The new society, like the old, did not have its own enforcement mechanisms. It was still formally an advisory body, reliant upon the cooperation of district, village, and congregational authorities. However, the Agricultural Society was to be far more important and controversial than the Forestry Society. The Forestry Society's jurisdiction extended to a part of agricultural activity that was always secondary; tree plantations never occupied more than a tiny proportion of Mennonite land and labour. The Agricultural Society 'advised' on all the principal economic activities of Mennonites, and indeed, on the very activities that defined the Mennonite world view. As James Urry explains, 'Ownership of land, or at least access to it, lay at the core of Mennonite life. The ethos of religious community was symbolised in agrarian imagery.'[49]

With the establishment of the Agricultural Society, Cornies entered the most important phase of his campaign to transform Mennonite society. He focused his activities on three principal themes: (1) more efficient allocation of limited Mennonite resources, (2) more efficient exploitation of those resources, and (3) rural industrialization. These were explicitly economic goals, but it would be incorrect to assume that they were a product of a strictly secular world view. To Cornies, efficiency, prosperity, and morality were inextricably linked. He confidently believed that if the Agricultural Society 'steadfastly directed its own business and tended to the well-being of its brothers,' the end result could only be '*morality*, industry and love of orderliness ... upon which prosperity must follow.'[50]

Cornies still operated within the congregational system in 1836. Bernhard Fast, Peter Wedel, and other leading figures in the Old Flemish congregation remained his close allies, and he relied on their support to implement the policies of the Agricultural Society. However, it was Cornies and not the congregational elders who now provided leadership.

More efficient allocation of Mennonite resources was bound to be a controversial issue. As explained in Chapter 3, Mennonites had no control over the allocation of their surplus land, while the reserve land not yet allocated was primarily useful only as pasture. Thus, the society looked to reallocate existing farms more efficiently. Forestry Society regulations threatened that people who disobeyed society orders would be dispossessed of their land, and their farms would be given to young families willing to follow directives. On this basis, in at least one instance, Cornies apparently succeeded in convincing the district administration to evict a householder, seventy-year-old Cornelius Fast, from his farm.[51] Cornies justified the eviction on the grounds that 'Fast could not have maintained himself further on his farm, even without the [matter of] his not fulfilling the plantings, in that he is a man of almost 70 years without means.' A second important factor in the decision was that 'a good, industrious farmer came along,' willing to take over the farm and work it properly.[52] At the heart of this policy was Cornies's belief that the welfare of Mennonites as a community had to supersede the welfare of individuals. This policy grew out of his understanding that the supply of land was not limitless, so only by its efficient allocation and use could the prosperity of the whole community be maintained.

Individual and community rights had always balanced uneasily in Mennonite theology. Sixteenth- and seventeenth-century lessons of martyrdom had taught Mennonites the need to stand together, and in many of its manifestations Anabaptism is a communitarian theology. Mennonites had never shared a belief in community of goods with other Anabaptists, like the Hutterites, but the duty of the individual to the welfare of the community remained (and still remains) an important element of Mennonite belief. Although Cornies is often represented as an opponent of traditional Mennonite values, and indeed as the very symbol of secularizing trends in nineteenth-century Mennonite society, his policies clearly placed the welfare of the Mennonite community above the welfare of individuals.

Once the Agricultural Society was created, Cornies expanded his efforts to evict inferior farmers from their land and replace them with younger families that promised to abide by society policies. Farmers who failed to keep up the condition of their farms, whether as a result of alcoholism, marital problems, sloth, disease, or age, were pressured to turn over their land to younger families. These, it was expected, would be better able to meet the demands of Mennonite society as expressed by the Agricultural Society.[53] Cornies drafted contracts defining the duties of families taking over farmsteads and pressed congregational officials to insist that such families sign them. When the Guardianship Committee placed Cornies in charge of establishing the new villages of Waldheim and Gnadenfeld (1835) and Landskrone (1839), he used the opportunities to rigorously apply his new standards to the new villages, modelling village plans on those he had already conceived for Akkerman.[54]

Cornies's moral imperative that the limited supply of land be used efficiently was accompanied by a concerted effort to develop more efficient agricultural methods. As chairman of the Sheep Society in the 1820s, Cornies had learned the value of improving the quality of agricultural production. When he turned his attention to other branches of agriculture, he carefully experimented with improved crops, improved implements, and improved techniques. Better ploughs and harvesting machinery, more wells, and irrigation dams to flood hay fields all received his close attention. Two agricultural changes marked a crucial turning point in Molochna Mennonite agriculture: the introduction of a four-field cropping system and black fallow.

Traditional arable husbandry in New Russia employed a long-fallow system, with fields cropped for several consecutive years and then left fallow for several more. This minimized the intensive labour of breaking new ground. However, because the long cropping period exhausted the soil, fields had to be left fallow for extended periods. As population density increased, cropping periods lengthened, fallow periods shortened, and productivity on the increasingly exhausted soil inevitably dropped.

In January 1837 Cornies ordered all Mennonite villages to implement a four-field cropping system in combination with manuring.[55] At first Cornies had intended to use the fallow field to plant potatoes, but he soon ordered the use of black fallow instead.[56] Most Molochna farmers used to allow their fallow fields to reseed with native grasses by invasion, thus providing grazing for livestock while the land lay fallow. The disadvantage of this was that grasses used up soil nutrients, as well as moisture, and retarded soil recovery. The Agricultural Society ordered householders to prevent livestock from grazing fallow fields and to plough them regularly throughout the summer to prevent the growth of grass and weeds.[57] This permitted fallow fields to recover more quickly and thus made land use more efficient, although at the expense of far more labour.[58] As Cornies described it in 1839, 'Occupation with field cultivation now binds everyone to his house and his soil; there are few easy, comfortable days which occurred so frequently with sheep-raising, and it is literally fulfilled here that man must eat his bread by the sweat of his brow.'[59]

As a result of these new methods, output/seed ratios in the Mennonite settlement increased significantly – wheat ratios, for example, averaged 4.75:1 from 1828 to 1835 and 7.08:1 from 1836 to 1848 – but the truly dramatic increase in production came as a result of increased yields per desiatina.[60] The four-field system put a greater proportion of the arable land under crops, while black fallow resulted in increased retention of moisture in the soil so that more seed could be planted per desiatina. On one Münsterberg farm this resulted in an average annual increase in wheat output from 131 chetverts per desiatina in the period 1828 to 1835 to 309 chetverts per desiatina in 1836 to 1848 (see Figure 5.1). All this, combined with a steady increase in sown land after 1836, produced an almost fourfold increase in the average gross wheat output of Mennonites between 1835 and 1848 (see Table 5.1).

Among Cornies's many accomplishments, none was more important for his ability to steer the Molochna economy than his close attention to markets. Cornies read a wide range of European and Russian agricultural periodicals. His most important source for keeping abreast of markets, however, was the Moscow wool merchant T.S. Blüher.[61] Cornies met Blüher in Moscow in 1824 while en route to St Petersburg to buy breeding stock for his sheep farm. The two men developed a fast friendship and corresponded on a broad range of subjects, but wool markets were always at the forefront. Cornies shipped his wool directly to Blüher, bypassing the middlemen who bought up most wool produced in Ukraine. He frequently sent Blüher samples of various kinds of wool, asking the merchant to explore marketing possibilities. He also asked Blüher's advice on silk marketing.[62] As a result of such contacts, when international wool markets began to decline in the late 1830s Cornies was among the first to recognize the trend. This decline, coupled with the growing European demand for grain, was an important motivating factor in the increased attention Cornies and the Agricultural Society paid to arable husbandry in the late 1830s.

Figure 5.1   Average wheat harvest per desiatina on one Münsterberg farm, 1808–1861

Source: 'Vypiska iz pravil'noi khoziaistvennoi tetradi otsa I syna Menonistov Neiman v kolonii Munsterberge na Molochne, o poseve I urozhae khleba,' *PJBRMA*, n.d., file 1308. A five-year running average has been employed.

Arable husbandry used to be a marginal commercial proposition in the Molochna region because the lack of a local port meant that grain had to be hauled overland to distant markets. Grain's low ratio of value to weight and problems of spoilage discouraged commercial production. In 1836 the state opened a port at Berdiansk, just sixty-five kilometres east of Molochna. This transformed the regional economy, opening the way to explosive economic growth. Where once every commercially minded farmer who could afford it would invest in sheep, suddenly grain became an important option. Already in 1837 Cornies observed that 'a few landowners are even expressing the opinion that field cultivation would be more worthwhile than sheep breeding. The plough, which formerly belonged to the lower classes, is rising appreciably to become an honourable implement, as has long been desired.'[63]

Economic Transformation and Landlessness

Cornies's attention to markets allowed him to encourage the production of commercial crops appropriate to international market conditions. Besides wheat, the most important among such crops in Molochna

TABLE 5.1
Gross grain production (chetverts) in the Molochna Mennonite settlement, 1828–1848

	Wheat	All grain		Wheat	All grain
1828	8,630	43,105	1838	36,034	86,752
1829	8,889	56,373	1839	18,389	53,240
1830	5,546	26,835	1840	29,320	80,818
1831	13,999	71,446	1841	23,943	77,636
1832	9,922	38,079	1842	24,992	76,178
1833	297	719	1843	33,149	103,171
1834	6,300	18,033	1844	48,629	122,811
1835	14,409	61,236	1845	21,719	41,928
1836	15,427	54,268	1846	67,583	179,415
1837	31,924	103,210	1847	84,804	180,381
			1848	20,486	39,908

Source: 'Verzeichnis über Aussaat und Ernte im Molotschner Mennonisten-Bezirk in den Jahren 1828 bis 1848,' n.d., *PJBRMA*, file 1308.

was flax. Introduced in 1836, flax seed became a major export crop, with over 95,000 chetverts shipped through Berdiansk in 1860 alone.[64] The seed, used to produce linseed oil, was a valuable export crop, but at least as important from Cornies's perspective was the use of flax straw for local linen production. 'Many hands lie idle [here], especially during the winter,' he wrote in 1836, 'and they could find other useful activity if the needed flax were cultivated, spun and manufactured into linen in the district.'[65] It is here that the community-based motives of Cornies's actions are most evident, for he was very concerned with providing employment for the growing numbers of landless Mennonites.

The rise of landlessness in Molochna has already been discussed in Chapter 3. By 1839, 47 per cent of Mennonites were landless, and by 1847 this figure had risen to 53 per cent.[66] Hidden in this statistic is an important change in the character of landless families. They had always been younger than landed families, for it was only natural that newly married couples lived with parents until they were able to establish their own household. Cornies himself numbered among the landless in 1813 when he, his wife, and their infant son still lived with Johann Sr.[67] However, while in 1847 landless families were still younger – and consequently smaller – than landed families, the gap between the two was narrowing. The average landless family in 1813 had 3.64 members, compared with 5.59 members in landed families.[68] By 1834 landless families on average had 4.12 members, while by 1847 they averaged

4.48 members.[69] Although they remained smaller than landed families, the trend was clear – landlessness was increasingly becoming a hereditary condition, as young families grew old without being able to acquire land.

Cornies was keenly aware of this development, and much of his activity in his last ten years was directed towards resolving the problems it posed for Mennonite society. The ideal solution, allotting land to the landless, was not an option. There was simply not enough viable land to be had, excepting of course the surplus land over which Mennonites had no direct control. Cornies had long been concerned that the rapid growth of the Mennonite population and the lack of available land for them in the Molochna basin might soon make out-migration necessary. As early as 1826 he cautioned his Prussian friend David Epp about future prospects for Mennonite immigration to New Russia from the Vistula: 'Time is rushing by, as on the wings of the eagle, [to a period] when Russia will no longer want fine immigrants, because from the interior of the Empire, where the overcrowded population is causing a great dearth of land, thousands are streaming to the southern and eastern steppe. Where ten or fifteen years ago one saw nothing but sky and steppe on a journey of several days, now the most poverty-stricken villages of 1,000 to 2,000 souls have been established.'[70]

In 1831 the Guardianship Committee proposed offering to landless Molochna Mennonite families forty-desiatina allotments southwest of the Molochna on the Tashenak River. Cornies advised that few were likely to accept such an offer when they could still 'receive better land for settlement, and get more land as well' in Molochna.[71] However, with the rapid occupation of surplus land by new villages in the late 1830s and 1840s Cornies became an enthusiastic supporter of the newly proposed Judenplan project, which in the 1850s established mixed villages of Mennonites and Jewish peasants on crown land outside the original Mennonite allotment.[72] The Russian state intended the project to provide Mennonite farmers as models to educate Jewish settlers who were inexperienced with agriculture. For Cornies the Judenplan offered a desperately needed outlet for the landless.

The drought of 1848 temporarily increased the urgency of land shortages in Molochna, and that year ninety-nine families left Molochna and purchased land in the Kiev and Volyniia guberniias.[73] The Agricultural Society vehemently protested such out-migration, complaining to the Guardianship Committee that unscrupulous Kievan and Volynian officials were luring Mennonites away with unfulfillable promises of cheap and plentiful land. Such Mennonites, the society complained, would soon return to Molochna, impoverished by this 'swindle,' and the Mennonite settlement would be forced to support them.[74] What became of these migrants is unclear. Apparently by the end of 1849 they had indeed returned to Molochna, but there is no further reference to them in statistical reports or Agricultural Society correspondence.

The alternative to out-migration was to provide gainful employment for the landless. This Cornies did with remarkable success. In 1836 he proposed the creation of a craftsmen's village alongside the village of Halbstadt.[75] To be called Neuhalbstadt, the new village was to be occupied by landless craftsmen and their families, of which there were 251 in the Molochna Mennonite settlement at that time.[76] Cornies wrote, 'These craftsmen, who live scattered around the District, only produce work that has been [specially] ordered, because most of them do not have sufficient means to purchase materials and to keep a supply of the products of their craft on hand to be sold.'[77] The idea of a craftsmen's village in Molochna was not original to Cornies. Prischib had been a craftsmen's village since its establishment by Germans in 1806.[78] In the context of the landlessness problem, however, Neuhalbstadt provides evidence of Cornies's views. As usual, he perceived the benefits of the project in a mixture of moral and economic terms: 'The goals of achieving the best development of the spiritual and physical strengths of those practising a craft, so that they can raise their own prosperity, and of the delivery of better and cheaper craft production for use by inhabitants who practise field cultivation, would be met if a portion of the craftsmen's class were settled together in one location, from which more industry and zeal to perfect their products would develop and the products themselves would be sold more easily. The agriculturalists, moreover, would be able to fill their needs better and more cheaply in one location from one or another.'[79]

Halbstadt was the obvious site for the new village. Its central location at the confluence of the Tokmak and Molochna rivers had already made it the home of a number of brandy, beer, and vinegar manufactures, several trading companies, the Klassen Cloth Factory, and the Gebietsamt offices. Residents of Halbstadt were less than enamoured with the idea, however, for the plan called for granting each craftsman a three-desiatina allotment to be carved from Halbstadt's reserve land. Halbstadters were to be compensated with land from the settlement's nearby communal sheep farm, but this exchange of flood-plain land for high-steppe pasture was a poor deal at best. Nevertheless, against their objections Cornies pushed the proposal through, and in 1841 ι craftsmen's village was established.[80] Neuhalbstadt would eventually gro\ to be the commercial and industrial centre of the Molochna basin, a position it retains to the present day.

Cornies also concerned himself with provisions for the much larger group of landless families dependent on cottage industry. In 1838 he received the Guardianship Committee's endorsement for a plan to set aside in every Molochna Mennonite village between four and six 300-square-sazhen (approximately 1.4 hectares or 3.5 acres) lots for 'poor young families of the artisan class,' whom he characterized as 'non-self-supporting [*nesostoiatel'nyi*].'[81] The holders of such small allotments were known as *Anwohner* – cottagers – and while there had always been Anwohner in the Mennonite settlement, the creation of distinct Anwohner districts now became a distinguishing characteristic of Molochna Mennonite villages. Such districts are frequently cited as evidence of the inequity of land allocation in Molochna Mennonite society. It is important, therefore, to note that they grew out of a deliberate effort to improve the lot of landless renters.[82]

A third project aimed at alleviating demographic pressures was the creation of the euphemistically named 'shared farms.' The Mennonite charter forbade subdivision of the standard sixty-five-desiatina farm allotments. This provision had important benefits for Mennonites because it forced them to maintain viably sized farms. During the landlessness crisis of the 1860s one of the most important concessions made to the landless was the creation of half-farms and quarter-farms, which sacrificed the economic benefits of maintaining full-farms in order to provide subsistence allotments to the landless (see Chapter 7). This concession is often cited as a victory of the landless over 'greedy' landowners, while in fact Cornies had been quietly circumventing the law against subdivisions since the mid-1840s.[83]

The first evidence of half-farms arose in 1845 when, in a widely distributed account of Mennonite administrative practices, Cornies described the rules governing 'those cases when two families want to share one farm.'[84] Such an arrangement was intended to permit two young families, who otherwise could not have afforded their own farm, to purchase one jointly. To circumvent the law against divided farms, one family was to be formally designated as owner, and the other as 'helper.' In practice, each family was to have its 'own equal share of the land, work its share independently, and be sole recipient of the produce of its share.'[85] Although the two families were officially supposed

ne and live as one household, the regulations
'lies are too large and cannot live in one house,
second house.'[86] There was even a provision for
their halves separately.[87] This shared-farm arrange-
oreshadowed the creation of half-allotments by some twenty
a common practice in the Molochna region by 1848, when
of 1,170 landed families (17 per cent) lived on shared farms.[88]

The document in which shared farms are described is a lengthy description of Molochna Mennonite administrative practices that Cornies compiled for Kiselev, the minister of state domains. It is a comprehensive blueprint of Cornies's vision of civil society in its fully mature form.[89] Kiselev was in charge of reforming the state peasantry, and his projects would eventually have an important influence on the Emancipation Edict that freed Russia's serfs in 1861. He and his senior aides were profoundly impressed with the order and industry of the Molochna Mennonite community and looked to it as a model for what might be accomplished in Russian state peasant villages throughout the empire. The description that Cornies provided Kiselev was thus widely distributed to the ministry's guberniia-level offices as a primer on efficient social management.[90] Cornies is often viewed as an agent of tsarist policy in Molochna, but this instance shows a second side of this relationship, in which Cornies acted as an agent for the dissemination of Mennonite policy throughout the Russian administrative system.

Of the thirty-five page, five-part, 126-point description, only slightly over three pages and twenty-six points addressed the duties and authority of district and village elders. The remaining thirty-two pages and 100 points described the duties, authority, and accomplishments of the Agricultural Society. Duties ascribed to district and village elders were limited to taxation and the enforcement of local laws. These conformed closely to the law of 1797 that defined the role of elders in all state peasant villages. Notably lacking in the description was any mention of congregational authority.

The document identified the Agricultural Society's role as reaching into every corner of Molochna life. It claimed that the society's authority, once based on the cooperation of congregational officials, was now explicitly based on the authority of the Guardianship Committee. The latter, the description implied, enforced the society's orders by decree. Although village elders were still responsible for enacting society orders, the document characterized elders as little more than liaisons between the society and individual householders. Even their election by the village was supposedly vetted by the society 'in consultation with representatives of the state, and in cases where they are unfit, the villages are forced to choose new ones.'[91]

The all-encompassing administrative system that Cornies envisaged in his report evidences the influence of contemporary European economic theory on his thought. The language of such theory had been creeping into Cornies's writing for several years, most notably in his increasing tendency to categorize members of Mennonite society into 'classes.' In the 1845 document phrases plucked from such theories jump from the page. For example, the Agricultural Society, Cornies claimed, ensured 'that [labourers] receive good pay, but only in measure to the work they perform,' and it prevented the development of 'any monopolies whatsoever.'[92] Yet Cornies was a Mennonite, too, and at the heart of his world view remained the good of the community. He charged the society with providing loans (at interest) to young, industrious Mennonites to permit them to establish themselves in trades, and with finding them allotments and helping them build homes.[93] 'In every case' the society was to 'ensure that the rich and strong do not oppress the poor and weak.'[94] As for settling families on new land, 'the objective,' Cornies wrote, was the profitable development of both the community and 'the very land that [the new settlers] till.'[95]

It is perhaps appropriate to pause briefly and reflect on the extent of Cornies's ambitions for Molochna Mennonite society as reflected in the 1845 document. This largely self-educated Mennonite farmer, living in an isolated river basin on the southern frontier of the Russian Empire, was fomenting a revolution – indeed, an industrial revolution. The complex integrated economy Cornies envisaged, with large and small industrial enterprises, cottage industry, commercial agriculture, primary and secondary schools, credit institutions, and a social safety net, was progressive by any standard. It was fully two generations ahead of any semblance of comparable developments in the rest of Russia. This was far more than a simple echo of contemporary economic thought in Western Europe, for the concern with public welfare, and particularly provisions to evict slipshod farmers from their land and give it to young, poor, but industrious families, represented a uniquely Mennonite contribution to liberal economics.

Not surprisingly, it was also a vision that was deeply distressing to conservative Mennonite congregationalists. By 1845 Cornies had altogether abandoned any pretence at enforcing his actions through congregational channels. In 1836 he had appealed to congregational officials for cooperation; now he issued decrees backed when necessary by the ready support of the Guardianship Committee. Always a decisive and domineering figure, Cornies had become authoritarian and even dictatorial in his actions, provoking bitter opposition from leaders of conservative congregations.[96]

The Waning of Congregational Authority

As in the 1820s, opposition to Cornies in the late 1830s and 1840s was led by Jacob Warkentin, elder of the Large Flemish congregation. The confrontation began in 1837, centring around the election of the district mayor.[97] The position had been filled since 1833 by Schönsee householder Johann Regier, a member of the Large Flemish congregation but also a supporter of the Forestry and Agricultural societies. By all accounts Regier was an able administrator, but unfortunately he was also an alcoholic whose sometimes disreputable conduct attracted the opprobrium of his congregation. Faced with the embarrassing possibility that the Large Flemish congregation might have to ban the district mayor, in 1837 Warkentin asked the elders of the other Molochna Mennonite congregations to support him in an appeal to the Guardianship Committee to have Regier and his senior assistant Toews removed from their positions. However, the other elders refused to do this.

As Regier's second term of office came to an end in 1838, Warkentin appealed directly to I.N. Inzov, head of the Guardianship Committee, to prohibit Regier from standing for re-election. Meanwhile, Cornies was busy behind the scenes, writing to Fadeev that, although 'the current Mayor Regier and his senior assistant Toews act and work to the community's best advantage in cooperation with the society purely out of conscientious conviction ... [Warkentin] wishes to put an end to this fruitful situation and is already making incognito preparations.'[98] Cornies appealed to Fadeev to 'as far as it is possible for you, through the Guardianship Committee ... make efforts so that Mayor Regier and his assistant Toews keep their positions for another term.'[99] Cornies prevailed, and in 1838 Regier was re-elected.

Two aspects of Warkentin's efforts to unseat Regier deserve attention. First is the political implications of the dispute. Regier was a political hot potato for Warkentin, for he was at once a member of Warkentin's congregation, the senior elected figure in the congregational administrative system, and a figure trusted by the Agricultural Society. The latter was rapidly consolidating its position as the most powerful civil agency in Molochna. If Regier were banned, Warkentin's weight in the balance of political power in the Molochna Mennonite settlement would undoubtedly decline.

The second aspect is Warkentin's willingness to appeal to the Guardianship Committee for support. Warkentin is commonly identified as the champion of congregational over civil authority in Molochna.[100] There is no reason to doubt that he, like Cornies, was motivated by a real concern for the welfare of Molochna Mennonite society. However, Warkentin's readiness to appeal to Inzov to obtain the dismissal of a mayor elected by the community at large and supported by the other elders shows that the era of independent congregational rule was effectively over.

At the next election, in 1841, Warkentin again opposed Regier. This time he tried new tactics, and put forward the widely respected Tiege resident Peter Toews as an alternative candidate.[101] The combination of Regier's alcoholism and Cornies's increasingly authoritarian manner helped Toews win the election handily. Cornies claimed that there had been voting irregularities and, supported by district secretary David Braun, he refused to accept the results. With the backing of Cornies and the Agricultural Society, Regier continued to act as mayor. Warkentin travelled to Odessa and protested to Evgenii von Hahn, newly appointed deputy to the aging Inzov. Von Hahn, now the real seat of power in the Guardianship Committee, ordered a new election. To Cornies's dismay, Regier then died and Toews won an easy victory.[102]

Warkentin and his supporters believed themselves to be the clear victors in this struggle for political supremacy in the Molochna Mennonite settlement. Rumours even circulated that Cornies was to be exiled to Siberia.[103] However, their jubilation did not last long. Without the cooperation of the district administration, Cornies's programs could not function, and the state was too reliant on Cornies to allow his political authority in Molochna to collapse. Later in 1841, during an inspection tour of Molochna, von Hahn confronted Warkentin, and accused him of meddling in official matters – and dismissed him from his position as congregational elder. At the same time, following the principle of divide and conquer, Hahn dissolved the Large Flemish congregation, and in its place created three smaller congregations.[104] This was a shocking violation of congregational autonomy, for Warkentin was in no sense a civil official, nor was the Large Flemish congregation a civil organization. Von Hahn's decision marked a stunning political victory for Cornies, and he would rule supreme in the Molochna basin

Figure 5.2   Livestock and agricultural implements in the Molochna Mennonite settlement, 1835

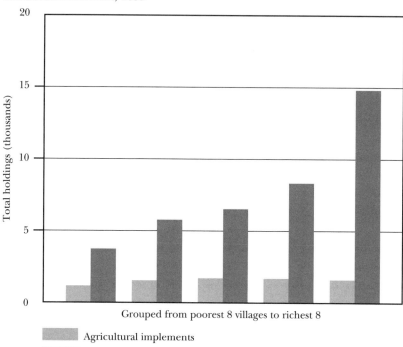

Source: 'S vedomostiami mestnykh kolonistakh nachal'stv o sostoianiia koloniia za 1835 god,' *RGIA, f.* 383, *op.* 29, *d.* 634.

until his death in 1848 (even extending his authority to the Khortitsa Mennonite settlement when he was made head of the Khortitsa Agricultural Society in 1846).[105]

Cornies's Economic Accomplishments

The dispute between Cornies and Warkentin should not be interpreted as a social conflict, for the leaders of the Large Flemish congregation were prosperous landowners whose concerns revolved around Cornies's intrusion into their right to run their own farms. This was, at heart, a political matter. Although significant economic differentiation had oc-

TABLE 5.2
Average annual trade at fairs and total exports from the port of Berdiansk, 1836–1860
(in paper rubles)

Trade at fairs		Berdiansk exports	
1843–45	263,283	1836	112,085
1846–50	549,748	1838	2,971,426
1851–55	1,252,326	1840	4,282,221
1856–60	1,392,249	1860	6,423,812

Sources: *Tavricheskaia Gubernskaia Vedomosti* 26 (1 July 1841); Khanatskii, ed., *Pamiatnaia Knizhka Tavricheskoi gubernii*, 434; *PJBRMA*, file 1858; 'Otchety tavricheskikh gubernatorov,' 1843–61, *f.* 1281, *op.* 4–6, and *f.* 1283, *op.* 1 (for 1854).

curred in Molochna by the mid-1830s (see Figure 5.2), there is no evidence to suggest that there was social conflict before the landless crisis of the 1860s, despite the fact that landlessness was growing rapidly already in the 1830s. This is a testament to the astonishing growth that the Molochna economy experienced between 1836 and 1855 and to Cornies's efforts to provide a role in this growth for all elements in Molochna Mennonite society.

Cornies's programs took advantage of the opening of the port at Berdiansk to usher in an era of rapid economic growth. The port, located sixty-five kilometres east of Molochna, provided an outlet for the region's produce, and for the first time made arable husbandry economically significant. Table 5.2 shows the remarkable pace at which exports from the port, and the closely related trade at fairs, grew. It should be noted that these data, and related statistics on industrial enterprises provided below (see Table 5.5), are two of the few extant sets of sources that show that the villages of the non-Mennonite Germans shared with the Mennonites in the economic boom.

The explosive growth of trade at fairs is the clearest evidence of economic growth in Molochna, and it requires more careful analysis. Fairs played a vital role in the Russian economy for a variety of reasons. First, because Russian peasants could not travel outside of their own districts, merchants had to come to them. At the same time, before 1863 townsmen were not permitted to operate shops in peasant villages, and fairs helped circumvent this rule. Finally, following changes to tariff laws in 1822, trade at fairs was duty free, making prices particularly attractive.[106]

Fairs served both the wholesale and retail sectors of the Russian market, trading in raw wool and cotton, textiles, manufactured goods, imported luxury goods, and livestock. They did not trade in grain, which grain brokers bought directly.[107]

In her study of the Nizhnii Novgorod fair, Anne Lincoln Fitzpatrick breaks the fairs into three categories. Small fairs, with a turnover of less than 10,000 rubles, catered to local needs and supplied peasants with manufactured goods and a market for the goods they themselves manufactured. Medium fairs, with a turnover of between 10,000 and 100,000 rubles, served as regional markets and included wholesale as well as retail trade. Large fairs, with a turnover in excess of 100,000 rubles, were mainly dedicated to wholesale trade and served as the principal agency for the wholesale market in the empire.[108] There were 5,653 fairs in Russia in 1860. Of these, 2 per cent had a trade volume of more than 100,000 rubles, while 85 per cent had a trade volume of less than 10,000 rubles.[109] Twenty-one of the largest fairs had a total turnover in excess of one million rubles each, led by the great Nizhnii Novgorod fair where trade exceeded sixty-one million rubles.[110]

In Ukraine there was a circuit of eleven very large fairs, each with a gross trade in excess of one million silver rubles. Largest of all, and second largest in the empire after Nizhnii Novgorod, was the January fair in Kharkov where turnover could top twenty-five million rubles.[111] Cotton was the staple of Ukrainian trade, with the exception of the June fair in Kharkov where wool took first place. Horses, cattle, and sheep also played a prominent role.[112]

In Melitopol and Berdiansk uezds there were twenty-nine fairs in 1843, the first year for which statistics are available. By 1846 the number had grown to fifty, and by 1860 it would reach sixty. The volume of trade at fairs in Melitopol and Berdiansk uezds hit its prereform peak in 1860 at over 1.9 million rubles. On average, fairs were large in these two uezds, and six of the fairs in 1860 fell into the over-100,000-ruble class, placing them among the largest 102 fairs in the entire empire that year.

The 9 May Bolshoi Tokmak fair was the great event of the year in Molochna. Mennonites and other German-speaking settlers, Orthodox state peasants, and Nogai mingled with Jewish hatmakers from Kherson, Tatar wine merchants from the Crimea, wool buyers from Kharkov, and hide buyers from Moscow. Booths selling wine, vodka, tobacco, perfume, makeup, glassware, and pottery did brisk business, while weary shoppers could stop to take in a performance by travelling comedy

TABLE 5.3
Goods imported through Berdiansk, 1860

Commodity	Quantity (puds[a])	Value (paper rubles)
Lumber, shovels, and miscellaneous tools	29,250	3,000
Furniture	927	2,700
Textiles	5,806	14,221
Oranges	135,977 pieces	6,000
Fruit and berries	3,207	8,242
Miscellaneous foodstuffs	2,879	4,863
Coffee	2,952	20,520
Peppercorn	316	1,550
Wine	58	120
Olive oil	481	3,600
Cigars	2	120
Tobacco	117	543
Matches	50	450
Coal and charcoal	4,920	19,500
Coinage		35,889
Soap	57	300
Miscellaneous	818	1,360
Total		122,978

[a] Unless otherwise specified.
Source: 'Verzeichnis der aus dem Hafen am Berdiansk im Jahre 1860, aus- und eingeführten,' 16 Feb. 1861, *PJBRMA*, file 1877, 2–7.

troupes. Wool took centre-stage, and each year fifty or more wool buyers arrived to obtain a share of local kurdiuch wool production. In 1845 the wool merchants took away over 80,000 puds of wool, and this was by no means atypical.[113]

The growth of fairs in the region is clearly linked to the opening of the port at Berdiansk. Tables 5.3 and 5.4 list the type and quantity of goods that passed through Berdiansk in 1860. Small quantities of luxury goods and a very small amount of cotton were imported through Berdiansk, but the amounts could hardly have satisfied demand; fairs filled this role. Turning to exports, it is apparent that a very significant proportion of grain production in the region was leaving through Berdiansk. The 608,730 chetverts exported through the port in 1860 probably represented the total of grain exported from the region that year.

Only 13,342 puds of wool were exported, which was less than a fifth of what was traded at Bolshoi Tokmak. The high average price of this

TABLE 5.4
Goods exported through Berdiansk, 1860

Commodity	Quantity		Value (paper rubles)
Butter	5,876	puds	32,318
Wheat	473,370	chetverts	4,800,330
Rye	10,043	chetverts	50,200
Barley	12,073	chetverts	42,254
Oats	5,888	chetverts	18,864
Mustard	12,306	chetverts	50,024
Flaxseed	95,050	chetverts	940,075
Flour	11,330	puds	16,800
Wool	13,342	puds	113,394
Rag wool	1,795	puds	2,300
Silk cocoons	55	puds	2,200
Cowhide	9,695	puds	190,778
Horse hair	112	puds	1,100
Tallow	35,877	puds	161,408
Bast	17,967	pieces	1,769
Total			6,423,814

Source: 'Verzeichnis der aus dem Hafen am Berdiansk im Jahre 1860, aus- und eingeführten,' 16 Feb. 1861, *PJBRMA*, file 1877, 2–7.

wool (8.5 rubles per pud) shows that it was merino wool, and given the over 1.1 million merino sheep in Melitopol and Berdiansk in 1860 the amount exported through Berdiansk cannot have represented much more than 15 per cent of production.[114] Thus, of the region's two primary agricultural products, wool passed northward through the fair system while grain went south through Berdiansk. As for other commercial goods, no doubt they came into the region through both Berdiansk and the fairs, and in fact the fairs must have acted as a distribution network for the goods that arrived in Berdiansk from abroad.

Fairs were not the only suppliers of manufactured goods to Melitopol and Berdiansk, for yet another sign of the growth of the local economy was the rapid growth of local industry. It is impossible to accurately track such growth, for the statistics are spotty, and the total volume of industrial production shown in Table 5.5 is probably seriously underreported. Such industry was primarily a phenomenon of the colonies, but not solely – the largest single industrial enterprise in the region was the tallow factory in Bolshoi Tokmak, while other Orthodox state peasant villages had tallow factories, brick and tile factories, tanneries, and so on.[115]

TABLE 5.5
Industrial production in Melitpol and Berdiansk uezds, 1843–1861

Year	No. of enterprises	Sales volume (paper rubles)	Year	No. of enterprises	Sales volume (paper rubles)
1843	14	92,638	1853	129	340,921
1844	48	118,497	1854	146	336,050
1845	218	158,622	1855	80	513,442
1846	147	195,255	1856	110	411,259
1847	311	369,314	1857	157	541,564
1848	364	460,041	1858	206	876,776
1849	200	228,249	1859	202	538,639
1850	232	235,197	1860	240	787,293
1851	237	271,240	1861	308	471,927
1852	214	274,806			

Sources: 'Otchety tavricheskikh gubernatorov,' 1843–61, *f.* 1281, *op.* 4–6; *f.* 1283, *op.* 1 (for 1854).

The clearest evidence that the fruits of this economic growth were enjoyed by landless as well as landed Mennonites comes from records of investment in sheep sharecropping. By the 1840s the philanthropic program that Cornies had established in the 1820s to encourage landed Mennonites to contribute to Nogai economic development (see Chapter 3) had also come to serve as an avenue for agricultural investment for landless Mennonites.

The serious slump in international wool markets, which bottomed out in 1847, in combination with a rise in grain prices, saw Mennonite landowners gradually shift from raising sheep to growing grain. As Table 5.6 shows, between 1835 and 1847 Mennonites increased the amount of their arable land by 55 per cent, while at the same time reducing their cattle and sheep holdings. Only the number of horses, needed as draft animals, stayed roughly constant.

The workings of the sharecropping system in the mid-1840s are detailed in two lists describing 188 contracts concluded between 1843 and 1847.[116] Ninety-three Mennonites took part, providing 10,279 sheep to Nogai. Just six contractors, including Cornies, supplied over one-third of the sheep, the remaining eighty-seven providing an average of just seventy-seven sheep each. As for the Nogai, no single sharecropper engaged in more than one contract, and no contract exceeded 120 sheep.

Farm inventories from 1847 are available for twenty-seven of the forty-four Molochna Mennonite villages, providing an economic profile of

TABLE 5.6
Land sown and livestock per Mennonite household, 1835 and 1847

	1835	1847
Per fullholder	(974 fullholders)[a]	(621 fullholders)[b]
Desiatinas sown	12.36	19.17
Horses	6.19	5.97
Cattle	7.93	5.88
Sheep	115.00	91.00

Sources: 'Tabellen. Über den Zustand der Molotschner Mennonisten Gemeinde in Zahlen im Jahre, 1835,' 1837, *PJBRMA*, file 1138, 1ob-37ob. This document provides only the number of chetverts of grain and other crops sown. The number of desiatinas sown has been calculated using figures from 'Verzeichnis des Molotschner Mennonisten Gebietsamtes über die Aussaat des Sommergetreides im Jahre 1857,' and 'Über die Winterssaat in der Kolonie des Molotschner Kolonisten Gebiet,' 1858, *GAOO*, *f*. 6, *o*. 4, *d*. 18086; 'Svedomostiami o blagosostoianii Molochanskago kolonistskago i menonistskago okruga,' 1847, *GAOO*, *f*. 6, *op*. 2, *d*. 10080.

[a] Includes complete data from all 42 villages.
[b] Includes data from only 27 villages.

thirty of the ninety-three Mennonite sharecropping contractors.[117] As Table 5.7 shows, on average contractors kept substantially more livestock of all kinds than other Mennonites, but sowed less land. As market forces pushed them to put more land under crops, they needed either to sell their livestock or to move it to different land. Sharecropping contracts furnished a way to keep part of the income from displaced sheep without incurring any direct costs for land rental, fodder, or labour at a time when investment was better directed into grain growing.

Most of these contractors continued to keep unusually large herds of sheep on their own land in addition to those they contracted to Nogai, but there were interesting exceptions. Peter Regier of Altona, who kept just seventy-eight sheep on his own land, contracted 852 sheep to Nogai, using sharecropping as a significant form of agricultural investment. In contrast, a few contractors were unusually poor, such as the brothers Heinrich and Gerhard Wiens, who shared a full holding in Blumenort and had only seven sheep between them apart from the 194 they contracted to Nogai.

A second important group of Mennonite sharecropping contractors can also be identified – the landless. Twenty contractors who lived in one or another of the twenty-seven villages for which full-holding inven-

TABLE 5.7
Land sown (in desiatinas) and livestock held by sharecropping contractors and other
Mennonites, 1847

	Sharecroppers	All Mennonites
Horses	6.16	5.97
Cattle	6.39	5.88
Sheep	111.81	91.00
Land sown	17.31	19.17

Source: 'S mesiachnymi vedemostiami o blagosostoianii kolonii berdianskago okruga
za Ianvar 1847,' *GAOO, f.* 6, *op.* 2, d. 10063.

tories exist were without land. Unfortunately, little more is known of
their circumstances. Peter Loewen of Altona was the single largest con-
tractor, supplying 978 sheep to Nogai sharecroppers. Even at deflated
1840s prices this must have represented an investment of over 20,000
rubles, making the landless Loewen a rich man. By comparison, the
other nineteen landless contractors averaged just sixty-five sheep under
contract, much fewer than most landowning contractors. The depres-
sion in wool prices permitted landless Mennonites to buy merino sheep
at deflated prices from landowners who were putting pasture lands to
the plough, while sharecropping permitted them to keep the sheep
without incurring direct costs beyond the original purchase price. Thus,
the sharecropping program, which began as a way to improve Nogai
sheep, became a way for landless Mennonites to invest in the agricultural economy.

Sharecropping made economic sense for Nogai, too. Because of the
five-fold gap between the price of merino and kurdiuch wool, Nogai
could make more money raising merinos with prices at their lowest
than they ever did raising kurdiuch sheep. One indication of the profit-
ability of raising merinos comes from a program introduced by Cornies
in 1843 to sell sheep to Nogai on credit.[118] A record of thirty sales
survives. Credit was interest free, averaging 277 rubles per purchase,
although whether in silver or paper rubles is unclear. The number of
sheep involved is also unclear. Nogai had no difficulty repaying the
loans, repaying all but twenty-five rubles within four years, and this
suggests that raising merino sheep was profitable.

Such positive evidence must be balanced by contrary indications of
problems for both Nogai sharecroppers and their Mennonite suppliers.
Cornies had always been less optimistic about Nogai progress in his
private correspondence than in official reports. As early as 1836 he

wrote to Fadeev: 'These people lack patience and perseverance, and ... knowledge of the methods of raising [merino] sheep.'[119] Some Mennonites apparently lacked 'patience and perseverance' with Nogai as well, for that same year Cornies asked the inspector of colonies to caution Mennonites not to 'mock or ridicule Nogai about their inability to accomplish what they have started.'[120] Cornies showed dissatisfaction with the terms of sharecropping contracts in 1837, proposing a revised twenty-two-clause contract that, if implemented, would have rigorously redefined Nogai obligations. It foresaw monthly inspections, and stipulated when sheep would be moved to pasture, when they would be mated, and when they would receive fodder. It also defined procedures for removing weak sheep from the flock and sharply redefined the treatment of sick sheep by specifying that 'regardless of whether the sheep are well or sick, [the sharecropper] may not slaughter them under any circumstances, and if he does he will have to pay for them, and beyond that will face punishment in court.'[121]

Nogai also had concerns, and in 1839 a group from Akkerman petitioned their 'esteemed benefactor' Cornies for help.[122] They described how their merinos had been afflicted since 1837 with a disease that reduced wool production and prevented successful breeding so that in 1837 and 1838 they had realized no profits. Because drought had destroyed fodder crops in 1839, they anticipated even greater losses. Therefore, they said, 'many of our people want to breed only [kurdiuch] sheep,' and they asked Cornies to intervene to help cure the disease and end their losses.[123]

In the 1840s Mennonite contractors began subtly manipulating the terms of contracts to their own advantage. They gradually increased the proportion of lambs included in contracts from 10 per cent to over 19 per cent, thus reducing wool production and, because ewes could not safely be bred before the age of 2.5 years, also reducing reproductive potential. At the same time they began supplying some male lambs in place of female lambs. A herd of fifty ewes – the standard contract number – needed only one ram, so for Nogai the ten to fifteen male lambs that began to be included in some contracts were superfluous, while the corresponding reduction in female lambs reduced the reproductive potential of the herd. Moreover, male sheep were less valuable wool producers because, while they produced more total wool, they produced less clothing wool, which brought a far higher price on international markets.[124]

The same conditions that made sharecropping a preserve of wealthy Nogai in the 1830s still applied in the 1840s, with important implications for the increase in differentiation in Nogai society. At root the problem was as much demographic as economic. There are no precise demographic data on Nogai in the 1840s, but already by 1837, when their population was 32,058 persons, Nogai holdings of 'good land' amounted to just 17.8 desiatinas per male soul. Located on the Azov Lowlands, it was the most arid land in the entire Molochna region, and it could not support their population on the basis of a pastoralist economy. If Nogai were to survive, let alone prosper, it was imperative that they turn to more intensive agricultural methods.

The transformation to arable husbandry would require employing the best Nogai land, located on the Molochna and Iushanlee river flood plains, for cropping. However, commercial sheep breeding demanded the use of precisely the same land as pasturage. This land had been designated as common pasture, and Nogai sharecroppers, with their disproportionately large flocks of merino sheep, were monopolizing it. Orthodox peasants in Molochna, faced with the same problem, decreased their commons, increased their arable land, and instituted land repartition on the arable portion. This ensured adequate access to land for the poor (see Chapter 6).[125] Poor Nogai may have tried similar tactics, for in November 1846 their Mennonite suppliers began requiring Nogai sharecroppers to provide written guarantees from village elders confirming their right to use the commons for contracted sheep. This implies that this right was in dispute.[126] That Nogai sharecroppers successfully obtained such guarantees suggests that, unlike Orthodox state peasants, the Nogai poor were unsuccessful in asserting their claims. Consequently, they could not follow the example of Orthodox peasants and turn to growing grain, for the land best suited to arable husbandry was also that best suited as pasture. The structure of Nogai–Mennonite economic relations thus encouraged a sheep monoculture at just the time when market demand dictated a transition to arable husbandry. Meanwhile, the introduction of pasture guarantees to Nogai sharecroppers was an important symbolic juncture in Nogai history, for it formally abrogated the customary nomadic right of common access to pasture.

Despite the negative potential of the sharecropping system, before 1848 it prompted no crisis in Nogai society. To that date the Nogai seemed to be sharing in Molochna's economic boom, dragged along on the coat tails of Mennonite prosperity. However, the crisis was looming, and as Chapter 7 will show, when it came its implications were as important for Mennonites as they were for Nogai.

Conclusion

When Johann Cornies died in 1848, few Mennonites mourned his passing. In the end he was more feared than loved, and as historian Harvey L. Dyck points out, only eight of the forty-four extant village histories that were written on the orders of the state shortly after Cornies's death have anything positive to say about him.[127] Yet it must be noted that these histories were written in the midst of the most severe drought since the Great Drought of 1832–4, a situation hardly likely to weigh in Cornies's favour in the minds of those who compiled the histories.[128] The fact that *this* drought, unlike the Great Drought, caused barely a stir in the Molochna Mennonite economy is a greater testament to Cornies's accomplishments than any tributes that village officials might have written. Heeding the lessons of 1832–4, Cornies had overseen a massive increase in agricultural and industrial productivity while consciously providing a place for landed and landless alike in this new, industrializing world.

The religious turmoil that accompanied the transformation has perhaps received more attention from historians than it warrants. It must be remembered that to a significant degree these were political disputes. There is little, if any, evidence that they were accompanied by social turmoil. Before condemning Cornies's actions, it is important to ask what other options there were. In the 1860s and 1870s Mennonites bought land and established daughter colonies, but this solution grew out of a real social crisis in a society that was already exploiting its other economic options to their fullest. Until internal solutions had been exhausted, it is hardly reasonable to expect that the Mennonite settlement would have taken more radical steps. Nor was land redistribution an attractive alternative, even setting aside the fact that it was forbidden by the Mennonite charter and certain to be even more vehemently opposed by conservative landowners than were Cornies's reforms. That option was tried by Orthodox state peasants, and the results (described in Chapter 6) served no one's interests.

The transformation of the Molochna Mennonite economy has important implications for the larger story of Russia's nineteenth-century economic development. Although Mennonites had special privileges,

their success was less a consequence of these privileges than of entre-
preneurship and leadership. The state adopted the Molochna Mennonite settlement as a shining example for all Russian state peasants and
actively encouraged similar reforms in other places. However, the state
could not replicate either Mennonite attitudes or Cornies's leadership,
even among neighbouring peoples in the Molochna basin, and it would
be several decades before the rest of Russia would follow the Molochna
Mennonites down the road towards the industrial revolution. The
Molochna Mennonite story is an object lesson about what could be
accomplished even within the institutional and political constraints of
prereform Russia.

CHAPTER SIX

The Path Taken by the Orthodox State Peasants: Land Repartition

The combination of isolation from markets and state authority and a sparsely populated, arid, grassland environment led Orthodox state peasants in the Molochna River Basin to adopt a subsistence economy that emphasized animal husbandry and gardening. The opening of the port at Berdiansk and the creation of the Ministry of State Domains altered their existence fundamentally. Ironically, the new ministry, which was intended to improve the conditions of the peasantry by easing land shortages in interior guberniias and ending administrative inefficiencies, increased state interference in the affairs of Molochna state peasants, while threatening to reduce their land allotments. At the same time, continued growth of both human and livestock populations placed strains on pasture lands that soon demanded a reckoning. Orthodox peasants once again proved their ability to adapt, turning to arable husbandry and exploiting newly accessible grain markets, while introducing land repartition to resolve the inequalities in land distribution that had become increasingly troublesome as their population grew.

The decision to impose land repartitioning is a puzzling one. Until the 1830s economic development in Molochna state peasant villages, with its emphasis on pastoralism, had in many ways parallelled that in Mennonite villages. In the 1830s Orthodox peasants stood at a fork in their developmental road. One way led to industrialization, modernization, and perhaps prosperity. The other led to communal land repartition, backward agricultural practices, and economic stagnation. They chose the latter, inviting state intervention to institute radical land reforms. Although practical administrative factors played an important role in this parting of ways with the colonists, in the final analysis it was a decision that can only be credited to a native peasant perception that justice was rooted in access to land.

Reform from Above: The Ministry of State Domains

The creation of the Ministry of State Domains, and the new ministry's decision to reclassify Tavria guberniia as land-poor and reduce peasant allotment sizes, has already been described in Chapter 4. However, the ministry, and its forerunner, the Department of State Domains of the Ministry of Internal Affairs, also explored a number of other ways to improve peasant agriculture. Plans to establish tree plantations, encourage potato cultivation, and establish agricultural schools were all in the works in the 1830s and 1840s.

Colonist efforts to establish tree plantations dated from the first decade of the nineteenth century, but Orthodox state peasants had never shown any interest in following their example. In 1834 the Ministry of Internal Affairs entertained a proposal for the 'development of forests in sandy steppe places in the uezds of Tavria guberniia.'[1] The author of the report wrote that the peasants' failure to establish tree plantations to that date was 'partly because [they], for various reasons, [have] no desire to develop tree plantations, partly because the steppe is considered unsuited to growing trees.'[2] The proposal suggested establishing a forestry institute, purchasing necessary tools, hiring workers, establishing a system of supervision and inspection, and constructing depots for storing seed.[3] It proposed a budget of 5,000 paper rubles to meet initial costs, and a further 25,000 rubles for ongoing expenses.

The proposal suggested growing, first and foremost, grape vines, and then a mixture of birch, aspen, black poplar, acacia, and various ivies. Curiously, the author took no notice whatsoever of the colonist tree plantations already established in the region. By 1835 colonists had more than 400,000 trees on their plantations and private plots, none of which were birch, aspen, black poplar, or ivy. Of the varieties proposed for planting on peasant plantations, only grape vines and acacia were already under cultivation in the region. This blindness to the example of the colonists would not be quickly remedied. Even Petr Köppen at the Ministry of State Domains in St Petersburg, who of all people should have been aware of the colonists' accomplishments, took no note. When he wrote to Kiselev in 1839 in support of the forestry program he pointed to successful tree-planting experiments on the shores of the Caspian Sea, in Astrakhan, and in the Caucasus, but said not a word of the colonists.[4] The first mention of using colonist expertise came only in 1843, when von Rosen, head of the Ministry of State Domains in Tavria guberniia, wrote to Kiselev proposing that the ministry establish a forestry school under the supervision of Johann Cornies, who already operated an agricultural school for state peasants. Von Rosen believed that the school (which was opened in 1844) would overcome the main obstacle to establishing tree plantations, namely, peasant ignorance.[5]

Despite all of the state's efforts to encourage Orthodox peasants to grow trees, there is little evidence of success. In 1849, fifteen years after the initial proposal, there was only one Orthodox state peasant tree plantation in all of Melitpol and Berdiansk uezds, and it was located in the village of Terpeniia, which the Orthodox peasants had inherited from the recently exiled Doukhobors.[6] Although Cornies established a forestry school, it trained only a handful of peasants – in 1854 it had just four students.[7] Clearly, Orthodox peasants had little interest in growing trees. This is perhaps understandable, as they had spent the previous half-century learning to live without them.

The Ministry of State Domains' efforts to encourage potato cultivation met with only slightly greater success. Motivated by an empire-wide crop failure in 1839, Nicholas I in 1840 initiated a program to diversify food crops by promoting potato cultivation throughout Russia.[8] From the very outset, the Ministry of State Domains assumed that because of the 'hot climate and dry soils' in New Russia the program would have little application there.[9] Fragmentary data from 1856 and 1858 show that state peasants in Melitopol and Berdiansk uezds planted only four to five thousand chetverts of potatoes per year, about one-twentieth of a chetvert per capita.[10] Undoubtedly, the main reason for the peasants' reluctance to grow potatoes was that the state's assessment of the unsuitability of the climate in New Russia was entirely accurate; potatoes thrive on low temperatures, short days, and very wet soils.[11] The lack of rainfall in Melitopol and Berdiansk meant that, without irrigation, potatoes could not be grown effectively as a field crop. Like cabbage, potatoes could have been grown in watered gardens, but as the temperatures along the coast of the Sea of Azov climbed into the high twenties (Celsius) during the midsummer months, potato growth would have become stunted. Although colonists achieved some success growing potatoes – in 1858, for example, they planted 9,639 chetverts, or roughly one-half chetvert per capita, and reaped a harvest of 51,065 chetverts[12] – cabbages, which needed less water than potatoes and thrived in hot temperatures, were already a fixture in peasant diets. It is little wonder that Orthodox state peasants in Molochna all but ignored the potato program that brought large increases in production in northern and central Russia.

A third state program to improve agriculture was the creation of agricultural schools for state peasants. Seven such schools were founded in Russia in 1842, with the nearest to Molochna in Ekaterinoslav. Because the Ekaterinoslav school enrolled a total of only 150 students at any one time, and allocated just fifty-five positions to students from Tavria guberniia, it had little effect on state peasant farming practices.[13] Closer to home, in 1839 the Ministry of State Domains enlisted Cornies to train state peasants on his estate at Iushanlee.[14] Once again the number of students was very small. In 1846 the first graduating class had just eight students: three Nogai boys, two Ukrainian boys, and three Ukrainian girls. The five Ukrainian graduates immediately protested plans to send them back to their home villages, asking instead to be settled together in Terpeniia where they could remain close to Cornies's Iushanlee estate.[15] Again, the potential impact of these students on Orthodox peasant agriculture was minimal.

Reforms from Below: Negotiating with the State

While Orthodox state peasants showed little interest in state-initiated reform plans, like the Mennonites they were willing to turn to the state for support in implementing their own reforms. The 1833 request of the villages of Berestova, Nikolaevka, and Popovka to have the state repartition their land is described briefly in Chapter 4, but a more thorough examination of the problems that these villages faced, and the solutions that they and the state proposed, reveals how the Orthodox peasants negotiated reform with the state.

The request for repartition came in the midst of a long and complex dispute between the three villages. Trouble had begun in 1812 when a land surveyor named Razumov, who was assigned to map the district, misplaced the border between Berestova, Nikolaevka, and the Nogai land grant, giving the Nogai 10,000 desiatinas of land that ought to have belonged to the Orthodox state peasants. At least this was the Orthodox peasants' claim, but unfortunately for them, in 1815 their original 1803 land grant, the 1812 map, and their petitions protesting the mistake, burned in a fire at the land surveyor's office in Simferopol.[16] New petitions eventually earned their case a hearing by the Senate in St Petersburg, where in 1824 it was ruled that although the two villages were indeed short of allotment land – their formal allotment amounted to less than ten desiatinas per male soul – free access to vast supplies of open steppe more than compensated them, so that they 'cannot be regarded as land-poor.'[17]

The state's typically ill-informed belief that arid steppe land was adequate compensation for a lack of good bottom land left the Berestova and Nikolaevka villagers with a serious land shortage. They renewed their petitions, provoking a new survey of the district in 1831. The surveyor, one Golenkin, increased the Berestova allotment by giving the village 6,000 desiatinas of land belonging to the neighbouring village of Popovka. Predictably, Popovka responded with its own petitions, prompting another survey in 1832. This time a different surveyor, Odintsov by name, confirmed the new border between Berestova and Popovka – but granted 1,900 desiatinas of Berestova land to Nikolaevka. More petitions followed, and in 1833 a third surveyor, Kuznetsov, muddled things further by giving Popovka 6,000 desiatinas of Berestova land as compensation for the land lost by Popovka in 1831. This left Berestova, the original petitioner, with *less* land than it had at the start! To make matters worse, the land Kuznetsov awarded to Popovka was not the same unoccupied land that Popovka had been forced to give up in the first place, but instead contained several khutors, two windmills, an orchard, and a number of vegetable gardens. Berestova now appealed to the district court and successfully won back its land. But when the Popovka villagers vacated in the summer of 1834 they took with them all the standing grain and hay and stripped the khutors of everything movable. The Berestova village elders petitioned Governor General Vorontsov, protesting that 'Berestova obshchina has been left without grain and without hay, and if this depredation [*nasiliia*], instigated by the land surveyor, continues further, then the village of Berestova, which now has only the most insignificant quantity of land, as a result of its utter impoverishment will not be in a position to pay its taxes.'[18]

To resolve the problem Berestova proposed that the state consolidate the landholdings of seven villages – Berestova, Nikolaevka, Andreevka, Popovka, Chernigovka, Novogrigor'evka, and Petropavlovka – into one district, add 'as much Nogai land as possible' to their combined landholdings, and redistribute the land proportionately on the basis of male souls.[19] Almost four years later, in March 1837, the Ministry of Internal Affairs ordered Vorontsov to institute precisely this solution, and ceded the seven villages 10,000 desiatinas of Nogai land to supplement their holdings.[20]

After 1837 the Berestova case disappears from extant records, and to follow the process of repartition further it is necessary to turn to a different example. But first there are a number of elements of the Berestova case that beg further comment. To begin with, this is a particularly clear example of the state's lack of understanding of environmental conditions in Molochna. The Ministry of Internal Affairs continued to understand land as simply area, equating high steppe with river bottom, and consequently it failed to resolve what was, after all, a fairly straightforward issue of land shortages. It is also noteworthy that the state made no distinction between the landholdings of different villages. Surveyors glibly shuffled land from village to village without any indication that the village obshchinas or their individual residents had any tenure rights. From the state's perspective, peasants had a right to a minimum amount of land but not to any specific piece of land.

The peasants themselves obviously had a different point of view. They regarded both their village's land as a whole and the mills and khutors of individual villagers to be real property. They apparently understood such property rights to be based on their payment of taxes, for when the Berestova obshchina appealed to Vorontsov its final argument was that if its problems were not resolved it would not be able to pay its taxes. This threat is often repeated in other peasant petitions relating to land claims; it seems likely, therefore, that peasants knew from experience that it was effective.[21]

It is important, too, to emphasize that the peasants lacked a sense of common interest extending beyond the borders of their own villages. Popovka village's seizure of Berestova grain, occurring as it did on the heels of the Great Drought, might perhaps be credited to desperation, but even so it bespoke a complete disregard for people who, after all, lived just a few kilometres down the road. The limited horizons of Ukrainian and Russian peasants is not a new discovery, but it is striking how starkly it contrasts with Mennonite reactions to the drought. Beyond the rights of individual villagers, individual villages, and individual congregations, Mennonites possessed a sense of the common good and organized famine relief efforts to serve their whole community. Lest this be thought of as a uniquely Mennonite characteristic, foreign to Slavic peasants, it is worth recalling, too, the unity of the Doukhobor community in the face of exile.

Their lack of mechanisms to self-administer intervillage disputes left Orthodox state peasants dependent on the state to resolve the increasingly pressing problems of overcrowding and land shortages. The state's solutions are revealed in its plans to repartition the land of the largest village in Molochna, Bolshoi Tokmak.

The Bolshoi Tokmak repartition is exceptionally well documented, and it provides a unique look into conditions in one Orthodox state peasant village in Molochna. An examination of the Bolshoi Tokmak repartition reveals that the lack of corporate identity among villages was echoed within individual villages, as well. Rich peasants and poor ones, traders and artisans, were deeply divided over the basic issue of land rights. In resolving their differences they resorted to the old standby of the Russian and Ukrainian peasantry – land repartition – turning away from the path of development that they had shared until then with their colonist neighbours and following a road that would soon lead to economic stagnation.

Bolshoi Tokmak, established in 1783 on a rich stretch of bottomland on the Tokmak River, was in the 1830s the largest settlement in the Molochna River Basin by a substantial margin. Although formally designated as just another agricultural village, in 1844 it had fifteen windmills, two watermills, three oil presses, a large tallow factory, a candle-making factory, and a brick and tile factory. Its approximately 6,700 residents included nine blacksmiths, twenty-six shoemakers (six of them German colonists), five hatmakers, sixteen weavers, sixteen tailors (six of them Jews), seventeen millers, two butchers, fifteen potters, nine tanners, two carriage-makers (both German colonists), one watchmaker (German), and six coopers. A further 126 families were engaged part-time in one or another of these trades as an adjunct to farming.[22]

In practice Bolshoi Tokmak was no longer just one village, but consisted of a large central settlement – Bolshoi Tokmak itself – and seven satellite settlements. The satellites had originally been founded as khutors, but had evolved into villages in their own right. About a third of the population migrated from the central village to the khutors each spring, returning to Bolshoi Tokmak at the end of the agricultural season. It was this third that controlled most of the wealth of Bolshoi Tokmak. One khutor-dweller rented 1,000 desiatinas of land from a nearby estate-owner, while many others rented smaller amounts from various sources. On average the wealthy peasants owned three times as much livestock as the families who did not own land in the khutors.

Alongside the rich peasants there was also a group of poor peasants. According to Wilhelm Bernhard Bauman, the agronomist assigned by the Ministry of State Domains in 1844 to administer the Bolshoi Tokmak repartition, many peasants had only a 'hand's-breadth' of land under crops, and even had they held more land, their lack of draft animals meant they could not have farmed it.[23]

Poor peasants lacked draft animals because the rich were monopolizing the common pastures. Unlike the Mennonite villages, which stinted their commons, the Orthodox state peasants left their commons completely unregulated. Rich peasants kept large herds of livestock on their khutors during the winter, feeding them fodder. They then released their livestock onto the commons as soon as the snow receded.[24] This was a formula for disaster. The earliest stages of growth are critical for pasture plants, for it is then that their roots spread and gain the capacity to store food.[25] Overgrazing at this vital stage kills plants, and 'in such cases, less palatable or wholly unpalatable plants commonly take their place and thrive because livestock avoid them.'[26] In Bolshoi Tokmak the consequence of such overgrazing was the creation of a near-barren stretch of land extending a kilometre around the village.[27]

Under such conditions, cottage industry and agricultural wage labour became increasingly important for poor peasants. The transition to arable husbandry after the 1830s (described below) sharply increased the number of seasonal jobs in the region, and rich peasants in the Orthodox villages were themselves significant employers of poor peasants. Bauman records a curious system of wage fixing in which Orthodox state peasant obshchinas met annually to set a high daily wage rate for workers from outside of their obshchina. There was no fixed wage rate for members of the obshchina, but because wages for outsiders were inordinately high, employers were encouraged to hire obshchina members first. Rich peasants, Bauman reports, were thus forced to support the poor.[28]

Agricultural labour was the single most important source of wage labour in Molochna. Its relative significance is shown by the way that wages fluctuated sharply in accordance with the agricultural season, peaking at as high as 1.25 rubles per day in midsummer – a man with a horse or two oxen could earn twice that much – and falling to half that in the winter months.[29] Records from Cornies's estate at Iushanlee give some indication of the nature of labour opportunities in the region. Cornies typically employed between fifteen and twenty full-time workers, usually under contract for either six months or a year. Half of these were shepherds whom he hired from state peasant villages in Melitopol, Berdiansk, and various places in Ekaterinoslav guberniia.[30] The shepherds apparently came as members of artels, for each year a large group of them would come from a single village, all hired on the same day and for the same term. A few of Cornies's employees were labourers, and unlike the shepherds, they brought their families with them to

Iushanlee. Although the labourers were also under temporary contracts, two of them, Demid Fatsenko and Ilia Odinets, worked at Cornies's estate continuously throughout the five-year period 1846–50 for which records are available. Cornies also usually had three or four foreign (German) employees working as supervisors or specialists. Almost all of the contract workers were men, the exceptions being Helena Fietz, a German maid who came to Iushanlee via St Petersburg in 1848, and Olga Roshchvei from Bolshoi Tokmak, who came to Iushanlee with her family in 1846 under a one-year contract as a labourer.

Cornies also employed a significant number of temporary workers, particularly in peak agricultural seasons. In 1847 he paid for a total of 12,011 days of work from temporary workers.[31] Of this, 57 per cent (6,794 days) came in August and September, during the harvest and the second shearing season, and a further 17 per cent (2,043 days) came in April and May, during planting and the first shearing season. Unlike with contract workers, some 29 per cent (3,486 days) of the temporary workers were women. There is no indication where these temporary workers came from, but clearly there was an available labour force in the region. Otherwise the wage control system described by Bauman would not have been necessary. The female half of the temporary workforce must have been local, for migrant labourers were almost exclusively men. With the spread of repartition in the 1840s and 1850s the local supply of labour would have declined as once-land-poor peasants received allotments. Migrant workers from the overpopulated industrial regions were a fixture on the steppe by midcentury, and the artels Cornies hired are proof of their presence in Molochna, so no doubt they filled some of the temporary positions as well. Nogai, who continued to practise extensive forms of agriculture, also had surplus labour to offer, but oddly, although Nogai had frequently worked for Cornies as labourers in the 1820s, they seldom appeared on his paybooks in the 1840s.

As noted in Chapter 5, industry was primarily a feature of Molochna towns and colonies, but it was not solely a colonist phenomenon. The largest single industrial enterprise in the Molochna region was the tallow factory in Bolshoi Tokmak, which averaged gross annual sales in excess of 100,000 rubles in the late 1850s. A substantial part of the 35,877 puds of tallow exported from Berdiansk in 1860 must have come from this factory. Bolshoi Tokmak also had a large candle-making factory, as well as a brick and tile factory, and there were smaller brick and tile factories in several other Orthodox state peasant villages. Just who owned these enterprises is impossible to say, except for the tallow factory in Bolshoi Tokmak, which belonged to a Russian merchant by the name of Litiachin.[32] More important than ownership is the fact that these factories provided wages to Orthodox state peasants, although the extent of such industrial wage labour in the region can only be guessed at. Most enterprises were very small and probably only employed the families who owned and ran them from their homes. Likely, the large estates employed more agricultural workers than the nascent industries employed industrial workers.

Before looking in more detail at the repartition of Bolshoi Tokmak it must be re-emphasized how closely Orthodox state peasant economic development parallelled colonist development to the end of the 1830s. Under conditions of hereditary tenure a significant group of landowners – about half of the Mennonites and a third of the Orthodox peasants – controlled most of the land and wealth, basing their success on sheep breeding. A small group of craftsmen – about 11 per cent of Bolshoi Tokmak families and 8 per cent of Mennonite families – were providing goods and services to the booming economy. Finally, a large group from both communities were either landless or land-poor and worked as labourers or supported themselves by cottage industry. It also must be noted that these colonist and Orthodox peasant economies were, to a significant degree, intermixed; colonist estates and industries employed Orthodox peasants, while the Bolshoi Tokmak fair served as a wholesale clearing house for colonists as well as Orthodox peasants. Nevertheless, while landless colonists and land-poor Orthodox peasants worked alongside one another as employees of wealthy Mennonites, there is no record of colonists working for wealthy Orthodox peasants.

These parallel developments suggest that in the late 1830s the possibility existed for Orthodox state peasants in Bolshoi Tokmak to continue along the same path of industrialization and prosperity that Mennonites would follow. But they did not. In 1836 the Bolshoi Tokmak obshchina petitioned the Ministry of Internal Affairs to impose a land repartition, explaining the request on the grounds that the village's 'wealthy householders have acquired the very best and largest quantity of the land, and the poor are victimized.'[33] This sharp break with previous practice demands explanation.

Part of the answer lies in the fact that the Orthodox poor were not entirely landless. Although many of them only had a 'hand's-breadth' of land, every household shared full rights to the commons, while the state distributed additional land after each census to households that were land-short. Obviously the exhaustion of land reserves was an important impetus to demanding a redistribution of the existing supply, but as important was the fact that the poor, as landholders, shared a full vote in the village assembly. Landless Mennonites had no vote. The Orthodox peasant decision to repartition was not unanimous – the rich 'opposed it with all their strength, which caused disputes, fights, and not infrequently, ruinous lawsuits.'[34] But the land-poor held a majority in the village assembly, and they imposed their will.

While voting rights explain how the Orthodox poor could force repartition, there is more to the story than this. There is no indication that the Mennonite landless ever expressed any desire for repartition, even if they had possessed the ability to force it. Clearly, there was also a different understanding in the two communities of what constituted equitable land distribution.

Orthodox state peasant support for land repartition should not be interpreted as the product of an inherent peasant opposition to wealth. After all, until shortages arose no one complained that some were wealthier than others. Peasants believed that everyone was ultimately entitled to *enough* land, to a subsistence minimum. When there ceased to be enough surplus land to ensure this minimum, the poor demanded a larger share of existing supplies.

This Orthodox peasant attitude towards land had some important similarities to the state's attitude. To both, land was first and foremost a public resource and not real property. But there was an important distinction. While the peasants were prepared to repartition the arable land, they viewed home plots, khutors, windmills, and so on, as real property. There was no indication that poor peasants ever proposed dispossessing the rich of such things. The state was prepared to reassign land regardless of the fixed assets that stood upon it.

One final point about this process must be made. Just as the land dispute between the villages of Berestova, Nikolaevka, and Popovka had to be resolved by state intervention, the internal land dispute in Bolshoi Tokmak also demanded that the state intervene. Internal administrative mechanisms were evidently too weak to deal with such a controversial issue. In this context it is vital to note how important the creation of the Ministry of State Domains was. The Berestova case began in 1812 and was still not fully resolved in 1837. In contrast, the state domains ministry moved much more quickly in dealing with Bolshoi Tokmak, resurveying the region and formulating a plan for the repartition within

TABLE 6.1
Villages and male souls in Bolshoi Tokmak volost, 1844

Villages, grouped by obshchina	Male souls	Good land (desiatinas)	Poor land (desiatinas)
Bolshoi Tokmak	2,279	22,629	4,971
Nizhnii Karakulak	160	1,589	33
Sladkaia Balka, Il'chenko, and Verkhnii Karakulak	353	3,505	1,365
Ocherstvovata	262	2,601	56
Ospushkova and Skelivatova	290	2,879	202
Total	3,344	33,203	6,627

Source: Bauman, 'Zusammenstellung,' *PJBRMA, 1291.*

eight years of the first request. The state's renewed will to take direct charge of its peasants through the ministry provided poor Orthodox peasants with a lever against the rich, just as it provided a lever for local administrators against the Doukhobors. Once again, the similarity between Orthodox and Mennonite experiences is apparent. At almost exactly the same time that poor Orthodox peasants were turning to the Ministry of State Domains to resolve their internal problems, Cornies and Warkentin were lobbying the Guardianship Committee for support against one another. As with Mennonites, the willingness of the Orthodox peasants to use ministry authority to impose repartition does not indicate that the peasants were prepared to cede full control of their affairs to the state.

Proof of this peasant insistence upon maintaining control of their own affairs comes from the Bolshoi Tokmak repartition itself. In 1843 the Ministry of State Domains decided to use the Bolshoi Tokmak request for repartition as an opportunity to implement its newly conceived 'Project for the correct economic distribution of land in state peasant villages in the southern guberniias.'[35] After first sending a survey team to accurately map the area, in 1844 the state sent Bauman to inspect existing agricultural systems and recommend changes. Although Bauman's report is not extant, much of its content can be inferred from correspondence it generated, while essays he later wrote confirm and expand on the correspondence.[36]

In 1844 Bolshoi Tokmak volost consisted of eight villages divided into five obshchinas (see Table 6.1). They were populated by 3,344

TABLE 6.2
Land sown (desiatinas) per male soul in Berdiansk and Melitopol uezds, 1841–1861

Year	Land sown	Year	Land sown
1841	2.91	1852	3.65
1842	–	1853	3.90
1843	2.67	1854	3.75
1844	–	1855	5.25
1845	2.15	1856	2.37
1846	2.00	1857	3.12
1847	2.57	1858	4.69
1848	4.32	1859	3.89
1849	3.42	1860	4.61
1850	3.52	1861	3.50
1851	3.31		
Average			3.45

Sources: 'Otchety tavricheskikh gubernatorov,' 1843–61, *f.* 1281, *op.* 4–6; *f.* 1283, *op.* 1 (for 1854).

male peasants and possessed 33,203 desiatinas of good land, an average of 9.93 desiatinas per male soul. Bauman found that almost half of this land – an average of four desiatinas per male soul – was used as commons and occupied all of the area closest to the villages. Meanwhile, some peasants lived as much as six versts from their grain fields. There is no indication of how much land was employed as arable, but a long-fallow system was in place, and if the peasants employed one-third desiatina per male soul for their dwellings and gardens (as did peasants in Orekhov volost to their immediate north), then they were left with 5.6 desiatinas per male soul for arable.[37] The fifteen-year rotation (described in Chapter 3) would have left a third of this, slightly less than two desiatinas per male soul, available for sowing in any given year. But as Table 6.2 shows, the peasants had well over two desiatinas per male soul under crops by the mid-1840s. With this much land sown, peasants in Bolshoi Tokmak volost could no longer have maintained the old pattern of cropping for five years and fallowing for ten. Such a rotation would have permitted only one-third of the arable land under crops at any one time. The combination of increased population and increased cropping had set in motion a process that by the 1880s would see the cropping period throughout New Russia climb to between six and nine years and the fallow period drop to two to three years.[38] Bauman recorded that in some places in Bolshoi Tokmak the fallow period had already dropped to as little as two years, and at most it was six years, although the cropping period remained at five years.[39]

Although this process of intensification showed no signs of adversely affecting crop yields before 1861, in the long term it would over-tax the capacity of the soil. Modern studies suggest that where grass leys are used in fallow periods, the ley period ought to match the cropping period if soil degradation is to be avoided.[40] In a situation like that in Bolshoi Tokmak, where fallow fields were not planted to grass but were simply left to reseed by invasion, the necessary ley period would have been longer still. As Postnikov shows, despite technological advances in peasant agriculture, in the 1880s peasants in Molochna were obtaining yields little better than they had in the 1840s and 1850s, and indeed worse than in the exceptional years of the late 1850s. Postnikov points to the growing evidence of soil exhaustion resulting from such overcropping.[41]

Bauman recommended a series of fundamental changes in Bolshoi Tokmak. To begin with, he suggested that the commons be reduced from four to three desiatinas per male soul. The 6.5 desiatinas per male soul this would have left as arable land, he suggested, ought to be used in a four-field rotation following the practice Mennonites were already successfully employing in nearby villages. He also recommended that the arable land be moved to the river flood-plain area closest to the village. Because this would have resulted in grazing livestock far from permanent water sources, he proposed digging water reservoirs on the steppe. He thought that if these were dug to a depth of three to four arshins they would hold water right through the dry season. Finally, Bauman recommended establishing a tree plantation on land that the village at that time employed for gardens, a proposal apparently supported by Cornies, who is referred to in the report as being well known to the ministry for having 'mastered the methods of steppe forestry.'[42]

Appended to the report were recommendations by the nachal'niks of Bolshoi Tokmak volost and Berdiansk uezd.[43] The volost nachal'nik generally supported the report but recommended minor revisions, suggesting that the commons be reduced to only 1.5 desiatinas per male soul. He also recommended that peasants be granted an additional one desiatina per male soul for grazing in the rocky hills near the village of Karakulak.[44] He cautioned that the place Bauman had designated for a tree plantation was too dry, and suggested an alternative site on Chungul Creek, at some distance from the village.

The uezd nachal'nik likewise largely accepted Bauman's report, although he recommended that the pasture lands only be reduced by one-fifth. He objected to the volost nachal'nik's proposal to pasture sheep near Karakulak because, he said, the land there was too poor.

Elders from each of the five peasant obshchinas in the volost also submitted opinions on Bauman's proposal, and here it met with less enthusiasm.[45] The elders accepted the redistribution of their land on a proportional basis and did not object to the reduction of the commons to three desiatinas per male soul. However, they were not willing to alter the practice of long fallow, claiming that if they tried to place the land under more intensive cultivation it would 'become altogether hard and not yield crops.'[46] They also rejected the idea of moving the commons away from the village and from immediate access to the river, protesting that their livestock had to be pastured near fresh water. They explained that the proposed reservoirs would not work because, except for areas immediately around the villages of Bolshoi Tokmak and Ostrikova, the water in the volost was bitter and salty, and if it were held in reservoirs through the dry season it would grow progressively worse. Although they acknowledged that without other options the livestock would drink such water, they claimed that the result would be an increase in livestock disease.[47]

The Ministry of State Domains' summary of Bauman's report emphasized at the outset that the 'project for the correct economic distribution of land' could only be implemented with the voluntary agreement of the peasants. This was apparently not forthcoming. But the summary went on to dismiss peasant objections, claiming they stemmed from a 'fear of work' and implying that peasant agreement was not really necessary.[48] The summary did not, however, give any directions for implementing the project, and there is no evidence that any of Bauman's recommendations, apart from the basic repartition, ever took effect.

The imposition of repartition had far-reaching effects on Orthodox state peasant agricultural practices in Molochna. As Table 6.3 shows, the peasants' average gross harvests between 1840 and 1861 were over seven chetverts per male soul, despite three near-total harvest failures. From 1858 to 1860 yields averaged in excess of ten chetverts per male soul. By comparison, gross harvests over the period 1808 to 1827 had averaged just 3.82 chetverts per male soul. The increase was not achieved by higher yields, but by planting more seed. The output/seed ratio for 1840 to 1861 was just 3.55:1, slightly less than the 3.64:1 of the earlier

TABLE 6.3
Orthodox state peasant harvests (in chetverts) in Melitopol and Berdiansk uezds,
1841–1862

	Male souls	Grain sown	Grain harvested	Output/ seed ratio	Gross harvest per male soul
1841	53,524	89,995	349,767	3.89	6.53
1842	53,760	83,742	502,287	6.00	9.34
1843	53,794	50,305	738,963	14.69	13.74
1844	–	–	–	–	–
1845	79,418	171,082	297,286	1.74	3.74
1846–53	–	–	–	–	–
1854	89,822	202,264	745,912	3.69	8.30
1855	89,583	166,664	105,608	0.63	1.18
1856	89,745	127,772	169,287	1.32	1.89
1857	–	–	–	–	–
1858	89,791	252,582	1,240,493	4.91	13.82
1859	101,993	239,209	1,048,005	4.38	10.28
1860	102,481	232,373	1,102,589	4.74	10.76
1861	–	–	–	–	–
1862	88,762	223,443	226,908	1.02	2.56
Average				3.55	7.31

Source: 'Otchety tavricheskikh gubernatorov,' 1843–61, *f.* 1281, *op.* 4–6; *f.* 1283, *op.* 1
(for 1854).

period. Obviously, Orthodox peasants were not following the Mennonite example of applying technology to increase yields.

For the most part Orthodox peasants in Molochna grew the same
basic crops in the 1840s and 1850s that they had in the first three
decades of the century, namely, wheat, rye, buckwheat, and millet. Bar-
ley also entered the market, as did flaxseed, which (as noted in Chapter
5), became an important export crop.[49] Price records show significant
changes from the earlier period (see Table 6.4). In Molochna, prices
no longer were lower than in the rest of the guberniia, showing that the
port at Berdiansk had overcome the high transportation costs from
which the mainland uezds in Tavria guberniia had once suffered.[50]

The increase in the arable land in Orthodox state peasant villages
had important implications for the other Orthodox state peasant agricultural strategies. As peasants increased the amount of land under
crops, their livestock holdings began to shrink. The data available will
not permit a precise delineation of this process because livestock hold-

TABLE 6.4
Regression analysis of Melitopol and Berdiansk uezd grain prices, 1843–1861

	Wheat		Rye		Oats	
	Melitopol	Berdiansk	Melitopol	Berdiansk	Melitopol	Berdiansk
Constant	2.06	2.38	−0.07	0.91	0.21	1.59
SE Y Est	1.53	1.87	0.67	0.80	0.71	0.81
R^2	0.56	0.46	0.85	0.78	0.78	0.35
Observations						
(n)	70.00	55	76	54	70	53
DOF	68.00	53	74	52	68	51
X-coefficient(s)	0.67	0.67	0.90	0.78	0.85	0.40
SE of coef.	0.07	0.10	0.04	0.06	0.06	0.08
Dependent						
variable	Uezd					
Independent						
variable	Guberniia					

Sources: 'Otchety tavricheskikh gubernatorov,' 1843–61, *f.* 1281, *op.* 4–6; *f.* 1283, *op.* 1, (for 1854).

ings are only reported in aggregates, including colonist, Nogai, and estate livestock, and each of these groups kept far more livestock per capita than did the Orthodox state peasants. However, although total livestock holdings in Melitopol and Berdiansk were little different in 1861 than they had been in 1843, the number of merino sheep had increased sharply, while the number of domestic sheep stopped growing, and cattle and horses decreased sharply. State peasant sheep were almost exclusively domestic breeds. Thus, it is clear that their total livestock holdings per male soul were falling (see Table 6.5).[51]

Table 6.6, which shows livestock holdings excluding merino sheep per male soul, gives some indication of the progression. The figures in this table can only point at approximate trends, for colonists, Nogai, and estate owners are still included; probably Orthodox state peasant holdings were smaller yet. Nevertheless, these figures show a striking development. The holdings per male soul after 1854 ranged between 1.98 and 2.28 animal units (AUs). At the peak of the earlier period, in 1827, AUs per male soul reached 2.24, a figure almost identical to the earliest recorded years from the later period. Although the lack of data for the years 1828 to 1843 makes it impossible to be certain, it may well be that the highest level of state peasant livestock holdings had already been reached by 1827.[52]

TABLE 6.5
Livestock per male soul in Melitopol and Berdiansk uezds, 1843–1861

	Horses per male soul	Cattle per male soul	Domestic sheep	Imported (merino) sheep	Sheep per male soul	Animal units per male soul
1843	0.79	3.48	292,500	462,108	9.66	5.09
1844	0.74	3.51	441,088	652,217	10.63	4.85
1845	0.37	3.47	439,500	597,981	9.75	4.46
1846	0.66	3.33	447,000	657,760	10.02	4.72
1847	0.15	0.32	36,798	489,868	4.78	1.36
1848	0.32	1.37	177,443	547,153	6.90	2.42
1849	0.37	1.71	353,838	470,903	7.89	2.80
1850	0.17	0.54	37,633	158,442	1.67	0.82
1851	0.24	0.56	60,083	497,292	5.05	1.54
1852	0.37	1.45	164,882	536,285	5.98	2.42
1853	0.50	2.07	270,277	862,630	8.97	3.76
1854	–	–	–	–	–	–
1855	0.46	1.93	270,290	770,242	7.99	3.47
1856	0.45	1.77	271,611	748,077	7.79	3.33
1857	0.50	2.06	310,287	881,239	8.92	3.90
1858	0.49	1.85	288,388	823,688	8.22	3.63
1859	0.46	1.94	462,270	894,576	9.58	3.70
1860	0.43	1.77	393,673	1,103,945	12.50	4.57
1861	0.56	1.67	327,252	960,018	9.55	3.66

Sources: 'Otchety tavricheskikh gubernatorov,' 1841–61, *f.* 1281, *op.* 4–6; *f.* 1283, *op.* 1, (for 1854).

The shift to arable husbandry in the 1840s was not solely or even primarily a reaction to market demand, for the introduction of repartition had an important impact on the increase in the area under plough. In theory, repartition redistributed all land in the obshchina equally, but in fact the unregulated commons were monopolized by rich peasants, so repartition only had real significance on the arable land. Rich peasants, who owned large flocks of sheep as well as disproportionately large amounts of the arable land, were under no pressure to exploit their share of the arable land intensively. As long as sheep remained profitable, the rich could continue to concentrate their efforts on them and treat the arable in the same casual manner that their forefathers had. At the same time, even if their abuse of the commons was causing its rapid deterioration, as long as rich peasants owned khutors they did not need to worry. Indeed, by grazing their herds on

TABLE 6.6
Animal units (AUs) per male soul, excluding merino sheep

1843	3.66	1852	1.40
1844	3.45	1853	2.14
1845	3.21	1854	0.00
1846	3.35	1855	2.04
1847	0.35	1856	1.94
1848	1.31	1857	2.27
1849	1.86	1858	2.10
1850	0.51	1859	2.24
1851	0.58	1860	2.28
		1861	1.98

Sources: 'Otchety tavricheskikh gubernatorov,' 1841–61, f. 1281, op. 4–6; f. 1283, op. 1, (for 1854).

the commons early in the year they spared their own land during the critical early season.

Rich peasants also had the ability to buy fodder to feed their livestock during the two or three months each winter when grazing was impossible. The purchase of fodder was beginning to significantly affect the cost of animal husbandry by the 1840s. In 1848 Russian regional historian A.A. Skal'kovsky wrote that fodder had always been regarded as free on the steppe because, as long as large areas of grasslands remained unpopulated, peasants could simply go out and harvest what they needed.[53] However, for the first time, in the 1840s the state began keeping records of the price of fodder. While such records are too fragmentary to allow cost accounting, that they were kept at all shows that the free fodder was disappearing. For poor peasants who did not own khutors and could not afford to lease land or buy fodder, the monopolization and destruction of the commons by the rich meant the carrying capacity of the commons was reduced to the point where survival dictated raising grain. When repartition returned land to those peasants who had been reduced to farming only a 'hand's-breadth' of land, it did not return to them control of the commons, which remained open to unrestricted use. Therefore, they turned to raising grain on the part of the land they did control. Because the proportion of the total of Orthodox state peasant landholdings that was in the hands of the poor rose through repartition, the total area of land under crops rose as well.

It must be noted, however, that because the commons continued to occupy the area closest to the village, the shift to arable husbandry did not place the prime flood plain land under crops.[54] Instead, peasant allotments were located on the high steppe and thus were heavily dependent on inconsistent Molochna weather. This had important long-term implications, for the intensive cultivation of the high steppe was certain to lead to soil exhaustion. The poor had little choice in this matter. Their allotments, exclusive of the commons, were only four or five desiatinas per male soul, which was too little land to support a family by raising livestock. To survive they had to take their chances with the weather and grow grain.

Conclusion

In Molochna, Orthodox state peasants, like Mennonites, shifted to growing grain in the 1840s. Unlike Mennonites, however, their actions were driven by land shortages rather than changing market demand. With the implementation of repartition, Orthodox peasants headed down a radically different road than colonists, one that would ultimately lead to economic stagnation.

The decisions taken by Orthodox peasants in Molochna in the 1830s and 1840s are fully consistent with James C. Scott's moral economy paradigm. Driven by the spectre of famine, peasants made the avoidance of dearth their first priority, implementing a policy that placed subsistence ahead of wealth. This begs the question of why Mennonites, who were, after all, themselves peasants – at least they had been when they arrived in Molochna – took such a sharply different path. The moral economy paradigm seems to possess little utility in answering this question.

In looking elsewhere for answers, the differing roles played by the two communities in allocating land must be reiterated. Prior to repartition Orthodox state peasants had much less collective control over their own land than did colonists, who controlled their own surplus lands, and consequently developed a system of self-administration over community resources. Orthodox state peasants were entirely dependent on the state to grant new land as their population grew. For colonists, the surplus land system provided an impetus to establish an internal administrative system and lent legitimacy to the participants in that system. Although Mennonite society was faced with many internal political disputes about who would control the system of internal administration of common resources, there was never any doubt that it would be Mennonites themselves who ultimately held the reins of control. Even when Mennonite leaders sought Guardianship Committee support against their political opponents they did not invite direct state participation in deciding internal matters, but rather sought the authority to make community decisions themselves. Orthodox peasants, meanwhile, lacked any such internal administrative system, so when problems arose they were constrained to invite outside assistance. The state granted Cornies the authority to manage Mennonite resources, but it sent its own representative to Bolshoi Tokmak to decide how state peasant resources should be divided.

As a consequence there arose in Mennonite society a corporate identity, what is commonly called the 'Mennonite commonwealth.' Mennonites, whether landless or landed, identified with the commonwealth and accepted, however grudgingly, decisions taken by community leaders about how the common good should best be served. The wealth of some was legitimized because it served all, and the poverty of others was made bearable by the promise that the poor would eventually share in the growing wealth of the whole community. Private enterprise blossomed in the name of communal good.

Orthodox peasants, meanwhile, had no common resources, and consequently there was no impetus for the creation of a corporate identity. When demographic pressures made land scarce they had no choice but to turn to the state, for they lacked any legitimate system to reallocate resources by themselves. Although their rejection of most of Bauman's recommendations reveals their desire to maintain independence from the state, when they invited state intervention they surrendered a critical element of their independence. Ironically, the peasants' lack of a corporate identity led to the rejection of private enterprise and the arbitrary outside imposition of how communal resources were to be shared.

CHAPTER SEVEN

Consolidation and Alienation

The livestock epidemic of 1847 and harvest failure of 1848 were less severe than the Great Drought of 1832–4. Nevertheless, they mark an important turning point for the Molochna region, for they forced consolidation of trends that had been developing over the preceding fifteen years. For Orthodox state peasants, after 1848 there was no going back to the old, pastoralist way of life. The rate of repartitions rose, and more and more state peasant land went under the plough. For the interlocked economy of the Nogai and Mennonites, the 1850s were a time of crucial new developments. Encouraged by Mennonite investment, Nogai had continued to base their economy almost exclusively on pastoralism in the 1840s. Therefore, when the 1847 epidemic hit they had nothing to fall back on. In the 1850s the Nogai fell into dependency on Mennonites until finally, impoverished and alienated, in 1860 they fled Molochna altogether.

The Nogai exodus had important, unanticipated implications for Mennonites. Landless Mennonites had come to rely heavily on land leased from Nogai. When the Nogai departed, the state ceded this land to new immigrants from Bulgaria, and one-time Mennonite leasers turned back to the their settlement, looking for a share of Mennonite land. The landlessness crisis that followed was thus closely linked to the long history of Nogai–Mennonite economic relations.

The End of Pastoral Economy

Uezd-level harvest data are not available for the period 1846–54, but guberniia figures, provided in Table 7.1, tell the story. Orthodox state peasant harvests in 1848, including those of the Nogai, barely returned

TABLE 7.1
Harvests (in chetverts) and output/seed ratios in Tavria guberniia, 1845–1861

Year	Orthodox state peasants			Colonists		
	Sown	Harvested	Yield	Sown	Harvested	Yield
1845	255,417	460,082	1.80	28,137	76,182	2.71
1846	231,419	1,528,900	6.61	25,602	310,973	12.15
1847	301,405	1,210,156	4.02	27,064	329,748	12.18
1848	308,779	313,628	1.02	29,027	60,962	2.10
1849	248,478	736,800	2.97	25,673	122,289	4.76
1850	260,465	440,649	1.69	28,767	107,556	3.74
1851	245,807	922,142	3.75	29,463	308,838	10.48
1852	273,165	2,261,932	8.28	34,990	374,020	10.69
1853	314,633	1,700,944	5.41	40,596	343,827	8.47
1854	282,077	1,086,430	3.85	41,587	364,827	8.77
1855	–	–	–	–	–	–
1856	–	–	–	–	–	–
1857	240,179	1,570,238	6.54	39,767	394,556	9.92
1858	354,725	1,646,376	4.64	37,811	393,644	10.41
1859	344,133	1,493,226	4.34	50,008	383,323	7.67
1860	322,053	1,574,925	4.89	60,569	382,618	6.32
1861	283,404	1,548,380	5.46	52,285	482,226	9.22

Source: 'Otchety tavricheskikh gubernatorov,' za 1843–61, *f.* 1281, *op.* 4–6; *f.* 1283, *op.* 1, (for 1854).

the seed planted. Colonist harvests, while better, were also desperately low. Livestock levels are provided in Chapter 6 (Table 6.6). In 1848 livestock holdings in Berdiansk and Melitopol uezds fell to just 0.82 animal units (AUs) per male soul, and Orthodox state peasants were particularly hard hit.

With wool prices already at an all-time low there was little impetus to reinvest in livestock, and so the Orthodox state peasants and Nogai did not replace their decimated herds. Colonists also increased the pace of transition to arable husbandry. The progression in colonist villages is shown in Table 7.2. By 1861 they were already pushing their ploughed fields beyond the flood plains and onto the steppe, placing more and more marginal land under crops. By 1889 colonists would be using about 70 per cent of their land as arable.

This process did not affect all villages equally, because later settlers received much worse land than the early ones. Already by 1835 the only land available for new villages was far up secondary streams in more

TABLE 7.2
Colonist transition to arable husbandry, 1837–1861

| | Sown + fallow land (as % of all allotted land) | | | | Livestock per capita (in animal units) | | |
	1835	1840	1848	1861	1835	1841	1866
Mennonites	26	37	52	59	3.50	3.04	1.53
Colonists	20	—	44	51	1.82	3.12	1.62
Total	24	—	49	56	2.69	3.08	1.56

Sources: 'Tabellen über den Zustand der Molotschner Kolonisten,' 1835, *PJBRMA*, file 1138, 1ob-37ob; 'Verzeichnis über Aussaat und Ernte im Molotschner Menonisten Bezirk in den Jahren 1828 bis 1848,' 1849, *PJBRMA*, file 1308, 25–6; A. Klaus, *Nashi Kolonii: Opyty i materialy po istorii i statistike inostrannoi kolonizatsii v rossii* (St Petersburg: Nusval'ta, 1869), Appendix 3 and Appendix 7; Franz Isaak, *Die Molotschner Mennonisten: Ein Beitrag zur Geschichte derselben* (Halbstadt: Braun, 1908), 32; 'Otchety Tavricheskikh Gubernatorov ... za 1861,' 1862, *RGIA*, f. 1281, *op.* 6, *d.* 47; Detlef Brandes, *Von den Zaren adoptiert: Die deutschen Kolonisten und die Balkansiedler in Neurussland und Bessarabien, 1751–1914* (Munich: R. Oldenbourg, 1993), 227, Table 29.

and more arid locations. A founding member of the village of Gnadenfeld, established on the Apanlee River in 1835, described how her family had 'come to a barren steppe without any roads and paths. No tree, no bush, only tall, dry, bitter grass and prickly camel fodder grew on the dry, cracked ground ... There were no wells, only an almost dry stream which provided water for man and beast ... Those not near the stream found no water except at great depths. This proved to be bitter, salty water unsuitable for drinking, cooking, and washing. The entire village of Gnadenfeld had only three wells with suitable water. For almost fifty years the villagers hauled their drinking water from these wells.'[1]

For Orthodox state peasants, post-1848 developments followed the path already established in previous years. Prior to 1840 just six land repartitions had ever occurred in all of Tavria guberniia; there were nineteen repartitions in the 1840s and forty-four in the 1850s.[2] Following the pattern described for Bolshoi Tokmak (in Chapter 6), arable land increased accordingly. By the 1880s roughly three-quarters of all peasant land was under crops. Common pastures disappeared altogether in some places, leaving peasants dependent on leased pastures and fodder crops to feed their draft animals.[3]

Interlocking Development – The Nogai–Mennonite Story

For Nogai and Mennonites the 1850s saw important changes. The livestock epidemic signalled the end of sheep sharecropping. From 1848 to 1850 there were just forty-one new contracts and after 1850 there were none. This is probably because the destruction of Nogai herds was enormously costly to everyone involved. Nogai, who no longer received income from existing herds, could not afford the start-up costs of undertaking new contracts. For Mennonites, their capital investment disappeared with the death of the sheep, and even if they could afford to replace them – a doubtful proposition, particularly for the landless – the risks, freshly demonstrated by the epidemic, must have been forbidding.

Meanwhile, in early 1848 for the first time the Nogai borrowed money, not sheep, from Mennonites. The interest-free loans were small, averaging just seventy-three rubles, due in full from six months to two years later. Records of thirty-one loans survive, although there is no indication of whether they were repaid on time or indeed repaid at all.[4] Other sources show that Nogai had great difficulty repaying their debts after 1848. Johann Cornies died in 1848, but that year and the next his heirs again sold sheep from his Iushanlee estate to Nogai on credit.[5] The amount, 21,134 rubles, was almost three times what had been granted in 1843 (see Chapter 5). All but twenty-five rubles of the 1843 loans were repaid by 1847, while repayment of the 1848 and 1849 loans stretched over nine years and in the end 5,844 rubles, over a quarter of the total, were never repaid. Records from 1848, 1849, and 1851 show that other Mennonites also sold sheep, worth over 28,000 rubles, on credit to Nogai, and although there are no payment records it is unlikely they were any better repaid than Cornies.[6]

The most compelling evidence of a crisis in Nogai society after 1848 comes from the two model villages, Akkerman and Aknokas. In January and February 1851 thirty-three Nogai from the model villages leased an average of 3.6 desiatinas each to Mennonites for between 3.5 and 4.5 paper rubles per desiatina. The rental payments went directly to the treasury to cover Nogai tax arrears.[7] The rental price was high – pasture land still rented for as little as 1.38 rubles per desiatina in Molochna in 1851[8] – but this was because the land in question was river flood plain, the most valuable land in the region.[9] Prerevolutionary Russian historian A.A. Sergeev suggests that leasing out land to pay tax arrears was common to all Molochna Nogai in the 1850s, although he credits it to laziness, writing, 'The Nogai were indifferent to agriculture and gardening and rented their land ... on the easiest of terms.'[10]

TABLE 7.3
Economic differentiation in Shuiut Dzhuret, 1836, and Akkerman and Aknokas, 1850

| | Shuiut Dzhuret | | Akkerman and Aknokas | |
	Sheep owning	Other	Sheep owning	Other
Percentage of households	22.00	78.00	48.00	52.00
Sheep/household	50.00	0.00	119.46	0.00
Horses/household	12.11	4.59	8.70	2.04
Cattle/household	9.11	2.09	3.07	1.12

Sources: 'Imennyi Spisok Pogorevshim Khoziaievam Melitopol'skago Okruga Dzhuretskoi Volosti Derevni Shuiut-Dzhureta,' 1836, *PJBRMA*, file 374, 1–14ob; 'Vedomost' o sostoianii Sel. Aknokas v 1850 godu,' and 'Vedomost' o sostoianii kolonii Akkermana. 1 Maia 1850,' 1850, *PJBRMA*, file 1463, 2, 4-4ob.

An 1850 report on the condition of the two model villages shows that while some residents were still wealthy, many had been reduced to abject poverty. Differentiation in the model villages in 1850 was an extreme version of that in the Nogai village of Shuiut Dzhuret in 1836. A much larger percentage of households in Akkerman and Aknokas owned sheep, and the rich in Akkerman and Aknokas were much richer than those in Shuiut Dzhuret, while the poor were poorer (see Table 7.3). The report details the economic condition of some Nogai involved in lease transactions. Unfortunately, inconsistent spellings of Nogai names and the use of only first names in some contracts make it impossible to identify all participants, but ten of the thirty-three can be identified. Eight of these ten were poor, owning no sheep and on average fewer than three head of livestock, while the other two owned eighty-four sheep between them, putting them at the bottom end of the sheep-owning households. As might be expected, Nogai who leased their land out to pay tax arrears were poor. The loss of use of their best land could only make them poorer, and confirming this, records for Akkerman from 1853 show that the amount of land leased to Mennonites had climbed to an average of 12.75 desiatinas per participating household, while the number of households involved grew from thirty-three to thirty-seven of the households in the village.[11] As for Mennonites who leased the land, unlike with sharecropping contracts in the 1840s, the majority of identifiable renters – seventeen of twenty-four – were landless, while none of the landed renters were owners of an exceptionally large sheep herd.

While poor Nogai in Akkerman and Aknokas were losing control of their land, a parallel process also appeared – in thirty-eight extant contracts Mennonites contracted to Nogai as sharecroppers.[12] The contracts called for Nogai to provide ploughed land, which the Mennonites were to sow. Nogai would harvest the crops, and the product would be split evenly. Twenty-nine of the thirty-eight Nogai involved can be identified, thirteen of them coming from the wealthy sheep-owning group. Only thirteen Mennonites can be identified, and of these just three held full holdings. Thus, in some instances wealthy Nogai were becoming landlords to poor Mennonites, showing that consequences of the 1847 epidemic were also dire for landless Mennonites.

Evidence of conditions in the Nogai villages in the 1850s is much scarcer than for earlier decades. Travellers to the region continued to report that the model villages were shining examples of order and prosperity – a description sharply contradicted by the data already presented above.[13] In 1855 Alexander Petzholdt described somewhat less idyllic conditions in the Nogai village of Baurdak, just south of Akkerman and Aknokas. He was dismayed by the haphazard layout of the village, its homes built of manure-and-straw bricks with crooked chimneys and badly thatched roofs.[14] Yet even here there was no hint of the deeply rooted problems that were soon to provoke a wholesale exodus of the Nogai to Turkey.

Russian officials were under no misconception about the decline in Nogai conditions. In 1853 the governor of Tavria reported to the Ministry of State Domains that 'the Nogai ... are almost completely identical to the Tatars.'[15] This contrasted sharply with the 1842 report that 'Nogai are far better than the Tatars, and are progressing by the year.'[16] The optimism that had permeated official reports before 1848 was gone. Nogai too, were no longer optimistic, and in the 1850s their leaders increasingly aligned themselves with the Crimean Tatars, ultimately joining in the Tatar exodus to Turkey in 1860.

A full explanation of the Nogai exodus from the Molochna basin requires a brief detour into the subject of relations between the Russian state and the Crimean Tatars. These relations had never been good, and they deteriorated rapidly in the 1840s and 1850s, reaching bottom during the Crimean War when suspicions of Tatar collaboration with Turkish forces caused the state to consider evicting large numbers of Tatars from their homes and relocating them inland.[17] Tatar dissatisfaction with the tsarist state centred on Russian nobles who had acquired large parcels of Tatar land, often through dishonest means.[18] The last straw for the Tatars was the Ministry of State Domains' rejection in 1859 of Tatar petitions for new land grants to ameliorate their poverty.[19]

There is no evidence to suggest that the Nogai were subject to the same suspicions as were the Crimean Tatars during the war. Like other residents of the southern guberniias, however, they were obliged to contribute to the war effort, sending 940 head of cattle to feed the troops at Sevastopol and supplying seventy-five wagons to transport materials.[20] Such contributions must have been a heavy burden for the already struggling Nogai. Just as significantly, war-induced shortages drove grain prices to new heights in 1854 and 1855, and while grain producers profited, grain buyers suffered as a result of the inflation. Land values soared along with wheat prices, but the best Nogai land had already been leased to Mennonites at prewar prices, and Nogai were left to buy grain produced on their own fields at prices that far outstripped the rents they received.

After the war Nogai leaders aligned themselves closely with their Crimean Tatar neighbours. In 1857 a group of Nogai murzas joined in Tatar petitions for increased land grants. Justifying their claims with stories of the services that their forefathers had provided the state, the Nogai protested that 'not having private land, we not only have been reduced to poverty, but a great many among us are compelled, in order to obtain subsistence, to work as simple servants.'[21] In ruling to reject the Nogai petition the Ministry of State Domains concluded that, although many of the murzas possessed legitimate proof of the noble status granted their ancestors by Catherine II in the eighteenth century, those ancestors were already long dead and claims based on their service had no significance.[22] With a stroke of the pen the murzas that remained were reduced to state peasants with no claim to special privileges.

In the fall of 1859 some 16,000 Nogai from the Caucasus obtained permission to emigrate to Turkey. They travelled overland to the Molochna basin, wintered with their Molochna cousins, and then in the summer of 1860 journeyed on to the Crimea where they continued by ship.[23] When they left, the Molochna Nogai went with them. In 1859 there were 35,149 Nogai in Molochna. By October 1860 there were 105. By January 1862 there were twenty.[24] Nogai land, including that leased by Mennonites, reverted to the state, which assigned much of it to Bulgarian colonists.

This brings to an end the story of Nogai in Molochna, but it leaves the Mennonites at a critical juncture. By 1860 roughly 60 per cent of all

Molochna Mennonite families were landless. In 1863 their demands for land resulted in a crisis that ultimately provoked state intervention on their behalf. The resultant 'landlessness crisis' has long been a significant issue both for Mennonites and for historians of Mennonites.

The full story of the landlessness crisis, which lingered on for decades, is beyond the scope of this study. Briefly, the Nogai exodus and the large, uncontrolled illegal influx of peasants into Molochna following the emancipation proclamation of 1861, compounded with a serious harvest failure in 1862, drove landless Mennonites to demand that they be allotted all unassigned surplus land in the Mennonite settlement. Opponents and proponents of this proposal engaged in heated disputes in the German-language press, as well as in a battle of appeals to the Russian state. Ultimately, a number of concessions were made to the landless including the distribution of reserve lands in half-holdings (32.5 desiatinas) and quarter-holdings (16.25 desiatinas) and, in the 1870s, community-funded purchases of land in other regions, which created the so-called daughter colonies.

For Mennonites the crisis, which saw poor landless Mennonites pitted against wealthy landed Mennonites in a bitter struggle over rights to land and to a voice in the administration of their communities, has been seen as a black mark that challenges Mennonite perceptions of their own society as being just and egalitarian. In this tradition, in the early twentieth century the great Mennonite historian Peter M. Friesen wrote, 'Like a misfortune [the crisis] lies on the soul of the community because there has not taken place a thorough cleansing of the corporate body through conscious repenting.'[25]

More recently, Mennonite historians have come to regard the crisis as a watershed event after which social and economic differentiation within Mennonite society became dominant forces. Such historians have not escaped the moralizing tone of earlier writers. David G. Rempel, whose pioneering work in the 1960s to 1980s revitalized the study of Russian Mennonite history, characterized the actions of the landed as 'unconscionable.'

For other historians the landlessness crisis has been seized upon as a particularly clear instance of class conflict in an industrializing society. James Urry, whose *None but Saints* has become the standard work on the first century of Mennonite settlement in the Russian Empire, writes that the 'land struggles revealed the ugly and unacceptable face of the economic and social transformations that had occurred since first settlement in Russia.'[26]

The crisis caused important changes in Mennonite economic life, and the deepness of the resentments it stirred is indisputable. It may be argued, however, that the severity of the initial dispute has been substantially inflated in subsequent accounts, while its resolution represented less a sharp discontinuity in Russian Mennonite life than a demonstration of the strength of reform traditions in the Molochna community.

In looking closely at the sources upon which assessments of the landlessness crisis have been made, it quickly becomes evident that much of the historiography has very shaky foundations. Too frequently it is based on statements made by participants in the crisis who had clearly vested interests in how it would be resolved. Letters to newspapers and petitions to the Guardianship Committee, written in the heat of the crisis, have been accepted as de facto confirmation of the claims of the landless, while isolated accounts of rapacious subleases of pasture land have been interpreted as evidence of widespread profiteering by all landowners.

One source has particularly influenced all subsequent interpretations: Franz Isaac's *Die Molotschnaer Mennoniten* reproduces several key letters and petitions from disputants in the crisis. Isaac's account is invaluable because it preserves many documents that are not available elsewhere. It is also very biased in favour of the landless. *Die Molotschnaer Mennoniten* tells the story almost exclusively in the words of the landless; it provides just two petitions from the landed, and these, introduced by Isaac as 'slanderous letters' (*Schmähschriften*), show the landed position at its worst.[27]

It is Isaac, too, who provides two of the most damning pieces of evidence regarding the attitudes of the landed during the crisis: district mayor (*Gebietsvorsteher*) David Friesen's alleged statement that the landless 'will never receive so much as a half desiatina of land,' and the contention that the wealthy were leasing large tracts of land for 2 kopecks per desiatina and subletting it to the landless for 3 to 4 rubles per desiatina.[28] These contentions, provided without references and tucked into a footnote, have come to symbolize the greed of all Molochna Mennonite landowners. As will be shown below, the credibility of these contentions is dubious at best.

As a first step in re-examining the crisis it is necessary to question whether the terms by which the principals in the dispute are usually identified are accurate. Neither 'the landed' nor 'the landless' identifies any group in Molochna with precision. The landless Molochna

Mennonites can be divided into two groups: the *Einwohner* (cottagers, or renters) and the *Anwohner* (owners of houses, but not of agricultural land allotments). In 1860 of the landless families 69 per cent were *Einwohner* and 31 per cent were *Anwohner*. Although the petitions of the landless supposedly represented all of these people, it seems apparent that the two groups did not form a united front. After all, the resolution of the crisis saw land allotted to the *Anwohner* only. The *Einwohner*, who come closest to representing a true proletariat in Molochna, gained little or nothing.

As for the landed, they too can be divided into two groups: estate owners and owners of sixty-five-desiatina full holdings. The estate owners were the principle target of the landless, who never challenged the rights of the run-of-the-mill fullholders to their basic sixty-five-desiatina allotments. Moreover, and despite assumptions implicit in the historical literature, there is no explicit evidence that the fullholders united as a corporate body to oppose the claims of the landless. Indeed, there is important evidence that implies quite the opposite.

This evidence comes from *Die Molotschnaer Mennoniten* and is a good example of how Isaac and others have distorted the record of the crisis. Isaac relates that a third important interest group of Molochna Mennonites, the merchants, largely supported the landless. Yet the petition Isaac produces in support of this contention comes not just from merchants but from 'merchants *and landowners*.'[29] Because there is no record of the signers of the petition (the original is not extant; the version reproduced by Isaac is the only record), it is impossible to be certain who these landed were. Still, as this petition makes clear, this was not a crisis that pitted all the landed against all the landless. Rather, it was a dispute between some of the landless and some of the landed.

The landed in question were the wealthy estate owners. Here again it is necessary to be cautious. Philip Wiebe, Johann Cornies's son-in-law and one of the wealthiest estate owners in the Molochna basin, was a leading defender of the rights of the landless during the crisis. Still, the identifiable leaders of the landed, including most notably district mayor Friesen and chairman of the Agricultural Society Peter Schmidt, were clearly from the wealthiest strata of Molochna Mennonite society.

If there is some justification for the accusation that some wealthy landowners were dealing unfairly with the landless, the broader accusation that the structure of the Mennonite economy was intentionally unjust and exploitative of the landless is patently untrue. Chapter 5 describes the efforts of Cornies, and those who supported him, to industrialize and to diversify agriculture in Molochna in order to provide employment to the landless. Cornies was constantly cognizant of the needs of the whole community, and his decisions were heavily influenced by Mennonite ethical norms.

The primary criticism levelled against the landed is that they failed to distribute surplus and reserve lands. These two categories of land have already been defined in Chapter 3, but it may be convenient to review them. Reserve land was crown land set aside for future settlement by new Mennonite immigrants. Mennonites had no direct control over the unoccupied portion of this land.[30] In addition to the reserve, to allow for natural population growth the state gave each Mennonite village surplus land equal to one-sixth its allotment land for future distribution.[31] This land was owned by the village collectively, and its allocation fell fully within the discretion of landed Mennonites. On the eve of the landlessness crisis, surplus land in Molochna amounted to 15,820 desiatinas – enough to grant just 243 of the 2,356 landless families allotments at the state-mandated sixty-five-desiatina norm.[32]

Although it is clear that the surplus land offered no solution to the landlessness crisis, that the landed failed to distribute it at all demands closer attention. There was not enough surplus land to provide a real solution, and (as pointed out in Chapter 3) it was of marginal quality anyway. Nevertheless, its monopolization by the landed was obviously perceived as unjust by the landless, and this acted as a rallying flag for disaffection of the landless.

The failure to allocate surplus land to the landless has been credited to the fact that landed Mennonites granted themselves cheap leases on it, instead, thus monopolizing it. Such landed lessees are condemned for in turn subletting the leased land at much higher rates to the landless. There is an element of truth in these allegations, albeit a small one. Three Mennonite landowners leased a total of 8,360 desiatinas of the surplus land. The remainder was divided between the Neuhalbstadt cloth factory (3,000 desiatinas) and the communal sheepfold (4,460 desiatinas). Whereas the three private lessees may have been the targets of landless wrath, there are no grounds for tarring all landed Mennonites with the exploiters' brush, and the idea that the landed as a group refused to redistribute the surplus out of financial self-interest clearly is without merit.

As for the accusation that landed lessees sublet land to landless Mennonites at unconscionably high rates, in truth surviving records show that, with few exceptions, Mennonite lessees paid lower rent to Mennonite landholders than they did to Nogai.[33] It should be noted, too, that Isaac's contention that the wealthy lessees paid just 1 to 2 kopecks per desiatina is simply unfounded. Although records for the 1860s are unavailable, in 1849 the Gebeitsamt already charged approximately 62 kopecks per desiatina for surplus land.[34] While the large landholders were undoubtedly turning a profit on the venture, the low rates they gave to Mennonite renters do not bear out the charge of profiteering.

Not only is there little merit to the charges against landed Mennonites – there is also no evidence whatsoever of disaffection among the landless *before* the Nogai exodus. As already argued in Chapter 5, it seems probable that the landless, whatever their dissatisfaction with not owning land, accepted the existing system as just. The ability of landless Mennonites like Peter Loewen to become wealthy without land helps to account for this lack of internal opposition to the landlessness situation. The economy was working, there were options for the landless, and the Molochna Mennonite settlement was economically and politically stable.

What threw the Molochna Mennonites into crisis was not deep-seated class alienation, but the sudden loss of thousands of desiatinas of land.[35] As a result of inflation after the Crimean War, landless Mennonites who held cheap long-term leases on Nogai land experienced an economic boom. At the same time, rising agricultural prices made land rental more attractive to landless Mennonites who until 1855 had been employed in cottage industry or as wage labourers, encouraging them to redirect their efforts into agriculture. This created labour shortages and drove wages up even for those landless Mennonites who remained dependent on wage labour and did not turn to leasing land. No doubt the sudden reversal of fortunes when the Nogai left was an important contributing factor to the activism of the landless during the landlessness crisis. Moreover, because increased competition for labour raised the operating costs of large landowners, a few such landowners welcomed the labour glut that followed the Nogai exodus and resisted the distribution of Mennonite land to the landless. The landlessness crisis, then, grew out of immediate, short-term conditions brought on by a combination of the declining condition of the Nogai and the economic turbulence sparked by the Crimean War.

The crisis did indeed see Mennonites divide into landed and landless factions, leading to the legalization of the subdivision of allotments, but (as pointed out in Chapter 5) this was hardly revolutionary. In the 1840s Cornies had already created a system to permit half-allotments.

Of far greater significance for the resolution of the crisis was the creation in the 1870s of daughter colonies (new colonies established on land purchased or leased by the original colonies). It should be noted again that the problem was not solved by establishing new villages on reserve land, but rather by buying new land. Although there was some unoccupied reserve land, it was far too arid to be suitable for establishing new villages.

Two further points must be made about the resolution of the landlessness crisis. First, it is not surprising that the loss of access to thousands of desiatinas of land provoked a crisis. Indeed, it would be astonishing had it not. The ability of Mennonite society to weather such a storm is a testament to the strength of the system that Cornies had engineered. Second, the solution – finding land for a relatively small portion of the landless in newly created daughter colonies or on half- and quarter-allotments – suggests that, far from rebelling against the traditional ideals of Mennonite society, the 'rebels' sought inclusion in the Mennonite mainstream. This was hardly a rebellion against the Mennonite commonwealth.

Conclusion

The interlocking story of Nogai and Mennonite economic development has several important lessons. To begin with, contrary to the image portrayed in most Mennonite sources, Mennonites were neither isolated from surrounding populations, nor simply paternalistic benefactors to backward neighbours. Whatever Cornies intended, Mennonite–Nogai relations soon came to be governed by pragmatic economic considerations, with the Nogai providing a significant avenue for Mennonite investment. Some Nogai grew rich in consequence, but most grew poor, and by encouraging animal husbandry to the exclusion of arable husbandry, in contradiction of shifting market demand, Mennonites unintentionally set the Nogai up for a fall.

It must be emphasized that traditional Nogai pastoral practices had already led to the brink of disaster through overgrazing as early as 1825. Something had to change. Cornies's programs were intended to guide that change along manifestly successful Mennonite paths. Even after Cornies's death, when the 1847 epidemic wiped out Nogai herds, Mennonites, although hard hit by the disaster themselves, gave interest-free loans to Nogai. Too, the Mennonite solution to the problem, namely, transition to arable husbandry, was not necessarily a panacea. Nogai land was the poorest in the Molochna region and only a relatively small proportion of it, along the banks of the Molochna and Iushanlee rivers, was truly suited to crop agriculture. The Bulgarian settlers who inherited the land in the 1860s quickly pronounced much of it uninhabitable, and they were only persuaded to stay by a large-scale state-funded well-digging program.[36] Still, some Nogai land was suited to arable husbandry, and indeed was ploughed and planted in the 1850s – mainly by landless Mennonite renters.

Placed in the context of Mennonite–Nogai economic relations and the post-1848 Nogai economic collapse, the Nogai exodus itself appears at least partly a product of Mennonite landlessness. Because the landlessness crisis occurred in the 1860s, the significance of landlessness in earlier decades has received only passing attention, but the Nogai story suggests it needs to be reassessed.[37] The role of Mennonites as models to surrounding settlers was hotly debated in the 1830s and 1840s. Progressive Mennonites, led by Cornies and supported by the state, argued that the terms of the Mennonite charter obliged them to act as model settlers. Conservative Mennonites responded that Mennonite faith was founded on separation from 'the world,' and thus precluded active involvement with other settlers.[38] Participation by landless Mennonites in Cornies's sharecropping program is a pointed reminder that the conservative ideal of living as 'the quiet in the land' was only possible for those *with* land. For the 53 per cent of Molochna Mennonites without land by 1848, the insular ideals of conservative congregations offered but cold comfort.

CHAPTER EIGHT

Conclusion

Orthodox state peasants, sectarians, Islamic Nogai Tatars, and German-speaking Mennonites, Catholics, and Lutherans arrived in the Molochna River Basin facing virtually identical challenges. Isolated from the state's authority, and from markets, they confronted harsh environmental conditions on the arid treeless steppe. With the exception of the Nogai they had no experience with agriculture under such conditions. All proved adaptive, turning to animal husbandry to solve their common problems.

Within a few decades they faced a second common challenge: adaptation to demographic growth and land shortages. Nogai reached the crisis point first. Their land grant was the poorest in the region, and as pastoralists by tradition, they had arrived in the Molochna region with large herds. Consequently, by 1825 their herds exceeded the carrying capacity of their land and they faced the need to change.

By the mid-1830s Orthodox state peasants faced the same dilemma. In 1835 the average Orthodox state peasant land allotment in Molochna was just 12.81 desiatinas per male soul, already less than the 15 desiatinas per male soul that made a region 'land-rich' in the state's eyes. Nor was there free crown land in the region to make up the shortfall; although some 97,000 desiatinas of crown land in Melitopol uezd remained unassigned in 1835, it was scattered in the most remote and arid places and had little value to the existing population.[1]

Foreign colonists, too, faced land shortages. By 1839 fully 47 per cent of Mennonites were landless and other foreign colonists had only avoided the same problem by using up their entire supply of surplus land.

This study began with the question of why these different ethnocultural groups, facing common conditions, parted ways and followed sharply divergent developmental paths in reaction to demographic pressures. My answer is primarily based on a comparison of Mennonites, Orthodox state peasants, and Nogai. In part this reflects the fact that far more documentary evidence survives for these three groups than for other Molochna settlers, but it also accurately represents the role of the Doukhobors, who were exiled to the Caucasus at just the point in time when land shortages became critical. As for non-Mennonite German-speaking colonists, relatively little direct evidence survives about them, but what does survive strongly suggests that their development in the 1840s and 1850s paralleled that of the Mennonites.

The Great Drought of 1832–4 gave particular urgency to the need to change agricultural practices in Molochna. Johann Cornies even saw a positive side to the drought, thinking it would force Mennonites to 'reconsider many things, deal with them and carry them out better, in order to prevent similar disasters in the future.'[2] Because it affected the entire empire, the drought pushed the state to renew efforts to reform state peasant administration, particularly contributing to the decision to create the Ministry of State Domains in 1838. The new ministry played an important role in the Molochna region by selectively lending its authority to settlers' demands for change.

With the need for change apparent, the critical question became the forms that it would take. Studies of peasants both in Russia and elsewhere identify them as 'risk averse,' preferring economic and social solutions that minimize the risk of starvation in times of dearth to innovative solutions that offer potentially higher returns, but at greater risk. The characteristic Russian peasant manifestation of 'risk averse' practices is communal land repartition. What makes the Molochna case particularly interesting is that at the critical juncture in the 1830s, when Orthodox peasants fell into the expected pattern and instituted communal repartition, Mennonite peasants chose a different path.

A key element in this argument is that Mennonites, when they came to the Molochna region, closely conformed to standard definitions of peasants. They had lived in insular, self-sufficient agricultural communities, played no role in the state administrative system, and had been subject to state expropriations that, as a result of religious prejudice, often were even more severe than those experienced by their non-Mennonite peasant neighbours. In Mennonite historiography these characteristics are commonly ascribed to Mennonite religious beliefs. Consequently, the process of economic change in the nineteenth century that saw Mennonites in Russia transform themselves from peasants into farmers, labourers, craftsmen, and industrialists is interpreted as a process of secularization rather than de-peasantization.

Religion clearly played a key role in the development of the Molochna Mennonite settlement. Common religious beliefs were important to the growth of an independent administrative system, while the sense of facing an alien world as a small religiously and ethnically cohesive group helped foster a sense of community. Meanwhile, the congregational system provided a medium for political activity. The importance of religion in forging community identity is further reinforced by the Doukhobor example. Doukhobors, too, developed a sense of community in Molochna, forming a 'Doukhobor commonwealth' strong enough to resist the state's efforts to convert them to Orthodoxy, even at the expense of accepting exile.

Nevertheless, the Mennonite religious ideal called for the colonists to live in a manner that is almost indistinguishable from peasanthood. That ideal, and their condition as peasants, underwent fundamental changes in Molochna as a result of the self-administrative system that Mennonites developed – a system that included among its most important functions the administration of land allocation and use. To understand the changes Mennonites in Molochna underwent it is necessary to temporarily set aside religious issues and think of Mennonites, not as a religious group in the process of secularizing, but as peasants in the process of 'de-peasantizing.'

A critical factor that helped Mennonites break out of peasanthood was their abundance of land in their first years in the Molochna basin. Land was the central productive factor in an almost exclusively agricultural economy, and its abundance meant that there was no need to create special systems to enforce its equitable distribution. This permitted particularly ambitious Mennonites to accrue wealth and invest in commercial ventures. The accrual of wealth served as a ratchet to economic growth and modernization, allowing investment in improved breeds of sheep, agricultural machinery, and land. This was not just the Mennonite story: Orthodox state peasants, Doukhobors, and even Nogai were also getting rich in Molochna in the first decades of the nineteenth century. Indeed, before the 1830s peasant economic development in Molochna had only minor ethnocultural variations.

Why, then, did Mennonites continue along the path of de-peasantization in the 1830s, while Orthodox peasants reverted to peasanthood? Mennonite economic success in Russia has traditionally been explained as a consequence of the state endowing them with more land than Orthodox peasants. This 'land explanation' can be quickly dismissed. Although initial Mennonite allotments of sixty-five desiatinas per family did give the average Mennonite family more land than the average Orthodox peasant family, by the 1830s rapid demographic growth in the Mennonite settlement had already eroded this advantage. Although *landed* Mennonite families still had more land per male soul than Orthodox families, by 1839 land per Mennonite male soul, *including the landless*, had dropped to 10.98 desiatinas, and by 1847 the figure had dropped to 9.35 desiatinas. By comparison, in Bolshoi Tokmak volost, the most populous state peasant district in the Molochna, average land holdings in 1844 were 9.93 desiatinas per male soul. Even the distribution of land within the two communities was similar. In 1844 about one-third of all Bolshoi Tokmak peasants had large holdings in the khutors, 11 per cent engaged in trades, and 55 per cent owned 'only a hand's-breadth' of land. In the Mennonite settlement in 1847, 47 per cent owned full or shared allotments, 8 per cent were tradesmen, and 45 per cent were landless. Clearly, neither the size nor distribution of land allotments will serve to explain the parting of ways.

A second factor often offered in explanation of Mennonite economic success is that the state gave more aid to Mennonites when they arrived in Molochna than it did to Orthodox peasants. This too is a misperception, probably rooted in the fact that aid to Mennonites is well documented, while aid to Orthodox immigrants has heretofore gone unnoticed. State policy towards Orthodox immigrants to New Russia explicitly recognized the need to treat them 'with precisely the same care as are foreign immigrants.'[3] Orthodox settlers received subsidies, loans, and tax deferrals during their first years in Molochna, just as Mennonites did. More importantly, whatever the role of subsidies in the early years, up until the 1830s Orthodox settlers followed a developmental path closely paralleling the Mennonites; this belies the suggestion that state subsidies at the time of immigration account for later Mennonite successes.

Changes in state policy in the 1830s played an important role in the parting of ways, but the state took an increasingly active role in both the Mennonite settlement and the Orthodox state peasant villages. State backing, for example, was critical in the outcome of internal political disputes between Warkentin and Cornies in the 1830s and 1840s. The increased role of the state helped make change possible, but the state cannot take credit for the nature of the change. Even the Doukhobors could resist the state's efforts to convert them, albeit at the expense of

accepting exile. Peasants, whether Doukhobor, Orthodox, or Mennonite, had substantial control over *how* state authority entered into local
decisions.

   This leads to the contradictory idea that in the Molochna basin, the
more sophisticated the mechanisms of community self-administration
before the land shortage crisis, the less communitarian the outcome
after the crisis. The most notable administrative difference between
Mennonites and Orthodox peasants before the crisis was that Mennonites controlled their own surplus land. As a result, involvement in the
public life of the community was critically important for Mennonite
landowners. Perhaps the clearest sign of the importance Mennonites
vested in involvement in the administration of the settlement was the
constant intercongregational disputes they engaged in. In a very important sense these disputes were political, revolving around who would
decide how Mennonite resources would be used. The disputes should
thus be viewed as evidence of a healthy Mennonite political world with
functional problem-solving mechanisms, rather than as a sign of instability. As Cornies insisted in 1840: 'Here in our community there is a
constant battle and this happens because the people here are alive. If
they were dead, there would be no battles, but then nothing good
would be achieved either, for that which is dead is not productive.
What Parliament in England is on a large scale, that is what the Molochna
Mennonites are on a small one.'[4]

   Although the state, by way of the Guardianship Committee, played a
significant role in Mennonite disputes in the Molochna River Basin, the
critical issue was which Mennonite faction would lead the settlement.
There was never any question that the reins of control would stay in
Mennonite hands. Indeed, contrary to conventional interpretations that
Cornies represented a statist fifth column in the Molochna settlement,
the relationship between the state and Cornies can be interpreted in
quite the opposite light. Cornies conceived an administrative system
completely outside of the Russian state's experience, and the state tried
to adopt it as a model for other state peasants. In a sense, this was a case
of the state becoming 'Corniest,' and not the other way around.

   Cornies's role in the development of Molochna Mennonite society
demands special attention, for he was a remarkable figure who left a
permanent imprint on the settlement. The explanation for Mennonite
development I have offered thus far suggests that developments in Mennonite society were based on objective economic conditions; this leaves
little room for Cornies's personal contributions. There is some truth to

this, for other Mennonite settlements in places outside of Cornies's control shared in the Mennonite success story. Cornies was a product of a system that allowed brilliant men to shine, and had he not risen to the task it seems likely that someone else would have. Still, Molochna was the most progressive of Mennonite settlements in Russia, constantly attracting the praise of the state, and this leading position must be credited to Cornies.

There were three important factors in the development of the Molochna Mennonite community: a self-conscious religious identity, a land tenure system that permitted Mennonites to take control of their own public resources, and the guiding hand of Cornies. As important as religion and Cornies's genius were, arguably it was control over common resources that played the decisive role. Administration of the settlement's surplus land encouraged Mennonites to develop a system of civil administration to parallel the congregational system. The civil administration system in turn took responsibility for the welfare of the entire Mennonite community. Mennonites created mechanisms to protect the interests of their poor without sacrificing the land tenure rights of individual community members. Wealthy progressive Mennonites then led the way to agricultural innovations that served the whole community.

The Orthodox state peasant solution to land shortages was far different from the Mennonite one. Orthodox peasants arrived in Molochna with a system of communal land administration already in place. But in Molochna the function of such self-administrative structures eroded because there was neither a shortage of land to necessitate communal administration nor a surplus to encourage it. The peasants' Orthodox faith provided no basis for developing a distinct community identity, for unlike Mennonites, Orthodox peasants were only passive participants in church affairs. The lack of corporate structures meant that when the land crisis came, Orthodox peasants lacked formal community problem-solving mechanisms to resolve them. In effect, theirs was a community without politics. The 'depredations' the village of Popovka committed against the village of Berestova in 1834 were the result of this lack of strong internal administrative structures. As a consequence of this deficiency, when the crisis hit, peasants had no choice but to turn to outside authorities to resolve their problems. It must be emphasized that this was not a reflection of the peasants' desire to have the state take control of their lives. Indeed, peasants in Bolshoi Tokmak resisted most of the reforms proposed by Wilhelm Bauman in 1844. Yet they could not resolve their central problem for themselves, and in the end they had no choice but to turn to the state. The result, namely, repartition, amounted to the imposition of communalism as a cure for the lack of community.

Stepping back from local specifics, the Molochna story has important implications for broader questions regarding the Russian state peasantry. Clearly, in Molochna the image of state peasants as 'the state's serfs' will not do, for foreign colonists, Nogai, Doukhobors, and Orthodox peasants, with their widely differing experiences, were all formally designated as state peasants. Molochna is not representative of the experience of all state peasants everywhere in the empire. Nevertheless, like the Molochna settlers, the majority of Russia's state peasants lived on the empire's peripheries. If the experiences of Siberian or Central Asian state peasants were not the same as those of state peasants in New Russia, the Molochna story nevertheless obliges us to recognize that it cannot be assumed that *any* state peasants fit neatly into a single socioeconomic mould. By 1858 state peasants made up half of Russia's peasant population and almost 40 per cent of the total population of the empire. They represented a vast, potentially innovative and productive human resource for Russia, and their role in Russia's development demands far closer attention than it has heretofore received.

Finally, the Molochna story highlights the barriers that hindered the state from effectively administering its peasants. The oasis that the state imagined to exist in the Molochna basin was a gross simplification of an environmentally, economically, politically, socially, and ethnically complex region. The state's inability to understand such complexities left it with little chance to administer Molochna effectively. Instead of guiding regional development it could only react when harvests failed or whole communities sank into poverty and fled. Even when the state attempted to become more closely involved, it relied so heavily on local administrators that its authority was reduced to little more than an unwieldy club, lent to whichever local figure or group was strong enough to swing it. Thus, Doukhobors, although 'among the best of the government's colonies,' were needlessly exiled.

The oasis was a mirage, and the government in far-off St Petersburg, thirsty for control of its peripheries, was only too eager to be deceived by it. The real Molochna combined the 'dry cracked ground' of Gnadenfeld and the lush orchards of Iushanlee, the Byzantine complexities of Mennonite intercongregational disputes and the crude expropriations of Orthodox peasant 'depredations.' Isolated from the state, constrained by the environment, pressured by demographic growth and changing markets, settlers had no choice but to draw upon their own traditions, experiences, and conceptions of justice and equity, as they fled, formed communes, or created commonwealths on the rolling steppes of the Molochna River Basin.

Appendix

TABLE A.1
Population of Melitopol uezd, 1804–1861, and Melitopol and Berdiansk uezds,
1842–1861

Year	Orthodox and sectarian state peasants	Sectarians	Nogai	Mennonites	Germans	Total
1804			16,003			
1805				1,532	872	
1806	21,763		17,122	1,547		
1807	25,023		17,088	1,744	956	44,811
1808	26,801		16,468	1,854	1,011	46,134
1809	30,412		16,975	1,919	998	50,304
1810	34,363		17,427	2,070	2,602	56,462
1811				2,107	2,912	
1812	51,395			2,253		
1813	52,863			2,329	3,582	
1814	44,346	2,273	31,778	2,413		
1815	48,563		31,394	2,479	3,817	86,253
1816	50,637		29,780	2,572	4,053	87,042
1817	40,563	2,412	32,712	2,670	4,172	82,529
1818	41,074	2,498	32,677	2,942	4,376	83,567
1819	43,757		32,924	3,047		
1820	44,010		33,710	3,641		
1821	41,447	2,514		4,922		
1822	50,446		32,685	5,364		

Table A.1 continued

Year	Orthodox and Sectarian State Peasants	Sectarians	Nogai	Mennonites	Germans	Total
1823	50,981		32,016	5,634		
1824	50,989		30,919	5,925		
1825	51,804		29,729	6,094		
1826	53,083		30,395	6,454		
1827	45,170		30,623	6,984		
1828	49,571			7,194	7,050	
1829	49,324		30,676	7,500	7,268	94,768
1830	50,444		30,881	7,662	7,492	96,479
1831	56,768		30,721	8,212	7,698	103,399
1832				8,344	7,921	
1833	81,180[a]			8,639	8,196	98,015
1834					8,830	
1835	81,173[a]			9,271	8,732	
1836				9,561		
1837		7,270	32,058	9,945		
1838				10,794	9,273	
1839				11,202	9,642	
1840				11,491	9,792	
1841				12,036	10,085	
1842	145,152[a]			12,206		
1843	152,932[a]			12,545		
1844	195,381[a]			12,833		
1845	204,224			13,279	11,228	228,731
1846	216,340[a]			13,832	11,464	241,636
1847	216,379[a]			14,265	11,583	242,227
1848	203,314[a]			14,636		
1849	202,533[a]			14,854		
1850	230,444[a]			16,024		
1851	215,735			16,357		
1852	227,335[a]			16,656		
1853	245,647[a]			17,420		
1854	252,831[a]			17,580		
1855	254,788[a]			17,764		

Table A.1 continued

Year	Orthodox and Sectarian State Peasants	Sectarians	Nogai	Mennonites	Germans	Total
1856	253,937[a]			18,427		
1857	258,462[a]			17,953	15,384	291,799
1858	261,726[a]			19,335	17,275	298,336
1859	239,054[a]		35,143	19,804	17,878	311,879
1860	235,340[a]		105	20,569	18,377	274,391
1861	263,225[a]		20	21,918	18,158	303,321

[a] Including Nogai.

Sources: *GAOO, f.* 1, *op.* 190, *d.* 12, 15; *f.* 1, *op.* 191, *d.* 29, 62; *f.* 6, *op.* 1, *d.* 302, 626, 973, 1024; *f.* 6, *op.* 4, *d.* 18086; *f.* 1, *op.* 200, *d.* 52; *f.* 1, *op.* 219, *d.* 3, n.p.; 'Otchety tavricheskikh gubernatorov,' 1823–27, *RGIA, f.* 1281, *op.* 11, *d.* 133; 'S otchetami mestnykh kolonistskim nachal'stvo so sostoianii kolonii za 1827,' *f.* 383, *op.* 1, *d.* 837; 'S otchetami mestnykh kolonistskim nachal'stvo so sostoianii kolonii,' 1828–35, *f.* 383, *op.* 29; 1842–61, *f.* 1281, *op.* 4–6; *f.* 1283, *op.* 1 (for 1854); 'Tabellen: über den zustand der Molotschner Kolonisten,' 1848, *PJBRMA*, file 1138, 1ob-37ob; 'Verzeichnis über die bevolkerüng im Molotschner Mennonisten Gebiet,' 1849, *PJBRMA*, file 1402, 2; *GADO, f.* 134, *op.* 1; *d.* 138, 310, 402, 786, 837; *GAKO, f.* 26, *op.* 1, *d.* 969, 994, 2478, 2503, 3283, 3308, 4137, 5017, 5369, 5394; Brandes, *Von den Zaren Adoptiert*, 340, Table 53; Goerz, *The Molotschna Settlement*, 45; Benjamin Heinrich Unruh, *Die niederländisch-niederdeutschen Hintergründe der mennonitischen Ostwanderungen im 16., 18. und 19: Jahrhundert* (Karlsruhe: Heinrich Schneider, 1955), 304–29; Urry, *None But Saints*, 287, Appendix II; Sergeev, 'Ukhod Tavricheskikh Nogaitsev,' 201–5.

TABLE A.2
Livestock in Melitopol uezd, 1805–1842, and Melitopol and Beriandsk uezds, 1843–1861

	Horses				Cattle				Sheep				Total animal units
	Orthodox and sectarians	Nogai	Colonists	Total	Orthodox and sectarians	Nogai	Colonists	Total	Orthodox and sectarians	Nogai	Colonists	Total	
1805	1,213				12,608			15,051					
1806	1,419				13,931			18,497					
1807	1,772	11,422			17,051	24,539			25,471	15,448			
1808	2,060	11,805			22,285	44,050			33,038	12,375			
1809	2,446	17,934			25,752	57,470			40,447	19,731			
1810	3,054	35,738			31,140	69,915			49,096	26,029			
1811	3,298	52,909	5,253	61,460	33,377	106,216	3,743	143,336	56,367	42,361	3,152	101,880	108,000
1812	3,637	43,713			35,545	96,355			64,705	45,809			
1813	3,625	37,600	5,540	46,765	25,134	83,335	5,422	113,891	65,036	48,708	3,378	117,122	90,923
1814	4,065	40,127			37,394	90,720			72,748	54,318			
1815	4,452	42,214			37,803	94,884			75,405	65,825			
1816	4,738	45,176			39,072	104,400			78,990	75,359			
1817	5,010	51,556			40,409	123,194			83,327	98,492			
1818	5,427	59,667			42,513	138,080			88,516	116,566			
1819	6,977	68,172			49,756	153,112			96,111	132,392			
1820	8,150			53,747				100,075					
1821	8,239			52,514				99,174					
1822	8,413			52,684				98,550					
1823	6,997	48,041			60,857	158,512			110,929	131,703			
1824	8,879	53,853			84,768	160,398			126,826	137,100			

Year	C1	C2	C3	C4	C5	C6	C7	C8	C9	C10	C11	C12
1825	6,976	32,740		71,629		135,915			107,190	125,297		
1826	6,965	36,389		65,667		157,664			112,115	134,353		
1827	6,681	54,045		62,133		107,121			128,086	112,669		
1828			10,188		14,199				99,029			
1829			11,563		14,726				113,247			
1830		26,462				89,648			104,194	134,174		
1831		28,799	13,294		18,018	88,790			109,557	148,381		
1832			13,403		20,279							
1833												
1834			10,259		10,945					114,346		
1835												
1836												
1837		13,058				21,966			68,512			
1838												
1839												
1840												
1841												
1842												
1843							271,550	61,900			754,608	273,968
1844							360,942	75,673			1,093,305	376,269
1845							369,600	38,850			1,037,481	354,447
1846							366,800	72,900			1,104,760	379,549
1847							34,847	16,246			526,666	110,486
1848							143,643	34,030			724,596	199,732
1849							178,574	39,063			824,741	234,184

TABLE A.2 continued

	Horses				Cattle				Sheep				Total animal units
	Orthodox and Sectarians	Nogai	Colonists	Total	Orthodox and Sectarians	Nogai	Colonists	Total	Orthodox and Sectarians	Nogai	Colonists	Total	
1850				19,909				63,705				196,075	69,841
1851				27,009				61,878				557,375	132,401
1852				42,935				170,226				701,167	211,599
1853				62,995				261,501				1,132,907	333,038
1854													
1855				60,167				251,300				1,040,532	311,852
1856				58,784				231,592				1,019,688	299,004
1857				67,001				274,376				1,191,526	350,311
1858				66,159				250,534				1,112,076	326,098
1859				65,520				274,725				1,356,846	377,361
1860				51,803				211,555				1,497,618	366,651
1861				75,072				225,324				1,287,270	348,054

Sources: GADO, f. 134, op. 1, d. 138, 310, 332, 356, 402, 981, 251, 343, 431, 692, 701, 711, 712, 753, 786, 893, 936; GAOO, f. 6, op. 1, d. 197, 5284; GAKO, f. 26, op. 1, d. 994, 2503, 3308, 4137, 5017, 5394; 'Otchety Tavricheskikh Gubernatorov,' 1808–1810, 1811–16, 1822–7, 1841–61; RGIA, f. 1281, f. 1281, op. 11, 4–6; f. 1283, op. 1 (for 1854); A.A. Sergeev, 'Nogaitsy na Molochnykh vodakh (1790–1832). Istoricheskoi ocherk,' Izvestiia Tavricheskoi Uchenoi Arkhivnoi Kommissii 48 (1912; Cornies, 'Landwirthschaftliche Notizen,' 1837, PJBRMA, file 992; Brandes, Von den Zaren Adoptiert, 201, Table 24; Unruh, Die niederländisch-niederdeutschen Hintergründe, 304–29.

Appendix 193

TABLE A.3
Nogai grain production (in chetverts), 1804–1831

	Population	Sown	Harvested	Output/seed ratio	Harvested per person
1804	16,003	–	–	–	–
1806	17,122	–	–	–	–
1807	17,088	–	–	–	–
1808	16,468	8,485	68,700	8.10	4.17
1809	16,975	8,692	39,895	4.59	2.35
1810	17,427	17,922	75,953	4.24	4.36
1811	–	–	–	–	–
1812	15,024	17,296	69,067	3.99	–
1813	–	23,405	63,920	2.73	–
1814	31,778	8,604	31,882	3.71	1.00
1815	31,394	10,946	45,458	4.15	1.45
1816	29,780	28,509	263,710	9.25	8.86
1817	32,712	39,270	217,839	5.55	6.66
1818	32,677	42,860	282,099	6.58	8.63
1819	32,924	48,100	203,695	4.23	6.19
1820	33,710	22,470	77,023	3.43	2.28
1821	–	23,031	69,930	3.04	–
1822	32,685	15,645	86,460	5.53	2.65
1823	32,016	19,702	15,774	0.80	0.49
1824	30,919	–	–	–	–
1825	29,729	11,791	27,123	2.30	0.91
1826	30,395	7,497	61,448	8.20	2.02
1827	30,623	10,943	38,005	3.47	1.24
1828	–	13,210	51,330	3.89	–
1829	30,676	21,723	108,131	4.98	3.52
1830	30,881	22,782	47,524	2.09	1.54
1831	30,721	18,506	102,566	5.54	3.34
Average				4.65	3.56

Sources: 'Otchety Tavricheskikh Gubernatorov,' 1808–1827, *RGIA*, f. 1281, *op.* 11; Annual reports of Demaison to the governor of Tavria: *GAKO*, f. 26, *op.* 1, *d.* 994 (1814), *d.* 2503 (1817), *d.* 3308 (1818), *d.* 4137 (1819), *d.* 5017 (1820), *d.* 5394 (1821); Sergeev, 'Nogaitsy na Molochnykh vodakh,' 61 (1828–31); Cornies, 'Landwirthschaftliche Notizen,' 1837, *PJBRMA*, file 992, 1–5ob.

Notes

Chapter One: Introduction

1 'Kritik betreffend die Schwarzebrache in Süd-Russland,' n.d. [1848?], *PJBRMA*, file 1308 (emphasis in original). In the 1860s another anonymous Russian writer would apply almost precisely the same description to Russian Mennonite colonies in the Volga region – see James W. Long, *From Privileged to Dispossessed: The Volga Germans, 1860–1917* (Lincoln: Nebraska University Press, 1988), 76.

2 Quoted in Heinrich Goerz, *The Molotschna Settlement*, trans. Al Reimer and John B. Toews (Winnipeg: CMBC/Manitoba Mennonite Historical Society, 1993), 28.

3 The most detailed record of the physical geography of the Molochna that I am aware of is B.G. Karpova, 'Formy poverkhnosti i stroenie zemnoi kory v predelakh Novorossii,' in *Rossiia. Polnoe geograficheskoe opisanie nashego otechestva*, (hereafter, *Rossiia*), ed. V.P. Semenov-Tian-Shanskii (St Petersburg: A.F. Devriena, 1910), 14: 1–48. The *Encyclopedia of Ukraine, s.v.* Azov Lowland, and Azov Upland, is also a valuable source, while a brief but useful summary can be found in John Friesen, *Against the Wind: The Story of Four Mennonite Villages (Gnadenthal, Grünfeld, Neu-Chortitza, and Steinfeld) in Southern Ukraine, 1872–1943* (Winnipeg: Henderson Books, 1994), 13–17.

4 On flora, see V.G. Karatygina, 'Rastitel'nyi i zhivotnyi mir,' in *Rossiia*, 14: 72–125.

5 On climate, see P.A. Fedulova, 'Klimat,' *Rossiia*, 14: 49–71; M.Y. Nuttonson, *Ecology and Crop Geography of the Ukraine and the Ukrainian Agro-Climatic Analogues in North America* (Washington, DC: American Institute of Crop Ecology, 1947).

6 'Raboty po snabzheniiu vodoi pereselentsev, proizvedennyia v Tavricheskoi gubernii v 1862 godu,' *ZhMGI* 83 (July 1863), 316.

7 'Vedomost' o glubine kolodtsev v kazhdoi kolonii Molochanskogo menonitskogo okruga,' 1842, *PJBRMA*, file 841.

8 'Po predstavlenniiu glavnago popechitelia kolonistov iuzhnago kraia Rossii po sporu menonitov s dukhobortsami o granitsakh ikh vladeniia,' 29 February 1828, *RGIA, f.* 383, *op.* 29, *d.* 480.

9 An excellent introduction to the historiography is Richard White, 'American Environmental History: The Development of a New Historical Field,' *Pacific Historical Review* 54:3 (1985), 297–335.

10 Donald Worster, *The Wealth of Nature: Environmental History and the Ecological Imagination* (New York: Oxford University Press, 1993), 48–9.

11 A particularly clear example of a study in which the environment is the subject is Elinor G. K. Melville, *A Plague of Sheep: Environmental Consequences of the Conquest of Mexico* (Cambridge: Cambridge University Press, 1994). On the issues of boundaries between disciplines, see Barbara Leibhardt, 'Interpretation and Causal Analysis: Theories in Environmental History,' *Environmental Review* 12:1 (1988), 23–36.

12 Goerz, *The Molotschna Settlement*; Franz Isaac, *Die Molotschner Mennoniten. Ein Beitrag zur Geschichte derselben* (N.P.: Halbstadt und Braun, 1908); The quotation is from James Urry, *None But Saints: The Transformation of Mennonite Life in Russia, 1789–1889* (Winnipeg: Windflower Communications, 1989), 26.

13 Notable recent work that begins to place the Mennonites more firmly in their Russian context includes Leonard G. Friesen, 'Mennonites and Their Peasant Neighbours in Ukraine Before 1900,' *Journal of Mennonite Studies* (hereafter *JMS*) 10 (1992), 56–69; Harvey L. Dyck, 'Landlessness in the Old Colony: The *Judenplan* Experiment 1850–1880,' in John Friesen, ed., *Mennonites in Russia 1788–1988: Essays in Honour of Gerhard Lohrenz* (Winnipeg: CMBC, 1989), 183–202, and James Urry, 'Mennonites, Nationalism and the State in Imperial Russia,' *JMS* 12 (1994), 65–88.

14 The standard history of the Doukhobors is George Woodcock and Ivan Avakumovic, *The Doukhobors* (London: Faber and Faber, 1968), while other important works on Doukhobors in the Molochna include Gary Dean Fry, 'The Doukhobors, 1801–1855: The Origins of a Successful Dissident Sect' (PhD dissertation, American University, 1976), and A.I. Klibanov, *Istoriia religioznogo sektantstva v Rossii (60-e gody XIX v.–1917 g.)* (Moscow: Nauka, 1965), 85–121. The best general source on German colonists in New Russia is Detlef Brandes, *Von den Zaren adoptiert: Die deutschen Kolonisten und die Balkansiedler in Neurussland und Bessarabien 1751–1914* (Munich:

Oldenbourg, 1993), which also contains an exhaustive bibliography on the subject.

15 E.I. Druzhinina, *Kuchuk-Kainardzhiiskii mir 1774 goda (ego podgotovka i zakliuchenie)* (Moscow: Nauka, 1995); *Severnoe Prichernomor'e v 1775–1800 gg.* (Moscow: Nauka, 1959); *Iuzhnaia Ukraina v 1800–1825 gg.* (Moscow: Nauka, 1970); and *Iuzhnaia Ukraina v period krizisa feodalisma 1825–1860 gg.* (Moscow: Nauka, 1981).

16 Druzhinina, *Iuzhnaia Ukraina v 1800–1825 gg.*, 128.

17 Olga Crisp, 'The State Peasants under Nicholas I,' in *Studies in the Russian Economy before 1914* (London: Macmillan, 1976), 73.

18 Ibid., 76.

19 Vadim Aleksandrovich Aleksandrov, 'Land Re-allotment in the Peasant Commune of Late-Feudal Russia,' in Roger Bartlett, ed., *Land Commune and Peasant Community in Russia: Communal Forms in Imperial and Early Soviet Society* (New York: St Martins, 1990), 39. For comparable assessments, see, e.g., Crisp, 'The State Peasants under Nicholas I,' 94; George L. Yaney, *The Systemization of Russian Government: Social Evolution in the Domestic Administration of Imperial Russia, 1711–1905* (Urbana: University of Illinois Press, 1973), 133.

20 N.M. Druzhinin, *Gosudarstvennye krest'iane i reforma P.D. Kiseleva*, 2 vols. (Moscow: Nauka, 1946 and 1958).

21 T.A. Koniukhova, *Gosudarstvennaia derevnia Litvy i reforma P.D. Kiseleva 1840–1857 gg. (Vilenskaia i Kovenskaia gubernii)* (Moscow: Moskovskogo universiteta, 1975); I.A. Antsupov, *Gosudarstvennaia derevnia Bessarabii v XIX veke (1812–1870 gg.)* (Kishinev: Kartia Moldoveniaske, 1966).

22 George Bolotenko, 'Administration of the State Peasants in Russia before the Reforms of 1838' (PhD dissertation: University of Toronto, 1979).

23 Eric R. Wolf, *Peasants* (Englewood Cliffs, NJ: Prentice-Hall, 1966), 3–4.

24 For a thorough discussion of standard definitions of peasants, see Frank Ellis, *Peasant Economics: Farm Households and Agrarian Development* (Cambridge: Cambridge University Press, 1988), 4–13.

25 James C. Scott, *Domination and the Arts of Resistance: Hidden Transcripts* (New Haven: Yale University Press, 1990), x.

26 James C. Scott, *The Moral Economy of the Peasant: Rebellion and Subsistence in Southeast Asia* (New Haven: Yale University Press, 1976), 6–7.

27 See, e.g., Steven L. Hoch, *Serfdom and Social Control in Russia: Petrovskoe, a Village in Tambov* (Chicago: University of Chicago Press, 1986); Jeffrey Burds, 'The Social Control of Peasant Labor in Russia: The Response of Village Communities to Labor Migration in the Central Industrial Region,

1861–1905,' in Esther Kingston-Mann, and Timothy Mixter, eds., *Peasant Economy, Culture, and Politics of European Russia, 1800–1921* (Princeton: Princeton University Press, 1991), 52–100; Lynne Viola, *Peasant Rebels under Stalin: Collectivisation and the Culture of Peasant Resistance* (New York: Oxford University Press, 1996).

Chapter Two: Colonization and Administrative Policy

1 'Ukaz tavricheskogo pravitel'stva ... ob otvode zemli gosudarstvennym krest'ianam iz chernigovskoi gubernii,' 18 February 1824, *GAKhO, f.* 14, *op.* 2, *d.* 7, n.p.

2 Alan W. Fisher, *The Russian Annexation of the Crimea, 1772–1783* (Cambridge: Cambridge University Press, 1970), 135–42.

3 Judith Pallot and Denis J. B. Shaw, *Landscape and Settlement in Romanov Russia 1613–1917* (Oxford: Clarendon Press, 1990), 21–6.

4 See, e.g., Roger P. Bartlett, *Human Capital: The Settlement of Foreigners in Russia, 1762–1804* (Cambridge: Cambridge University Press, 1979), 23–30.

5 *PSZ* (1), 12099. Regarding the implementation of the Plan, see Bartlett, *Human Capital,* 109–118.

6 On the general subject of immigration to the region, see Bartlett, *Human Capital.*

7 P.S. Pallas, *Travels through the Southern Provinces of the Russian Empire, in the Years 1793 and 1794,* 2 vols. (London: A. Strahan, 1802), vol. 1, 531–5.

8 For the 1797 map, see *RVIA, f.* 846 *op.* 16, *d.* 23814, n.p. For short histories of villages and towns in the region, see V.I. Petrikin et al., eds., *Istoriia mist i sil Ukrains'koi RSR: Zaporiz'ka oblast'* (Kiev: Nauka URSR, 1970).

9 The lack of proper equipment during the original surveys is frequently referred to in the course of new surveys done in the 1830s and 1840s. See, e.g., *RGIA, f.* 383 *op.* 1, *d.* 190, *l.* 6ob.

10 *PSZ* (1), 1265.

11 V.M. Kabuzan, *Zaselenie Novorossii (Ekaterinoslavskoi i Khersonskoi gubernii) v XVIII-pervoi polovine XIX veka (1719–1858 gg.)* (Moscow: Nauka, 1976).

12 Kabuzan, *Narodonaselenie Rossii v XVIII–pervoi polovine XIX v. (po materialam revizii)* (Moscow: Nauka, 1963), 159–63, Table 17; Druzhinina, *Iuzhnaia Ukraina v 1800–1825,* 247, Table 19; Druzhinina, *Iuzhnaia Ukraina v period krizisa feodalizma,* 13, Table 1.

13 At least, my attempts to find the 1835 *reviziia* records in *RGIA, f.* 571, turned up only partial records. A full-scale demographic study, such as that conducted on the remainder of New Russia by Kabuzan, would quite possibly permit a reconstruction of the *reviziia*. For sources, see Table 2.1.

14 'Verzeichnis Über die Bevölkerung im Molotschner Mennonisten Gebiet. Von Januar 1806 bis derselben datum 1849,' *PJBRMA*, file 1402, 2.

15 Hoch, *Serfdom and Social Control*, 73.

16 Don Karl Rowney, and Walter McKenzie Pinter, 'Officialdom and Bureaucratization: Conclusion,' in Pintner & Rowney, eds., *Russian Officialdom: The Bureaucratization of Russian Society from the Seventeenth Century to the Twentieth Century* (Chapel Hill: University of North Carolina Press, 1980), 371.

17 S. Frederick Starr, *Decentralization and Self-Government in Russia, 1830–1870* (Princeton: Princeton University Press, 1972), 20.

18 A number of studies have addressed the Russian regional administrative system. On the State Peasant administration specifically, the most important are Druzhinin, *Gosudarstvennye krest'iane*, and Bolotenko, 'Administration of the State Peasants.' Important works on the broader administrative problem include Starr, *Decentralization and Self-Government*, and Yaney, *The Systematization of Russian Government*. Marc Raeff's voluminous writings are basic to an understanding of the ideological underpinnings of Russian administrative structures. See, e.g., Marc Raeff, *The Well-Ordered Police State: Social and Institutional Change through Law in the Germanies and Russia, 1600– 1800* (New Haven: Yale University Press, 1983).

19 Bolotenko claims that where land redistribution did not exist, neither did the obshchina. On this basis, he claims that it did not exist in Tavria guberniia prior to the 1820s or 1830s (Bolotenko, 'Administration of the State Peasants,' 31). However, peasants in non-redistributive state peasant villages in Tavria guberniia routinely identified themselves in their petitions as members of obshchinas.

20 Urry, *None But Saints*, 71–2.

21 Bolotenko, 'Administration of the State Peasants,' 195.

22 Ibid., 206.

23 Ibid., 209.

24 Ibid., 209.

25 Ibid., 209.

26 Ibid., 160–61. *Zemskii ispravnik* is often translated as 'police chief,' but 'district administrator' more accurately expresses the broad administrative functions of the position.

27 Starr, *Decentralization and Self-Government*, 40.

28 Properly called the 'Office of Guardianship of New Russian Settlers' until 1818.

29 On the ill-defined role of Governor-Generals, see Yaney, *The Systemization of Russian Government*, 72.

30 'O glavnykh osnovaniiakh novago polozheniia ob obezpechenii prodovol'stviia,' 1840, *RGIA, f.* 1589 *op.* 1, *d.* 693, *ll.* 70–132.

31 *PSZ* (1), 13017.

32 *PSZ* (1), 17127.

33 *PSZ* (1), 19203.

34 'Ob urozhae v nyneshniem godu khleba i o merakh k obezpecheniiu prodovolstviia zhitelei Krymskago poluostrova,' 1821, *GAKO, f.* 26, *op.* 1, *d.* 5394, n.p.

35 'Po zapiske o predpisanii kolonistskim nachal'stvam otnositel'no obespecheniia v prodovol'stvii kolonistov v neurozhainom gody,' May 1822, *RGIA, f.* 383, *op.* 29, *d.* 502, *ll.* 2–5ob.

36 Arcadius Kahan, 'The "Tsar Hunger" in the Land of the Tsars,' in Arcadius Kahan, *Russian Economic History: The Nineteenth Century* (Chicago: University of Chicago Press, 1989), 108.

37 For 1843 grain reserve figures, see 'Otchety tavricheskikh gubernatorov ... za 1843,' *RGIA, f.* 1281, *op.* 4, *d.* 49a, *ll.* 74ob–75. For the 1842 modification to the law see 'Instruktsiia o privedenii v deistvie vysochaishe utverzhdennago 16–go marta 1842 goda polozheniia ob obespechenii prodovol'stviem gosudarstvennykh krest'ian chastnymi zapasami,' 16 March 1842, *RGIA, f.* 1589 *op.* 1, *d.* 693, *ll.* 310–316ob.

38 'Vedomost' o summakh, otpushchennykh iz gosudarstvennago kaznacheistva na prodovol'stvie gosudarstvennykh krest'ian v 1833 i 1834 godakh, po sluchaiu neurozhaia,' *RGIA, f.* 1589, *op.* 1, *d.* 693, *l.* 39. The paper ruble, or assignant, traded at 3.65 to the silver ruble in 1834.

39 'Ob urozhae khlebov i trav v Tavricheskoi gubernii v 1858 godu,' *RGIA, f.* 1287, *op.* 3, *d.* 199, n.p.

40 'O glavnykh osnovaniiakh novago polozheniia ob obespechenii prodovol'stviem,' 1840, *RGIA, f.* 1589 *op.* 1, *d.* 693, *l.* 71.

41 'Mnenie upravliaiushchago Ministerstva Politsii generala ot infanterii grafa Viazmitinova, po predmetu zapreshcheniia vypuska khleba iz odnoi Gubernii v druguiu pri sluchae neurozhaia i nedostatka v prodovol'stvii,' n.d. (probably 1819), *RGIA f.* 1287, *op.* 1, *d.* 184, *ll.* 4–13ob.

42 *PSZ* (1), 19943.

43 *PSZ* (1), 24992; *PSZ* (1), 25302.

44 *PSZ* (1), 25856.

45 *PSZ* (1), 24992.

46 Petrikin, *Istoriia mist i sil Ukrains'koi RSR: Zaporiz'ka oblast'.*

47 'O pereselenii Smolenskikh kazennykh krest'ian v Novorossiiskii krai,' 1803–1822, *RGIA, f.* 1285, *op.* 1, *d.* 13a, *ll.* 19–23ob. Regarding the secularisation of church and monastery lands and the creation of economic

peasants, see V.I. Semevskii, *Krest'iane v tsarstvovanie Imperatritsy Ekateriny II,*
2 vols. (St Petersburg: Stasiulevich, 1881), 2:252–286.

48 'O pereselenii Smolenskikh ... krest'ian,' 1803–1822, *RGIA, f.* 1285, *op.* 1, *d.*
13a, *ll.* 19–23ob.

49 Ibid., *ll.* 87–87ob.

50 Ibid., *ll.* 87–87ob.

51 Contenius to Ministry of Internal Affairs, 22 August 1806, *RGIA, f.* 1285, *op.*
1, *d.* 73, *ll.* 7–9ob.

52 'Po predmetu pereseleniia kazennykh krest'ian v Novorossiiskii krai,'
September 1806, *RGIA, f.* 1285, *op.* 1, *d.* 73, *ll.* 32ob–34ob.

53 Ibid., *ll.* 32ob.–34.

54 'Po pis'mam khersonskago voennago gubernatora Diuka Rishel'e,' August
1806, *RGIA, f.* 1285, *op.* 1, *d.* 73, *ll.* 1–7.

55 On the origins of early colonists, see A. S. Kotsievskii, 'Krest'ianskaia
kolonizatsiia iuzhnoi ukrainy v pervoi treti XIX v.,' *Materialy po istorii
sel'skogo khoziaistva i krest'ianstva SSSR,* 4 (1964), 130.

56 *PSZ* (1), 21941.

57 On the influence of the climate on settlement sites, see Friesen, 'Mennonites and their Peasant Neighbours in Ukraine Before 1900,' 58. Seasonal
water flow in the rivers of the Molochna watershed are described in
'Opisanie rechek, protekaiushchikh v Novorossiiskoi gubernii v
Mariupol'skom uezde, pri kotorykh predpologaiutsia seleniia dlia
frantsuzskikh vykhodtsev,' 5 August 1797, *RGVIA, f.* 846, *op.* 16, *d.* 23814,
n.p.

58 Bolotenko, 'Administration of the State Peasants,' 30.

59 Wilhelm Bernard Bauman, 'Opisanie kazennago seleniia Tokmaka, v
Tavricheskoi gubernii,' *ZhMGI* 24 (1847), 3–4.

60 See, e.g., 'Spisok khutorov Dneprovskago i Melitopol'skago uezdov,
pereimenovannykh v sela,' 15 December 1839, *GAKhO, f.* 14, *op.* 2, *d.* 97,
n.p.

61 This organic development of multivillage obshchinas is noted by Moshe
Lewin in 'The obshchina and the Village,' in Roger Bartlett, ed., *Land
Commune and Peasant Community in Russia: Communal Forms in Imperial and
Early Soviet Society* (London: Macmillan, 1990), 20–35. Lewin, who calls
multivillage obshchinas 'complex communes,' provides a full examination
of the historiographical debate surrounding the obshchina.

62 See, eg, Johann Cornies, 'Notwendig zu beobachtende und in den Nogaier
Dialeckt zu übersetzen nötige Regeln, zur Zivilisie ung der nogaischen
Bewohner der aus einem Nogaier Aule gegründeten Muster Kolonien
Akkermann,' *PJBRMA,* file 364, 8–16ob.

63 See, e.g., an 18 November 1804 letter from Infantry General Rosenburg to Cavalry Colonel Trevogin, in which Rosenburg expresses his 'disgust, most of all, at the disorder' of nomadism. *GAKO, f.* 27, *op.* 1, *d.* 543, n.p. On Russian attitudes toward non-Christian peoples, see Michael Khodarkovsky, '"Ignoble Savages and Unfaithful Subjects": Constructing Non-Christian Identities in Early Modern Russia,' in Daniel J. Brower and Edward J. Lazzerini, eds., *Russia's Orient: Imperial Borderlands and Peoples, 1700–1917* (Bloomington: Indiana University Press, 1997), 9–26.

64 B.B. Kochekaev, *Nogaisko-russkie otnosheniia v XV–XVIII vv.* (Alma-Ata: Nauka, 1988).

65 Pallas, *Travels through the Southern Provinces of the Russian Empire*, 1: 533.

66 For the 1796 group, see Pallas to Tavria Governor Zubov, 19 March 1796, *GAKO, f.* 801, *op.* 1, *d.* 58, n.p. On the 1807 and 1810 groups, see K. B Khanatskii, ed., *Pamiatnaia knizhka Tavricheskoi gubernii* (Simferopol': Tipografiia Tavricheskogo gubernskogo pravleniia, 1867), 210.

67 'Otchety Tavricheskikh gubernatorov ... za 1810,' *RGIA, f.* 1281, *op.* 11, *d.* 131, n.p.

68 Pallas, *Travels*, 1:532–3.

69 Ibid.

70 A.M. Khazanov, *Nomads and the Outside World* (Cambridge: Cambridge University Press, 1984), 19.

71 Ibid., 51.

72 'Plan Novorossiiskoi gubernii Mariupol'skago uezda, protekaiushchikh rechek sniatyi v 1797 godu Avgusta 5 dnia,' *RGVIA, f.* 846, *op.* 16, *d.* 23814, n.p.

73 Baiazet Bey to Civil Governor Borozdin, 1803, *GAKO, f.* 27, *op.* 1, *d.* 543, n.p.

74 Demaison (ca. 1760–1826), who signed himself 'le Comte de Maison,' in his French-language correspondence, entered Russian service with the rank of College Assessor in 1802, when he became an inspector at the Aleksandrovskii state factory in Ekaterinoslav. He was made Chief of the Nogai Horde on 21 April 1808, a post he would hold until one year before his death in 1826. His complete service record can be found in *GAKO, f.* 26, *op.* 1, *d.* 5509, n.p.

75 Johann Cornies, 'Kratkii obzor polozheniia Nogaiskikh tatar, vodvorennykh v Melitopol'skom uezde Tavricheskoi gubernii,' *Teleskop* 33 (1836): 7–8.

76 These instructions are described in Tavria Civil Governor Borozdin to Tavria Guberniia Land-Surveyor M. A. Mukhin, 7 June 1809, *GAKO, f.* 377, *op.* 1, *d.* 595, n.p.

77 Borodin to Mukhin, 7 June 1809, *GAKO, f.* 377, *op.*.1, *d.* 595, n.p.

78 Service record of Demaison, *GAKO, f.* 26, *op.* 1, *d.* 5509, n.p.

79 Cornies, 'Einiges über die Nogaier-Tataren,' 6–7.
80 Demaison to Richelieu, 15 Feb. 1817, *GAKO, f.* 26, *op.* 1, *d.* 2607, n.p.
81 'Po zhalobam nogaitsev na nachal'nika svoego Demezona,' 1820, *GAKO, f.* 26, *op.* 1, *d.* 4906, n.p.
82 'Reshenie khersonskago voennago gubernatora,' 13 Aug. 1829, *GAKO, f.* 26, *op.* 1, *d.* 4906, n.p. It is hard to imagine that Demaison could have been entirely ignorant of the affair. According to the official decision, some 246,000 kg. of salt were illegally exported and sold, and the original complaint alleged that the amount was roughly 980,000 kg.
83 Demaison to Todorov, 3 Sept. 1821, *GAKO, f.* 26, *op.* 1, *d.* 5579, n.p.
84 Based on the seven years for which comparable data is available. See Table 3.4.
85 Theories on the Doukhobors' origins and early history are usefully summarized in Woodcock and Avakumovic, *The Doukhobors*, 17–34. See also Fry, 'The Doukhobors,' 30–78. The most influential Russian-language account is A. I. Klibanov, *Istoriia religioznogo sektantstva v Rossii (60–e gody XIX v.–1917 g.)* (Moscow: Nauka, 1965), 85–121. The latest assessment of Skovoroda's influence is Victor O. Buyniak, 'Skovoroda in early Dukhobor History: Fact or Myth,' in Koozma J. Tarasoff, ed., *The Spirit Wrestlers: Centennial Papers in Honour of Canada's Dukhobor Heritage* (Hull: Canadian Museum of Civilization, 1995), 9–20.
86 Woodcock and Avakumovic, *The Doukhobors*, 19.
87 Ibid., 20.
88 II Corinthians, III, 6. On Doukhobor attitudes to the written word, see Fry, 'The Doukhobors,' 22.
89 Woodcock and Avakumovic, *The Doukhobors*, 36.
90 Ibid., 31.
91 Fry, 'The Doukhobors,' 103.
92 Fry, 'The Doukhobors,' 218–20.
93 The intention to quarantine the Doukhobors was clearly understood at the time. See Robert Pinkerton, *Russia: or Miscellaneous Observations on the Past and Present State of that Country and Its Inhabitants* (London: Seeley and Sons, 1833), 168.
94 *PSZ* (2), 5:4010.
95 For the population in 1811, see *GAKO, f.* 26, *op.* 1, *d.* 994, n.p. In 1824 there were 2,055 males (*GAKhO, f.* 14, *op.* 2, *d.* 70, n.p.), while the total number of Doukhobors exiled to the Caucasus between 1841 and 1845 was 4,992 (*GAOO, f.* 1, *op.* 166, *d.* 32).
96 'Ukaz Tavricheskogo gubernskago pravleniia o razmezhevanii Doukhoborcheskikh zemel',' 17 February 1825, *GAKhO, f.* 14, *op.* 2, *d.* 70, n.p.

97 'Delo ob otmezhevanii zemli v obrochnoe soderzhanie dukhoborcheskimi seleniiami v Melitopol'skom uezde,' 4 August 1821, *GAKhO, f.* 14, *op.* 2, *d.* 70, n.p.

98 For a detailed description of these exchanges, see Fry, 'The Doukhobors,' 186–90.

99 Fry, 'The Doukhobors,' 189.

100 'Ukaz Tavricheskogo gubernskago pravleniia o razmezhevanii Dukhoborcheskikh zemel',' 17 February 1825, *GAKhO, f.* 14, *op.* 2, *d.* 70, n.p.

101 'Vedomost' o chisle sostoiashchikh v Melitopol'skom Uezde dukhoborcheskikh selenii,' March 1824, *GAKhO, f.* 14, *op.* 2, *d.* 70, n.p.

102 Dukhobor elders to Ministry of Internal Affairs, 18 March 1824, *GAKhO, f.* 14, *op.* 2, *d.* 70, n.p.

103 The classic formulation of the 'Mennonite Commonwealth' thesis is David G. Rempel, 'The Mennonite Commonwealth in Russia,' *Mennonite Quarterly Review* (hereafter *MQR*) 47 (1973), 259–308 and 48 (1974), 5–54. The growth of a group identity amongst the Dukhobors is an important theme in Fry's 'The Doukhobors.'

104 'Ukaz Ego Imperatorskago Velichestva,' 17 February 1825, *GAKhO, f.* 14, *op.* 2, *d.* 70, n.p.

105 O. Köppen, 'O polevodstve v Tavricheskoi gubernii,' 104.

106 P.I. Köppen, 'O raskol'nikakh, prozhivaiushchikh v Tavricheskoi gubernii' (hereafter 'O raskol'nikakh'), 1837, *GAOO, f.* 1, *op.* 200, *d.* 52, n.p.

107 The reserve land system in the Colonies is described in Rempel, 'The Mennonite Commonwealth in Russia,' *MQR* 48: 7.

108 *Modern Encyclopedia of Russian and Soviet History,* s.v. 'Molokane.' There is no good modern history of the Molokans. A useful but doctrinaire summary can be found in Klibanov, *Istoriia religioznogo sektantstva,* 122–83.

109 Köppen, 'O raskol'nikakh,' 42.

110 Woodcock and Avakumovic, *The Doukhobors,* 30.

111 Summarized in a report of the Tavria office of the Ministry of State Domains to the First Department of the Ministry of State Domains in St Petersburg, 1838, *RGIA, f.* 383, *op.* 1, *d.* 234, *ll.* 16–17ob.

112 Tavria office of the Ministry of State Domains to the First Department of the Ministry of State Domains in St Petersburg, 1838, *RGIA, f.* 383, *op.* 1, *d.* 234, *ll.* 16–17ob.

113 'O pereselenii malakanov i drugikh podobnykh im raskol'nikov iz Vladimirskoi v Tavricheskuiu guberniiu na otvedennye dlia vodvoreniia im tam zemli v chisle 30,000 desiatin,' 15 February 1828, *RGIA, f.* 1284, *op.* 195, *d.* 165, *ll.* 1–2.

114 See, e.g., Bartlett, *Human Capital*, 23–30.
115 The Mennonite Charter of Privileges is reproduced in Urry, *None But Saints*, 282–4.
116 On Russian recruitment policies, see Bartlett, *Human Capital*, 23–30; Urry, *None But Saints*, 51–6.
117 Villages of origin are given in Benjamin Heinrich Unruh, *Die niederlandisch- niederdeutschen Hintergründe der mennonitischen Ostwanderungen im 16., 18. und 19 Jahrhundert* (Karlsruhe: Heinrich Schneider, 1955), 304–29.
118 'Historische Übersicht! Der am rechten Ufer des Molotschna Flusses angesiedelten deutschen Kolonisten und dessen Zustand,' 1836, *PJBRMA*, file 375.
119 Lew Malinowski, 'Passage to Russia: Who were the Emigrants?,' trans. Emil Toews, *Journal of the American Society of Germans from Russia* 2 (1979), 27.
120 Urry, *None But Saints*, 55.
121 Ibid., 61.
122 Rempel, 'Mennonite Commonwealth,' 2:7.
123 Ibid., 2:7.
124 'Kameral Liste,' 1834, *GADO, f.* 134, *op.* 1, *d.* 981.
125 Urry, *None But Saints*, 38–40.
126 Ibid., 71.
127 Fred C. Koch, in his study of the Volga Germans, concludes that the Volga Guardianship Committee had quite the opposite effect, leading the Volga Germans to be 'retarded culturally and handicapped economically.' See Koch, *The Volga Germans: In Russia and the Americas, from 1763 to the Present* (Philadelphia: Pennsylvania State University Press, 1978), 42.

Chapter Three: Adaption on the Land-Rich Steppe, 1783–1833

1 Anne Booth and R.M. Sundrum, *Labour Absorption in Agriculture: Theoretical Analysis and Empirical Investigations* (Oxford: Oxford University Press, 1985), 78–97.
2 On the economic logic of wool production in isolated areas, see Bruce R. Davidson, 'The Development of the Pastoral Industry in Australia during the Nineteenth Century,' in Koster and Chang, *Pastoralists*, 79–102.
3 Friesen, 'New Russia,' 121 n. 39.
4 Iu. Witte, 'O sel'skom khoziaistve v Khersonskoi, Tavricheskoi i Ekaterinoslavskoi guberniiakh,' *ZhMVD*, no. 3 (1834), 110. Witte says the haylands produced the equivalent of from 1,960 and 2,450 kilograms of

hay per desiatina. Consumption was approximately 1.22 kilograms per sheep per day.

5 See 'Kammeral Liste,' 1825, *GADO f.* 134, *op.* 1, *d.* 786, n.p.; 'Kammeral Liste,' 1829, *GADO f.* 134, *op.* 1, *d.* 893, n.p.; 'Kammeral Liste,' 1834, *GADO f.* 134, *op.* 1, *d.* 981, n.p.. In the 1870s E. I. Falts-Fein kept 170,000 sheep on 82,046 desiatinas – 2.07 sheep per desiatina – in Dneprovsk (Friesen, 'New Russia,' 142).

6 Peter F. Ffolliott, *Dryland Forestry: Planning and Management* (New York: John Wiley and Sons, 1995), 20.

7 'Statisticheskii ocherk torgovli skotom v s. Petrburge,' *ZhMGI* 31 (1848), 20.

8 A.T. Semple, *Grassland Improvement* (Cleveland: CRC Press, 1970), 28.

9 Ibid., 58.

10 Elinor G.K. Melville, *A Plague of Sheep: Environmental Consequences of the Conquest of Mexico* (Cambridge: Cambridge University Press, 1994), 6–7.

11 Melville, *A Plague of Sheep,* 7.

12 Philip Burnham, 'Spatial mobility and political centralization in pastoral societies,' in *Pastoral Production and Society: Proceedings of the International Meeting on Nomadic Pastoralism* (Cambridge: Cambridge University Press, 1979), 351.

13 A.M. Khazanov, *Nomads and the Outside World* (Cambridge: Cambridge University Press, 1984), 127–32.

14 Khazanov, *Nomads and the Outside World,* 127; Lawrence Krader, *Social Organization of the Mongol–Turkic Pastoral Nomads* (The Hague: Mouton, 1963), 335.

15 Khazanov, *Nomads and the Outside World,* 132.

16 Jean-Pierre Digard, 'The Segmental System: Native Model or Anthropological Construction? Discussion of an Iranian Example,' in Wolfgang Weissleder, ed., *The Nomadic Alternative: Modes and Models of Interaction in the African-Asian Deserts and Steppes* (The Hague: Mouton, 1978), 315. See also Khazanov, *Nomads and the Outside World,* 127.

17 'Geschichte der Tataren und Nogaier aus derselben,' 1838, *PJBRMA,* file 494.

18 Philip Carl Salzman, 'Synthetic and Multicausal Approaches to the Study of Nomadic Peoples.' *Nomadic Peoples* 16 (1984), 315. See also Krader, *Social Organization,* 337.

19 Khazanov, *Nomads and the Outside World,* 140.

20 Ibid., 147.

21 Krader, *Social Organization,* 335–6; Khazanov, 'Characteristic Features of Nomadic Communities in the Eurasian Steppes,' in *The Nomadic Alternative,* 123.

22 Salzman, 'Synthetic and Multicausal Approaches,' 33.

23 Khazanov, *Nomads and the Outside World*, 152–7.

24 Johann Cornies, 'Einiges über die Nogaier-Tataren in Russland,' 1825, *PJBRMA*, file 69, 7–8.

25 Cornies, 'Kratkii obzor polozheniia nogaiskikh tatar, vodvorennykh v Melitopol'skom uezde Tavricheskoi gubernii,' *Teleskop* 33 (1836), 8.

26 Ibid., 294.

27 Mennonite and state peasant yields are based on data from 'Otchety tavricheskikh gubernatorov ... za 1816,' *RGIA, f.* 1281, *op.* 11, *d.* 133, part 1, *l.* 9–16, 66–69, 92–93, 113–116; 'Ob urozhae khlebov ... v 1817 g.,' *GAKO, f.* 26, *op.* 1, *d.* 2503, n.p.; 'Ob urozhae khlebov ... v 1818 g.,' *GAKO, f.* 26, *op.* 1, *d.* 3308, n.p.; 'Ob urozhae khlebov ... v 1819 g.,' *GAKO, f.* 26, *op.* 1, *d.* 4137, n.p.

28 Demaison's assistant, a Major Baraktarev, filled in until 1825. He was succeeded by a series of appointees, none of whom held the post long.

29 Cornies, 'Einiges über die Nogaier-Tataren,' 25. This unpublished essay, while in most essentials identical to Cornies' 1836 *Teleskop* article, is much more pessimistic about the future of the Nogais.

30 There is an extensive literature on the cultural role of livestock in pastoral societies. A useful introduction is John G. Galaty, 'Cultural Perspectives on Nomadic Pastoral Societies,' *Nomadic Peoples* 16 (October 1984), 15–30.

31 Daniel Schlatter, *Bruchstücke aus einigen Reisen nach dem südlichen Russland, in den Jahren 1822 bis 1828* (St Gallen: Huber und Comp., 1830), 188.

32 Cornies, 'Einiges über die Nogaier-Tataren,' 25.

33 Goerz, *The Molotschna Settlement*, 24.

34 Schlatter, *Bruchstücke*, 279–80.

35 Ibid., 108.

36 Ibid., 87, 285.

37 Ibid., 60.

38 'Vedomost'. O skotovodstve v Tavricheskoi gubernii za 1824 g.,' 1825, *RGIA*, f. 1281, *op.* 11, *d.* 133, part II, *l.* 38–9.

39 Schlatter, *Bruchstücke*, 60.

40 David H. Epp, *Johann Cornies*, trans. Peter Pauls (Winnipeg: CMBC/The Manitoba Mennonite Historical Society, 1995), 6.

41 Cornies, 'Einiges über die Nogaier-Tataren,' 49.

42 'Rechnung. Über die Pachtländer,' 1824, *PJBRMA*, file 68, 1–5ob.

43 Cornies to P.I. Köppen, 28 Dec. 1837, *PJBRMA*, file 236.

44 'Dogovora Zakliuchennye mezhdu I. Kornisom i Nogaitsami,' 1 November 1834, *PJBRMA*, file 307, 1–4ob.

45 In fact the sharecropper sometimes provides draft animals and even agricultural implements, but these form a small part of the total capital input. For a useful summary of sharecropping and its economic analysis, see Frank Ellis, *Peasant Economics: Farm Households and Agrarian Development* (Cambridge: Cambridge University Press, 1988), 141–59.

46 R. Pearce, 'Sharecropping: Towards a Marxist View,' in T.J. Byres, ed., *Sharecropping and Sharecroppers* (London: Frank Cass, 1983), 42–70.

47 For a useful summary, see Byres, 'Historical Perspectives on Sharecropping,' in *Sharecropping and Sharecroppers*, 7–40.

48 On the value of Nogai sheep, see Schlatter, *Bruchstücke*, 184–5. On merino sheep, see Cornies, 'Landwirthschaftliche Notizen,' 1837, *PJBRMA*, file 992.

49 The small-bodied, short-legged merinos were susceptible to cuts from sharp grass and bushes on the rangelands, less resistant to cold than native sheep, and had not developed immunities to many of the deseases carried by native sheep. On the relative merits of merinos and other sheep, see Friesen, 'New Russia,' 110–12, 127.

50 'Raboty po snabzheniiu vodiiu pereselentsev, proizvedennyia v Tavricheskoi gubernii v 1862 godu,' *ZhMGI*, no. 83 (1863), 316.

51 'Po tsirkuliarnomu predpisaniiu nekotorym Palatami Gosudarstvenykh Imushchestv ob ustroistve kolodtsev na bezvodnam obrochnykh uchastkakh,' 1840, *RGIA, f.* 383, *op.* 3, *d.* 2530, n.p.

52 'Putevye zametki pri ob'ezde Dneprovskago i Melitopol'skago uezdov Tavricheskoi gubernii, v 1835 godu,' *Listki izdavaemye obshchestvom sel'skogo khoziaistva iuzhnoi Rossii* (1838), 289–90.

53 August Von Haxthausen, *The Russian Empire: Its People, Institutions, and Resources*, 2 vols (London: Chapman and Hall, 1856), 2: 67.

54 Iu. Witte, 'O sel'skom khoziaistve v Khersonskoi, Tavricheskoi i Ekaterinoslavskoi guberniiakh,' *ZhMVD*, no. 3 (1834), 22.

55 V.E. Postnikov, *Iuzhno-russkoe krest'ianskoe khoziaistvo* (Moscow: Kushnerev, 1891), 193.

56 A. Schmidt, *Khersonskaia guberniia. Materialy geografii i statistiki Rossii sobrannye ofitserami general'nogo shtaba*, 2 vols, (St Petersburg: Voennoi Tipografii, 1863), 1:20; Witte, 'O sel'skom khoziaistve,' 66.

57 'O glavnykh osnovaniiakh novago polozheniia ob obespechenii prodovol'stviem,' 1840, *RGIA, f.* 1589 *op.* 1, *d.* 693, 70–132.

58 Colin Clark and Margaret Haswell, *The Economics of Subsistence Agriculture*, 4th ed. (London: Macmillan, 1970), 59. Clark and Haswell calculate the minimum at 210 kg. of grain per person per year.

59 Ibid., 64–5. 'Grain equivalents' refers to the conversion of calories obtained from other sources into units of grain in order to provide a standard unit of calculation.

60 E.I. Druzhinina, *Iuzhnaia Ukraina v period krizisa feodalizma 1825–1860 gg.*
(Moscow: Nauka, 1981),41. Druzhinina obtains this figure from an 1849
report in *RGIA, f.* 1281, *op.* 5, *d.* 60, n.p. For an earlier (1840), similar
account, see 'O glavnykh osnovaniiakh novago polozheniia ob
obespechenii prodovol'stviem,' 1840, *RGIA, f.* 1589 *op.* 1, *d.* 693,
70–132.

61 Patricia Herlihy, *Odessa: A History, 1794–1914* (Cambridge: Harvard
University Press, 1986), 68.

62 'Umen'shennyi plan kazennykh dach, sel i dereven' Orekhovskoi volosti
Berdianskago uezda, Tavricheskoi gubernii,' 1848, *GAZO, f.* 263, *op.* 1,
d. 50, n.p.

63 'Po otchetam grazhdanskikh gubernatorov o sostoianii gosudarstvennykh
krest'ian i o merakh uluchsheniia ikh byta,' 10 June 1847, *RGIA, f.* 1589, *op.*
1, *d.* 729, *ll.* 33–35ob; 'Otchety tavricheskikh gubernatorov ... za 1837,'
RGIA, f. 1281, *op.* 3, *d.* 47, *ll.* 2ob–100b.

64 R.E.F. Smith and David Christian, *Bread and Salt: A Social and Economic
History of Food and Drink in Russia* (Cambridge: Cambridge University Press,
1984). They obtained a further 29 per cent from potatoes, but these were
principally grown as a field crop.

65 The weather conditions leading to the harvest failure are described in
RGIA, f. 1281, *op.* 11, *d.* 133, part 1, *l.* 149.

66 'Ob urozhae v nyneshnem godu khleba i o merakh k obespecheniiu
prodovol'stviem zhitel'ei Krymskago poluostrova,' 1821, *GAKO, f.* 26, *op.* 1,
d. 5394, n.p. For a comparable report from neighbouring Dneprovsk uezd,
see 'Ob urozhae v nyneshnem godu khleba i o merakh k obespecheniiu
prodovol'stviem zhitelei Krymskago poluostrova,' 1821, *GAKO, f.* 26, *op.* 1,
d. 5394, n.p.

67 Friesen, 'New Russia,' 106–44.

68 Wilhelm Bernhard Bauman, 'Zusammenstellung der von mir in den
Steppen des südlichen Russlands gemachten Beobachtungen in Beziehung
des Ackerbaues,' 1847, *PJBRMA*, file 1291, 3.

69 Numerous examples of typical land allocation patterns in the British Isles
may be found in Alan R.H. Baker, and Robin A. Butlin, eds., *Studies of Field
Systems in the British Isles* (Cambridge: Cambridge University Press, 1973).
For French examples, see Marc Bloch, *French Rural History: An Essay in Its
Basic Characteristics*, trans. Janet Sonderheimer (London: Routledge and
Kegan Paul, 1966), centre-plates between pp. 142–143.

70 Witte, 'O sel'skom khoziaistve,' 66–7.

71 For a description of the infield/outfield system, see G. Whittington, 'Field
Systems of Scotland,' in Alan R.H. Baker and Robin A. Butler, eds., *Studies*

of Field Systems in the British Isles (Cambridge: Cambridge University Press, 1973), 532–5.

72 Köppen to Kiselev, 12 December 1838, *RGIA, f.* 1589, *op.* 1, *d.* 362, *ll.* 144–7. According to Long, Volga Germans voiced almost precisely the same objections ('Our forefathers have so farmed') to abandoning strip farming as late as the first years of the twentieth century – see Long, *From Privileged to Dispossessed,* 72.

73 This attitude is best evidenced in peasant reactions when land shortages arose – see Chapter 6.

74 George Woodcock and Ivan Avakumovic, *The Doukhobors* (London: Faber and Faber, 1968), 44.

75 Robert Pinkerton, *Russia: or Miscellaneous Observations on the Past and Present State of that Country and Its Inhabitants* (London: Seeley and Sons, 1833), 168.

76 Kolosov, 'Sekretnaia zapiska Melitopol'skago zemskago ispravnika' (hereafter 'Sekretnaia zapiska'), 1837, *GAOO, f.* 1, *op.* 200, *d.* 52, n.p.

77 Quoted in Fry, 'The Doukhobors,' 271.

78 A.A. Skal'kovskii, *Khronologicheskoe obozrenie istorii Novorossiiskago kraia 1730–1823. Chast II. s 1796 po 1823* (Odessa, 1838), 167.

79 Woodcock and Avakumovic write that in 1822 the Dukhobors cultivated an average of 100 acres per male soul, but this is almost certainly a reference to their total land holdings, rather than the amount actually cultivated. Data from the period 1817–1821 suggest they cultivated only about ½ *desiatina* per male soul (Woodcock and Avakumovic, *The Doukhobours,* 40; 'O poseve i urozhae khlebov,' 1817, *GAKO, f.* 26, *op.* 1, *d.* 2503, n.p.; 1818, *GAKO, f.* 26, *op.* 1, *d.* 3308, n.p.; 1819, *GAKO, f.* 26, *op.* 1, *d.* 4137, n.p.; 1820, *GAKO, f.* 26, *op.* 1, *d.* 5017, n.p.; 1821, *GAKO, f.* 26, *op.* 1, *d.* 5394, n.p.).

80 Quoted in Fry, 'The Doukhobors,' 271. For other accounts, see, e.g., Pinkerton, *Russia,* 167–8. The leasing of 902 merino sheep by Dukhobors to Nogai Tatars between 1832 and 1836 is recorded in 'Spisok akkermanskikh nogaitsev, vziavshikh u dukhobortsev po usloviiam shpanskuiu ovtsy,' 18 March 1839, *PJBRMA,* file 691, 7.

81 'Svedenie o stepeni i sostoianii stad tonkorunnykh ovets Tavricheskoi gubernii ... dlia 1840 goda,' *GAOO, f.* 22, *op.* 1, *d.* 580, *ll.* 110–111; on Dukhobor experiences in the Caucasus see Woodcock and Avakumovic, *The Doukhobors,* 62–83.

82 Woodcock & Avakumovic, *The Doukhobors,* 284–307.

83 Ibid., 45.

84 Ibid., 45.

85 'Glavnyi uchitel' Dukhobortsev,' 9 December 1816, *GAOO, f.* 1, *op.* 219, *d.* 3, *ll.* 200–200ob.

86 Orest Novitskii, *Dukhobortsy. Ikh istoriia i verouchenie,* 2 ed (Kiev: Universitetskaia tipografiia, 1882), 85.

87 'Po otchetam grazhdanskikh gubernatorov o sostoianii gosudarstvennykh krest'ian i o merakh uluchsheniia ikh byta,' 10 June 1847, *RGIA, f.* 1589, *op.* 1, *d.* 729, *ll.* 33–35.

88 Bauman, 'Zusammenstellung,' 8.

89 Judith Pallot and Denis J.B. Shaw, *Landscape and Settlement in Romanov Russia 1613–1917* (Oxford: Clarendon Press, 1990), 111; K. B. Khanatskii, ed., *Pamiatnaia knizhka Tavricheskoi gubernii* (Simferopol': Tipografiia Tavricheskogo gubernskogo pravleniia, 1867), 201.

90 Roger P. Bartlett, *Human Capital: The Settlement of Foreigners in Russia, 1762–1804* (Cambridge: Cambridge University Press, 1979), 211.

91 Zieber's report is described in a letter from the Ministry of Internal Affairs' Department of Agriculture to the Minister of State Domains, 26 July 1813, *GADO, f.* 134, *op.* 1, *d.* 343, n.p.

92 James Urry, *None but Saints,* 88. For an early report on the success of the program, see 'Doneseniia glavnogo sud'i kontoru v MVD o razvitii ovtsevodstva v koloniiakh,' 29 January 1809, *GADO, f.* 134, *op.* 1, *d.* 225, n.p.

93 For merino and mixed-breed wool, see 'Auszug über den Ertrag der Schafe auf dem Vorwerke Iushanlee von 1825 bis 1845,' 1845, *PJBRMA,* file 71, 1–19ob. For *kurdiuch* wool, see Schlatter, *Bruchstücke,* 185.

94 For a typical report on sheep-rearing, see 'Vedomosti Molochanskikh kolonii smotritelia ob ovtsevodstve,' 1815, *GADO, f.* 134, *op.* 1, *d.* 402, n.p. On the creation of the 'Organization for the Improvement of Sheep Breeding,' see Urry, *None But Saints,* 111.

95 See, e.g., Contenius to Guardianship Committee, 19 January 1823, *GADO, f.* 134, *op.* 1, *d.* 741, n.p.

96 On the German role in developing scientific forestry, see Robert Pogue Harrison, *Forests: The Shadow of Civilization* (Chicago: University of Chicago Press, 1992), 122. The general development of Russian forestry is recorded in the records of the forestry department of the Ministry of Agriculture (*RGIA, f.* 432), while forestry in Tavria Guberniia is recorded in the records of the Tavria Forstmeister (*GAKO, f.* 82, *f.* 94, and *f.* 798).

97 Guardianship Committee to Contenius, 15 January 1815, *GADO, f.* 134, *op.* 1, *d.* 225, n.p.

98 'Kammeral Liste,' 1826, *GADO, f.* 134, *op.* 1, *d.* 786, n.p.; 'Die in Jahr 1825 von den Molotschner Kolonisten angepflangten und unserzeugten Bäume

verschiedener Arten,' 1825, *GADO, f.* 134, *op.* 1, *d.* 786, n.p.; 'Kammeral Liste,' 1834, *GADO, f.* 134, *op.* 1, *d.* 981, n.p.

99 Urry, *None But Saints*, 112.

100 The 'Instruction' describing the Society's original responsibilities and authority is located in *PJBRMA*, file 166, 1–21.

101 Urry, *None But Saints*, 71.

102 Detlef Brandes, *Von den Zaren adoptiert: Die deutschen Kolonisten und die Balkansiedler in Neurussland und Bessarabien 1751–1914* (Munich: Oldenbourg, 1993), 78.

103 Data compiled from Unruh, *Die niederlandisch-niederdeutschen Hintergründe*, 304–29.

104 Mary S. Sprunger, 'Dutch Mennonites and the Golden Age Economy: The Problem of Social Disparity in the Church,' in Calvin Redekop, Victor A. Krahn, and Samuel J. Steiner, eds., *Anabaptist/Mennonite Faith and Economics* (Lanham, MD: University Press of America, 1994), 30. This collection of essays provides a valuable diversity of views on the subject.

105 'Vedomost' o blagosostoianii molochanskikh kolonistov za istekshii fevral' mesiats 1813 goda,' *GAOO, f.* 6, *op.* 1, *d.* 773, *ll.* 43–6.

106 'Vedomost' o blagosostoianii kolonii Molochanskago Menonistskago okruga za ianvar' mesiats 1839 goda,' 1 January 1839, *GAOO, f.* 6, *op.* 1, *d.* 5099, *ll.* 58–61.

107 Rempel, 'Mennonite Commonwealth,' 2:7.

108 Department of Agriculture of the Ministry of Internal Affairs to the Minister of Internal Affairs, 26 July 1813, *GADO, f.* 134, *op.* 1, *d.* 343, n.p.

109 'Vedomosti o prikhode i raskhode denezhnykh summ Novorossiiskoi opekunskoi kontory,' 1807–1818, *RGIA, f.* 383, *op.* 29, *d.* 667–682.

110 An identical practice emerged in Russia's Volga German colonies. See James W. Long, *From Privileged to Dispossessed: The Volga Germans, 1860–1917* (Lincoln: University of Nebraska Press, 1988), 4.

111 Dyck, 'Introduction,' *A Mennonite in Russia*, 61.

112 See, e.g., 'Regal über Ansiedlung der Jungen Mennonitischen Familien,' 1839, *PJBRMA*, file 563, 1–2ob.; James Urry, 'The Social Background of the Emergence of the Mennonite Brethren in Nineteenth Century Russia,' *Journal of Mennonite Studies* 6 (1988), 145–6.

113 See Cornies to Fadeev, 7 January 1830, *PJBRMA*, file 169.

114 Cornies to David Epp, 5 February 1831, *PJBRMA*, file 200.

115 Witte, 'O sel'skom khoziaistve,' 110; O. Köppen, 'Neskol'ko slov o razvedenii kormovykh trav v Tavricheskoi gubernii,' *ZhMGI* 83 (1863), 269–74.

116 Schlatter, *Bruchstücke*, 108.

117 'Kammeral Liste,' 1834, *GADO, f.* 134, *op.* 1, *d.* 981, n.p.

118 On land leases, see Urry, *None But Saints*, 109; O. Köppen, 'Neskol'ko slov,' 269–74.

119 O. Köppen, 'O polevodstve v Tavricheskoi gubernii i o vrednykh na nego vliianiiakh,' *ZhMGI* 83 (1863), 104.

120 'Rechnung. Über die Pachtländer,' 1824, *PJBRMA*, file 68, 1–5ob.; 'Rechnung. Über die Pachtländer,' 1833, *PJBRMA*, file 242, 68–95ob.

121 Based on Unruh, *Die niederlandisch-niederdeutschen Hintergründe*, 304–29.

122 Peter J. Klassen, *A Homeland for Strangers: An Introduction to Mennonites in Poland and Prussia* (Fresno: Center for Mennonite Brethren Studies, 1989), 13.

123 Molochna Mennonite Gebietsamt to Inspector Pelekh, 25 November 1836, *PJBRMA*, file 367, 4–5ob.

124 Witte, 'O sel'skom khoziaistve,' 67.

125 Urry, *None But Saints*, 144–5.

126 Ibid., 144.

127 The precise figures were 28% in 1815, 32% in 1839.

128 'S vedomostiami mestnykh kolonistikh nachal'stv o sostoianii kolonii za 1835 g.,' 1836, *RGIA, f.* 383, *op.* 29, *d.* 634, *ll.* 87–100. In 1835, the average German Colonist family had 7.56 members, compared to just 4.98 in Mennonite families.

129 Urry, *None But Saints*, 36–8.

130 Ibid., 47.

131 Ibid., 79–82, 99–103.

132 Delbert F. Plett, *The Golden Years: The Mennonite Kleine Gemeinde in Russia (1812–1849)* (Steinbach: Author, 1985), 156. In his review of *The Golden Years*, Urry questions this conclusion, but my own calculations suggest that the twenty-six families identified by Plett are an astonishingly representative cross-section of the larger community (Urry, 'All that Glisters ... ': Delbert Plett and the Place of the Kleine Gemeinde in Russian Mennonite History,' *JMS* 4 [1986]), 228–50. Note, however, that there are a number of errors in the data as reproduced by Plett, and those wishing to examine the matter more closely should base their investigations on the reproduction of the complete census in Unruh, *Die niederlandisch-niederdeutschen Hintergründe*, 304–29. A complete 1813 census, comparable to the 1808 census published by Unruh, exists in *GADO, f.* 134, *op.* 1, *d.* 356, but I was not permitted to copy it. A careful examination of this census, and a comparison between it and the 1808 census, may well offer some revealing insights into the socioeconomic basis of the Kleine Gemeinde.

133 Heinrich Balzer, 'Understanding and Reason: Simple Opinions Regarding the Difference between Understanding and Reason, Discussed According to the Teachings of the Gospel,' reproduced in Plett, *The Golden Years*, 244.
134 O. Köppen, 'O polevodstve,' 148.
135 Goerz, *The Molotschna Settlement*, 13.

Chapter Four: The Great Drought of 1832–1834

1 Cornies provides a running account of the drought in his correspondence. See Cornies to Schlatter, 11 March 1833, *PJBRMA*, file 276, 7–10; Cornies to Blüher, 10 June 1833, *PJBRMA*, file 276, 18–20; Cornies to Fadeev, 17 July 1833, *PJBRMA*, file 276, 24–26ob.; Cornies to Fadeev, 13 September 1833, *PJBRMA*, file 276, 33–35ob.; Cornies to Blüher, 22 June 1834, *PJBRMA*, file 300, 53–57ob.; Cornies to Fadeev, 18 September 1834, *PJBRMA*, file 300, 67–68ob.
2 Details of the drought and state relief efforts are described in 'Sravnenie neurozhaev 1833/34 i 1839/40,' 1840, *RGIA, f.* 1589, *op.* 1, *d.* 693, *ll.* 1–7ob.
3 Roderick E. McGrew, *Russia and the Cholera, 1823–1832* (Madison: University of Wisconsin Press, 1965), 3.
4 Ibid., 98.
5 Ibid., 67.
6 Cornies to Fadeev, 15 October 1830, *PJBRMA*, file 169, 42–43ob.
7 Cornies to Fadeev, 22 December 1830, *PJBRMA*, file 169, 64–67ob. Cornies implies that the Nogai paid their *nachal'nik* a bribe to file an October report denying the outbreak.
8 Cornies to Fadeev, 22 December 1830, *PJBRMA*, file 169, 64ob.–67ob..
9 Cornies to Fadeev, 7 January 1831, *PJBRMA*, file 200, 2–3.
10 Cornies to Fadeev, 29 July 1831, *PJBRMA*, file 200, 38–8ob.
11 Cornies to Schlatter, 11 March 1833, *PJBRMA*, file 276, 7–10.
12 Cornies to Blüher, 10 June 1833, *PJBRMA*, file 276, 18–20ob.
13 Cornies to Fadeev, 17 July 1833, *PJBRMA*, file 276, 24–26ob.
14 Cornies to Fadeev, 17 July 1833, *PJBRMA*, file 276, 24–26ob.
15 Cornies to Blüher, 15 February 1834, *PJBRMA*, file 300, 21–22ob.
16 Cornies to Blüher, 15 February 1834, *PJBRMA*, file 300, 21–21ob.
17 Cornies to Blüher, 22 June 1834, *PJBRMA*, file 300., 53ob–57.
18 Cornies to Johann Regier, 12 February 1834, *PJBRMA*, file 300, 16–17ob.
19 Cornies to Blüher, 15 February 1834, *PJBRMA*, file 300, 21–22ob.
20 'Sravnenie neurozhaev 1833/34 i 1839/40,' 1840, *RGIA, f.* 1589, *op.* 1, *d.* 693, *ll.* 1–7ob.

21 See Table 2.1.

22 'Verzeichnis über die Bevölkerung im Molotschner Mennonitischen Gebiet,' 1849, *PJBRMA*, file 1402, 2.

23 Cornies to Blüher, 22 June 1834, *PJBRMA*, file 300, 53ob–57. For Colonist livestock figures, see 'Otchet za 1832,' *RGIA, f.* 383, *op.* 29, *d.* 631, *ll.* 22–40, and 'Otchet za 1834,' *RGIA, f.* 383, *op.* 29, *d.* 633, *ll.* 139–51.

24 'Izvlechenie. Iz proekta o razdelenii Melitopol'skago okruga gosudarstvennykh imushchestv na volosti i sel'skie obshchestva,' 25 June 1841, *RGIA, f.* 383, *op.* 4, *d.* 3021, *ll.* 30–31ob.

25 'Izvlechenie. Iz proekta o razdelenii Melitopol'skago okruga gosudarstvennykh imushchestv na volosti i sel'skie obshchestva,' 25 June 1841, *RGIA, f.* 383, *op.* 4, *d.* 3021, *ll.* 30–31ob.

26 'Otchet o zaniatiiakh Tavricheskoi gubernskoi komissii dlia prigotovitel'nykh rasporiazhenii po priemu gosudarstvennykh imushchestv s 10 avgusta na 10 sentiabria 1838 goda,' *RGIA, f.* 1589, *op.* 1, *d.* 362, *ll.* 86–89ob.

27 'Po otnosheniiu Tavricheskoi kazennoi ekspeditsii. O molokanakh Melitopol'skogo uezda, zhelaiushchikh pereselit'sia v Zakavkazskie provintsii,' 1833, *GAKO, f.* 26, *op.* 1, *d.* 9830, n.p.

28 Details of the matter are summarized in a report of the Tavria office of the Ministry of State Domains to the First Department of the Ministry of State Domains in St Petersburg, 28 May 1841, *RGIA, f.* 383, *op.* 4, *d.* 3101, *ll.* 2–5.

29 'Otchet o zaniatiiakh Tavricheskoi gubernskoi komissii dlia prigotovitel'nykh rasporiazhenii po priemu gosudarstvennukh imushchestv s 10 avgusta na 10 sentiabria 1838 goda,' *RGIA, f.* 1589, *op.* 1, *d.* 362, *ll.* 86–89ob.

30 These proposals are described in great detail in volume 1 of Druzhinin, *Gosudarstvennie Krest'iane.*

31 Quoted in Druzhinin, *Gosudarstvennie Krest'iane,* 1:294.

32 Ibid., 1:521.

33 Ibid., 2:188.

34 First Department of the Ministry of State Domains to Kiselev, 31 May 1843, *RGIA, f.* 383, *op.* 1, *d.* 190, *ll.* 100–107ob.

35 Veselovskoe Sel'skoe Obshchestvo to Ministry of State Domains, 1841, *RGIA, f.* 383, *op.* 1, *d.* 190, *ll.* 51–52ob.

36 Tavria office of the Ministry of State Domains to the Ministry of State Domains in St Petersburg, 11 September 1841, *RGIA, f.* 383, *op.* 1, *d.* 190, *ll.* 32–32ob.

37 Governor General of New Russia to Ministry of State Domains, 2 January 1843, *RGIA, f.* 383, *op.* 1, *d.* 190, *ll.* 94–96ob.

38 George L. Yaney, *The Systemization of Russian Government: Social Evolution in the Domestic Administration of Imperial Russia, 1711–1905* (Urbana: University of Illinois Press, 1973), 203.

39 I have borrowed the concept of an ethnocultural 'commonwealth' from David G. Rempel's classic essay 'The Mennonite Commonwealth in Russia,' *Mennonite Quarterly Review* 47 (1973), 259–308 and 48 (1974), 5–54. The growth of a group identity among the Doukhobors is an important theme in Gary Dean Fry, 'The Doukhobors.'

40 'Po otnosheniiu Tavricheskoi kazennoi ekspeditsii. O molokanakh Melitopol'skogo uezda, zhelaiushchikh pereselit'sia v Zakavkazskie provintsii,' 1833, *GAKO, f.* 26, *op.* 1, *d.* 9830, n.p.

41 Summarized in a report of the Tavria office of the Ministry of State Domains to the First Department of the Ministry of State Domains in St Petersburg, 1838, *RGIA, f.* 383, *op.* 1, *d.* 234, *ll.* 16–17ob.

42 'Po otnosheniiu Tavricheskoi kazennoi ekspeditsii. O molokanakh Melitopol'skogo uezda, zhelaiushchikh pereselit'sia v Zakavkazskie provintsii,' 1833, *GAKO, f.* 26, *op.* 1, *d.* 9830, n.p.

43 For a thorough summary of the accusations and investigation, see Woodcock and Avakumovic, *The Doukhobors*, 49–52. A full record of the investigation is located in *GAOO, f.* 1, *o.* 219, *d.* 3.

44 Ekaterinoslav Arkhiapiskop Iov to Minister of Police, 18 August 1816, *GAOO, f.* 1, *o.* 219, *d.* 3, *ll.* 188–9.

45 Woodcock and Avakumovic, *The Doukhobors*, 49–51.

46 Official Nationality was not officially proclaimed until 2 April 1833, but the reactionary attitudes underlying it date from the start of Nicholas's reign. The standard treatment of the subject is Nicholas Riasanovsky, *Nicholas I and Official Nationality in Russia, 1825–1855* (Berkeley: University of California Press, 1967).

47 *PSZ* (2) 5:4010.

48 The Fifth Department project to survey the provinces is described in W. Bruce Lincoln, *In The Vanguard of Reform: Russia's Enlightened Bureaucrats, 1825–1861* (Dekalb: Northern Illinois University Press, 1982), 33.

49 Kolosov, 'Sekretnaia zapiska,' 82–92ob. Kolosov mentions his membership in the commission on page 88ob. of this report.

50 Ibid., 86–87ob.

51 Ibid., 90–91ob.

52 Ibid., 91–92ob.

53 Köppen's recommendation is quoted in a report from the Ministry of Internal Affairs to Vorontsov, 22 February 1838, *GAOO, f.* 1, *op.* 200, *d.* 52, n.p.

54 Kiselev to Bludov, 3 February 1838, *RGIA, f.* 1284, *op.* 197, *d.* 131, *ll.* 12–13.
55 Secret Section of the Ministry of Internal Affairs to Vorontsov, 22 February 1838, *GAOO, f.* 1, *op.* 200, *d.* 52, n.p.
56 'Zapiska, zakliuchaiushchaia v sebia predpolozheniia o merakh v otnoshenii molokanov i dukhobortsev Tavricheskoi gubernii,' 22 February 1838, *GAOO, f.* 1, *op.* 200, *d.* 52, n.p.
57 Vorontsov to Bludov, 21 March 1838, *RGIA, f.* 1284, *op.* 197, *d.* 131, *ll.* 22–24ob. On Vorontsov's attitude toward sectarians, see Anthony L.H. Rhinelander, *Prince Michael Vorontsov: Viceroy to the Tsar* (Montreal: McGill-Queen's University Press, 1990), 86–8.
58 Vorontsov to Bludov, 13 August 1838, *RGIA, f.* 1284, *op.* 197, *d.* 131, *ll.* 28–35ob.
59 Fry, 'The Doukhobors,' 286.
60 'Spisok dukhobortsev, naznachennykh k pereseleniiu v Akhaltsyskii uezd bez zhrebiia,' 26 March 1842, *GAOO, f.* 1, *op.* 151, *d.* 77, *ll.* 120–35.
61 'Spisok dukhobortsev, naznachennykh k pereseleniiu v Akhaltsyskii uezd po zhrebiiu,' 26 March 1841, *GAOO, f.* 1, *op.* 151, *d.* 77, *ll.* 136–48.
62 For a summary of all five parties, see 'Otchet o melitopol'skikh dukhobortsakh ... pereselennykh za Kavkaz,' n.d., *GAOO, f.* 1, *op.* 166, *d.* 32, *l.* 134. For the numbers that converted, see 'Spisok dukhobortsev, prisoedinennykh k pravoslavnoi tserkvi s 27 maia 1843 goda po 5 iiunia 1844,' and 'Spisok gosudarstvennykh krest'ian iz sekty Dukhoborcheskogo ... zhelaiushchikh obratit'sia v pravoslavie,' *RGIA, f.* 383, *op.* 5, *d.* 4319, *ll.* 89–91ob. and 162–3ob.; and 'Spisok prisoedinivshikhsia dukhobortsev k pravoslavnoi tserkvi s 1 iiunia 1842 goda po 27 maia 1843 goda,' *RGIA, f.* 383, *op.* 4, *d.* 3212, *l.* 70. The figure of twenty-seven families reported by Woodcock and Avakumovic apparently only includes the May 1843 to June 1844 list.
63 'Vypiska iz dela, proizvedennogo sledstviem o raznykh zlodeianiiakh, proiskhodivshikh v dukhoborskikh i molokanskikh poseleniiakh Melitopol'skogo uezda,' (hereafter 'Vypiska iz dela'), n.d., *PJBRMA*, file 392.
64 The report is now located in the *PJBRMA*, a collection of documents assembled by Peter Braun, a teacher and historian, between 1917 and 1920. The fact that the document is in the *PJBRMA* means that it almost certainly originated from a Mennonite source, and consequently can be expected to have been in Mennonite hands in the 1830s. The Soviet-era catalogue of the archive, echoed in the new English-language catalogue, dates it to 1836, a year probably derived from the most recent testimony in the document. See Ingrid I. Epp and Harvey L. Dyck, *The Peter J. Braun Russian*

Mennonite Archive, 1803–1920: A Research Guide (Toronto: University of Toronto Press, 1996).

65 Kolosov writes that the investigation was ordered by Vorontsov in 1834, and took place in 1835 and 1836. Secondary accounts often refer to a six-year investigation lasting from 1834 to 1839, but this presumably includes the review of the case by central authorities leading up to the exile decree. See, e.g., Baron Von Haxthausen, *The Russian Empire: Its People, Institutions, and Resources*, trans, Robert Farie, 2 vols. (London: Chapman and Hall, 1856), 1: 293; Woodcock and Avakumovic, *The Doukhobors*, 57. Novitskii says it lasted five years, from 1835 to 1839 (Novitskii, *Dukhobortsy: ikh istoriia i veroucheniia*, 144).

66 Novitskii, *Dukhobortsy: ikh istoriia i veroucheniia*, 145.

67 Case 12, 'Vypiska, iz dela,' 31–6.

68 Vorontsov to Bludov, 3 February 1838, *RGIA, f.* 1284, *op.* 195, *d.* 165, *ll.* 12–13.

69 Haxthausen, *The Russian Empire*, 1:293; Novitskii, *Dukhobortsy: ikh istoriia i verouchenii*, 144; Woodcock and Avakumovic, *The Doukhobors*, 57.

70 Case 14, 'Vypiska, iz dela,' 45–49ob.

71 Case 1, 'Vypiska, iz dela,' 1–2ob.

72 Case 10, 'Vypiska, iz dela,' 19–20.

73 The trials and tribulations of Iosif and Fomin are related in Case 12, 'Vypiska, iz dela,' 31–6.

74 Case 11, 'Vypiska, iz dela,' 20–31. Some testimony mentions a third victim, identified only as 'Ivan.'

75 See e.g. Woodcock and Avakumovic, *The Doukhobors*, 57.

76 This is explained in Case 2, 'Vypiska, iz dela,' 2ob.

77 Case 5, 'Vypiska, iz dela,' 9ob.

78 Haxthausen, *The Russian Empire*, 1:293.

79 Haxthausen, *The Russian* Empire, 1:293; Haxthausen, *Studien über die innern Zustande, des Volksleben und insbesondere die ländlichen Einrichtungen Russlands*, 3 vols. (Hanover, 1847), 1:409; Haxthausen, *Etudes sur la situation, la vie nationale et les institutions rurales de la Russie*, 2 vols. (Hanover, 1847), 1:376.

80 Novitskii, *Dukhobortsy: ikh istoriia i verouchenii*, 144.

81 Ibid., 145.

82 Woodcock and Avakumovic, *The Doukhobors*, 59.

83 Andreevskii to Vorontsov, 6 December 1840, *GAOO, f.* 1, *op.* 200, *d.* 52, n.p.

84 On arson in Canada, see Woodcock and Avakumovic, *The Doukhobors*, 308–31.

85 Steven L. Hoch, *Serfdom and Social Control in Russia: Petrovskoe, a Village in Tambov* (Chicago: University of Chicago Press, 1986), 160–1.

86 Report of the Secret Section of the MVD to Governor General of Novorossiia and Bessarabia Vorontsov, 22 February 1838, *GAOO, f.* 1, *op.* 200, *d.* 52, n.p.
87 Cornies' political role is described in Harvey L. Dyck, 'Russian Servitor and Mennonite Hero: Light and Shadow in Images of Johann Cornies,' *Journal of Mennonite Studies* 2 (1984), 9–41. On Cornies' anger about Dukhobor dealings with the Nogai Tatars, see 'Prikaz Dzhuretskomu volostnomu pravleniiu,' *PJBRMA*, file 691, 9–12.
88 Cornies to Fadeev, 28 July 1836, *PJBRMA*, file 388, 35–36ob.
89 See, e.g., Michael I. Aronson, 'Geographical and Socioeconomic Factors in the 1881 Anti-Jewish Pogroms in Russia,' *Russian Review* 39:1 (1980), 18–31.
90 Petition from the Doukhobors to Nicholas I, 22 March 1841, *GAOO, f.* 1, *op.* 151, *d.* 77, *ll.* 86–8. Note that this petition, by virtue of its existence, refutes Aylmer Maude's argument, echoed by Woodcock and Avakumovic, that the lack of Doukhobor protests tends to confirm their guilt. See Maude, *A Peculiar People: The Doukhobors* (New York: Funk and Wagnells, 1904), 149; Woodcock and Avakumovic, *The Doukhobors*, 59.
91 Quoted in Fry, 'The Doukhobors,' 278.
92 Joseph Elkinton, *The Doukhobors: Their History in Russia, Their Migration to Canada* (Philadelphia: Ferris and Leach, 1903), 261–2.
93 Kolosov, 'Sekretnaia zapiska,' 87ob.
94 Köppen, 'O raskol'nikakh,' 44ob.
95 'Zapiska, zakliuchaiushchaia v sebia predpolozheniia o merakh v otnoshenii molokanov i dukhobortsev Tavricheskoi gubernii,' 22 February 1838, *GAOO, f.* 1, *op.* 200, *d.* 52, n.p.
96 Ministry of State Domains to Inzov, 3 February 1842, *GAOO, f.* 1, *op.* 152, *d.* 16, *ll.* 28–39.
97 It is noteworthy that, under similarly crowded conditions, and at almost precisely the same time, sectarians in the Volga region were also exiled in an attempt to force their conversion. See Long, *From Privileged to Disposed*, 1.
98 Quoted in Woodcock and Avakumovic, *The Doukhobors*, 59.
99 Dukhobor elders to Nicholas I, 22 March 1841, *GAOO, f.* 1, *op.* 151, *d.* 77, *ll.* 168–71.
100 Dukhobor elders to Nicholas I, 1841, *GAOO, f.* 1, *op.* 151, *d.* 77, *ll.* 168–71.
101 Ministry of State Domains to Inzov, 3 February 1842, *GAOO, f.* 1, *op.* 152, *d.* 16, *ll.* 28–39.
102 Ministry of State Domains, Department of Agriculture, Tavria guberniia to Ministry of State Domains, First Department, St. Petersburg, 14 April 1842, *RGIA f.* 383, *op.* 1, *d.* 234, *ll.* 34–35ob.

103 'Po pros'be molokan Melitopol'skago uezda seleniia Astrakhanki ... o dozvolenii im pereselit'sia za Kavkaz,' 1841, *RGIA, f.* 1284, *op.* 199, *d.* 74, n.p.

104 See, e.g., 'Otchety tavricheskikh gubernatorov ... za 1847,' *RGIA, f.* 1281, *op.* 4, *d.* 35a, *ll.* 1–75.

105 The terms of the original lease are mentioned in correspondence regarding David Cornies's request to renew it in 1861. See Ministry of State Domains to Governor General of New Russia, 24 June 1861, *GAOO, f.* 1, *op.* 81, *d.* 90.

106 On Cornies's pursuit of land, see, e.g., Urry, *None But Saints,* 108–13.

107 Ministry of State Domains to Inzov, 3 February 1842, *GAOO, f.* 1, *op.* 152, *d.* 16, *ll.* 28–39.

108 Woodcock and Avakumovic, *The Doukhobors,* 59.

Chapter Five: Johann Cornies and the Birth of a New Mennonite World View

1 On changing perceptions of Cornies, see Dyck, 'Russian Servitor,' *passim.*

2 See Urry, *None But Saints,* 34–49; Redekop, Krahn and Steiner, *Anabaptist Faith and Economics*; Klassen, *A Homeland for Strangers.*

3 Urry, *None But Saints,* 41, 99.

4 Ibid., 99–102.

5 Ibid., 34–49; 99–100.

6 Ibid., 101.

7 Ibid., 105.

8 Ibid., 105–6.

9 Ibid., 101.

10 Ibid., 102.

11 Ibid., 111.

12 'Zhurnal registratsii iskhodiashchikh dokumentov,' 20 May 1821, *GADO, f.* 134, *op.* 1, *d.* 692, n.p.

13 Epp, *Johann Cornies,* 27.

14 Cornies to Schlatter, 12 March 1830, *PJBRMA,* file 169, 14–20ob.

15 Cornies to Schlatter, 22 December 1828, *PJBRMA,* file 129, 58–63ob.

16 Cornies to Schlatter, 12 March 1830, *PJBRMA,* file 169, 14–20ob.

17 Cornies to Van der Smissen, 18 September 1831, *PJBRMA,* file 200, 48–51ob.

18 Cornies to David Epp, March 1826, *PJBRMA,* file 82, 14–15.

19 Cornies, 'Einiges über die Nogaier-Tataren.'

20 'Pravila neobkhodimye k sobliudeniiu pri ustroistve iz Nogaiskoi derevni akerman v obraztsovuiu ili primernuiu koloniiu,' 1842, *PJBRMA,* file 818,

1–18. There are numerous other versions of this document scattered through the Cornies papers.

21 'Pravila neobkhodimye k sobliudeniiu,' 1842, *PJBRMA*, file 818, 1–18.

22 On cameralism, see Marc Raeff, *The Well-Ordered Police State: Society and Institutional Change through Law in the Germanies and Russia, 1600–1800* (New Haven: Yale University Press, 1983).

23 Urry, *None But Saints*, 55.

24 Harvey L. Dyck, introduction to *A Mennonite in Russia: The Diaries of Jacob D. Epp, 1851–1880*, ed. and trans. Harvey L. Dyck (Toronto: University of Toronto Press, 1991), 9.

25 E.K. Francis, *In Search of Utopia: The Mennonites in Manitoba* (Altona, MB: D.W. Friesen and Sons, 1955), 9–10. This attitude rested uneasily with the terms of the Russian Mennonites' Charter of Privileges, which specifically enjoined them to act as a model to other settlers. On divisions within the Mennonite community over their role in the greater society, see, e.g., Urry, *None But Saints*, 123–37.

26 Cornies, 'Einiges über die Nogaier-Tataren,' 50.

27 'Instruction für die Vereine in den Kolonien des Molotschner und Chortitzer Mennonisten Gebiets, zur fördersamen Verbreitung in derselben des Gehölz-, Garten-, Seiden-, und Wein-Baues,' 1830, *PJBRMA*, file 166, 1–21. Note that Khortitsa had its own Forestry Society.

28 See, e.g., Urry, *None But Saints*, 112.

29 'Instruction für die Vereine,' 1830, *PJBRMA*, file 166, 1–21.

30 'Instruction für die Vereine,' 1830, *PJBRMA*, file 166, 1–21.

31 See Harrison, *Forests*, passim.

32 Cornies to Fadeev, 24 July 1831, *PJBRMA*, file 200, 37–37ob.

33 For a complete list, see 'Catalog. Die Bücher des Vereins,' 1841, *PJBRMA*, file 797, 20–9.

34 Cornies to Fadeev, 24 July 1831, *PJBRMA*, file 200, 37–37ob; Baron von Rosen to the Department of Agriculture, 14 April 1847, *RGIA, f.* 383, *op.* 10, *d.* 9108, *ll.* 3–12ob.

35 Urry, *None But Saints*, 113.

36 'Instruction für die Vereine,' 1830, *PJBRMA*, file 166, 1–21.

37 'Po otnosheniiu Departamenta Sel'skogo Khoziaistva o vvedenii u russkikh pereselentsev khoziaistva i poriadka upravleniia menonitov,' 24 September 1845, *RGIA, f.* 383, *op.* 10, *d.* 7164, n.p.

38 'Instruction für die Vereine,' 1830, *PJBRMA*, file 166, 1–21.

39 Contenius to Guardianship Committee, 19 January 1823, *GADO, f.* 134, *op.* 1, *d.* 741, n.p.

40 Cornies to Schlatter, 12 March 1830, *PJBRMA*, file 169, 14–20ob.

41 Forestry Society to *Gebietsamt*, n.d. (probably 1834), *PJBRMA*, file 310, 41–41ob.

42 Forestry Society to *Gebietsamt*, n.d. (probably 1835), *PJBRMA*, file 343, 27–28.

43 Cornies to Fadeev, 15 January 1835, *PJBRMA*, file 315.

44 Forestry Society to *Gebietsamt*, 10 December 1836, *PJBRMA*, file 361.

45 Cornies to Fadeev, 13 September 1833, *PJBRMA*, file 251.

46 Cornies to Fadeev, 26 February 1836, *PJBRMA*, file 388.

47 Cornies to Fadeev, 26 February 1836, *PJBRMA*, file 388.

48 Cornies to Fadeev, 26 February 1836, *PJBRMA*, file 388.

49 Urry, *None But Saints*, 196. See also Calvin Redekop, 'The Mennonite Romance with the Land,' in Harry Loewen and Al Reimer, eds., *Visions and Realities: Essays, Poems and Fiction Dealing with Mennonite Issues* (Winnipeg: Hyperion, 1985), 83–94.

50 Cornies to Fadeev, 26 June 1839, *PJBRMA*, file 521 (italics added).

51 Cornies to Fadeev, 5 April 1833, *PJBRMA*, file 251, 11–12ob.

52 Cornies to Fadeev, 5 April 1833, *PJBRMA*, file 251, 11–12ob.

53 See, e.g., Cornies' notes from an inspection trip, 10–14 February 1836, *PJBRMA*, file 368, 1–8ob; Cornies to Tiegenhagen *Schulzenamt*, January 1839.

54 On Waldheim and Gnadenfeld, see Cornies to Fadeev, 28 January 1837, *PJBRMA*, file 432. On Landskrone, see Cornies to Fadeev, 26 June 1839, *PJBRMA*, file 521.

55 Cornies to Fadeev, 26 June 1839, *PJBRMA*, file 521.

56 Cornies to Fadeev, 28 January 1837.

57 An important technological factor in this process was the development of the bukker, a forerunner of the disk cultivator used by modern farmers to destroy surface weeds while minimizing the exposure of deeper soils to moisture evaporation. See Leonard Friesen, 'Bukkers, Plows and Lobogreikas: Peasant Acquisition of Agricultural Implements in New Russia before 1900,' *Russian Review* 53:3 (July 1994), 399–418.

58 Cornies to Fadeev, 28 January 1837, *PJBRMA*, file 432.

59 Cornies to Fadeev, 26 June 1839, *PJBRMA*, file 521.

60 'Verzeichnis über Aussaat und Ernte im Molotschner Mennonisten' Bezirk in den Jahren 1828 bis 1848,' n.d., *PJBRMA*, file 1308, 25–6.

61 Cornies' extensive correspondence with Blüher, which spanned twenty-three years (1825–1848), is scattered throughout the *PJBRMA*.

62 Cornies to Blüher, 18 January 1832, *PJBRMA*, file 236, 7–7ob.

63 Cornies to Fadeev, 26 April 1838, *PJBRMA*, file 496.

64 See Table 5.4.

65 Cornies to Fadeev, 28 January 1837, *PJBRMA*, file 432.

66 'Vedomost.' O blagosostoianii kolonii Molochanskago Menonitskago okruga za ianvar' mesiats 1839 goda,' *GAOO, f.* 6, *op.* 1, *d.* 5099, n.p.; 'S mesiachnymi vedomostiami o blagosostoianii Berdianskago okruga za ianvar' 1847,' *GAOO, f.* 6, *op.* 2, *d.* 10063, n.p.

67 'Vedomosti Molochanskago Menonitskago okruzhnago prikaza o khoziaistvennom sostoianii kolonii za 1813 god,' *GADO, f.* 134, *op.* 1, *d.* 356, n.p.

68 'Vedomosti o blagosostoianii molochanskikh kolonistov za istekshii fevral' mts. 1813 goda,' *GAOO, f.* 6, *op.* 1, *d.* 773, n.p.

69 'Kammeral Liste,' 1 January 1834, *GADO, f.* 134, *op.* 1, *d.* 981, n.p.; 'Vedomost.' O blagosostoianii kolonii Molochanskago Menonitskago okruga za ianvar' mesiats 1839 goda,' *GAOO, f.* 6, *op.* 1, *d.* 5099, n.p.; 'S mesiachnymi vedomostiami o blagosostoianii Berdianskago okruga za ianvar' 1847,' *GAOO, f.* 6, *op.* 2, *d.* 10063, n.p.

70 Cornies to David Epp, 14 August 1826, *PJBRMA*, file 82, 34–35ob.

71 Cornies to Fadeev, March 1831, *PJBRMA*, file 200, 16–16ob.

72 See Harvey L. Dyck, 'Landlessness in the Old Colony: The *Judenplan* Experiment 1850–1880,' in John Friesen, ed., *Mennonites in Russia 1788– 1988: Essays in Honour of Gerhard Lohrenz* (Winnipeg: CMBC, 1989), 183– 202.

73 'Kammeral Liste,' 1 January 1849, *PJBRMA*, file 1392, 1–7ob.

74 'Notizen wegen der Bittschriften einigen Mennoniten sich nach dem Kiewschen und Wolynischen Gouvernement zu übersiedeln,' 1849, *PJBRMA*, file 1429, 1–2ob.

75 Cornies to Inspector Pelekh, 25 November 1836, *PJBRMA*, file 367, 4–5ob.

76 Cornies to Inspector Pelekh, 25 November 1836, *PJBRMA*, file 367, 4–5ob.

77 Cornies to Inspector Pelekh, 25 November 1836, *PJBRMA*, file 367, 4–5ob.

78 'Vedomosti o blagosostoianii Molochanskikh kolonii ... za fevral' mesiats 1807 goda,' *GAOO, f.* 6, *op.* 1, *d.* 302, n.p.

79 Cornies to Inspector Pelekh, 25 November 1836, *PJBRMA*, file 367, 4–5ob.

80 Urry, *None But Saints*, 140–1.

81 Cornies to Pelekh, 12 January 1840, *PJBRMA*, file 612.

82 Urry, for example, writes that *anwohner* 'were often poor, forced to live on the edge of the village and the fringe of society because they had no choice' (*None But Saints*, 60).

83 For a critical view of the role of landowners, see Urry, *None But Saints*, 203–5.

84 'Po otnosheniiu Departamenta Sel'skago Khoziaistva o vvedenii u russkikh pereselentsev khoziaistva i poriadka upravleniia menonitov,' *RGIA, f.* 383, *op.* 10, *d.* 7164, *ll.* 92–127.

85 Ibid., Part 3, Item 3.
86 Ibid., Part 3, Item 2.
87 Ibid, Part 3, Item 6.
88 'Kameral Liste,' 1 January 1949, *PJBRMA* file 1392, 1–7ob.
89 'Po otnosheniiu Departamenta Sel'skago Khoziaistva o vvedenii u russkikh pereselentsev khoziaistva i poriadka upravleniia menonitov,' *RGIA, f.* 383, *op.* 10, *d.* 7164, *ll.* 92–127.
90 For example, the version cited here comes from the records of the Ministry of State Domains in Saratov guberniia.
91 'Po otnosheniiu Departamenta Sel'skago Khoziaistva o vvedenii u russkikh pereselentsev khoziaistva i poriadka upravleniia menonitov,' Part 2, Item 32, *RGIA, f.* 383, *op.* 10, *d.* 7164, *ll.* 92–127.
92 'Po otnosheniiu Departamenta Sel'skago Khoziaistva o vvedenii u russkikh pereselentsev khoziaistva i poriadka upravleniia menonitov,' Part 3, Items 22 & 27, *RGIA, f.* 383, *op.* 10, *d.* 7164, *ll.* 92–127.
93 Ibid., Part 3, Item 11.
94 Ibid., Part 3, Item 27.
95 Ibid., Preface to Part 4.
96 See Dyck, 'Russian Servitor.'
97 Urry, *None But Saints*, 127.
98 Cornies to Fadeev, 26 April 1838, *PJBRMA*, file 496. Fadeev had by this time already left the Guardianship Committee to take up a new post as Chief Guardian of the Kalmyk Horde, but he remained highly influential with Guardianship Committee members.
99 Cornies to Fadeev, 26 April 1838, *PJBRMA*, file 496.
100 Urry, *None But Saints*, 125.
101 Ibid., 128.
102 Ibid., 128.
103 Ibid., 128.
104 Ibid., 129.
105 Ibid., 135.
106 Anne Lincoln Fitzpatrick, *The Great Russian Fair: Nizhnii Novgorod, 1840–90* (London: Macmillan, 1990), 5.
107 Fitzpatrick, *Great Russian Fair*, 9. See also Herlihy, *Odessa*, 88–9.
108 Fitzpatrick, *Great Russian Fair*, 9.
109 B.N. Mironov, *Vnutrennii rynok Rossii vo vtoroi polovine XVIII–pervoi polovine XIX v.* (Leningrad: Nauk, 1981), 161.
110 Fitzpatrick, *Great Russian Fair*, 8–9.
111 See R. Gohstand, 'The Geography of Trade in Nineteenth-Century Russia,' *Studies in Russian Historical Geography* 2: 339–346.

112 *Tavricheskaia gubernskaia vedomost'* 4 (28 January 1838).
113 Wilhelm Bernhard Bauman, 'Opisanie kazennago seleniia Tokmaka v Tavricheskoi gubernii,' *ZhMVD* 26 (1848), 1–9.
114 According to Aksakov, merino sheep produced about 3.5 *funts* of wool per sheep (*Izsledovanie o torgovle*, 200). There were 1,103,945 merino sheep in the two uezds in 1860, so wool production would have been 3,863,808 *funts*, or 96,595 *puds*.
115 For a complete list of State Peasant crafts- and tradesmen in the Molochna in the 1840s, see 'Verzeichnis der Professionisten der Berdjanschen, Melitopolschen und Dneprowschen Kreise,' 1849, *PJBRMA*, file 1439, 1.
116 'Verzeichnis: Über die im November 1843 unter den Nogaier auf Condition gegebene Schafe,' 1843, *PJBRMA*, file 903, 1; 'Verzeichnis: Über die auf rechtmässige Weise unter den Nogaiern befindt. Schafe und deren Contract,' 1847, *PJBRMA*, file 1269, 26–37.
117 'S mesiachnymi vedomostiami o blagosostoianii kolonii Berdianskago okruga za ianvar' 1847,' *GAOO, f.* 6, *o.* 2, *d.* 10063, n.p.
118 'Nogaier Schaafschuld von 1844 an zu bezahlen mit der Bemerkung wie viel von Zeit zu Zeit dieselbe darauf abgetragen haben,' n.d., *PJBRMA*, file 916, 1–6.
119 Cornies to Fadeev, 30 December 1836, *PJBRMA*, file 236.
120 *Zemskii ispravnik* Kolosov to Inspector Pelekh, 14 February 1836, *PJBRMA*, file 691, 2–3.
121 'Ob iavlenii konditsii,' 1837, *PJBRMA*, file 406, 1–6.
122 Nogais to Cornies, 1839, *PJBRMA*, file 543, 1–12.
123 Ibid.
124 On ram vs. ewe wool and international demand, see Barnard, *Australian Wool Market*, 5–6.
125 Bauman, 'Zusammenstellung,' 1847, *PJBRMA*, file 1291, 1–18.
126 See guarantee to a contract between Regier and Adzhigulov, 3 November 1847, *PJBRMA*, file 1268, 1–2.
127 Dyck, 'Russian Servitor,' 13.
128 The 1848 drought is described in Chapters 6 and 7.

Chapter Six: The Path Taken by the Orthodox State Peasants: Land Repartition

1 'O razvedenii lesov v stepnykh uezdakh Tavricheskoi gubernii,' 7 November 1843, *RGIA, f.* 387, *op.* 1, *d.* 10407, *ll.* 20–4.
2 Ibid.

3 Ibid.

4 Köppen to Kiselev, 19 March 1839, *RGIA, f.* 387, *op.* 1, *d.* 10407, *ll.* 20ob–22.

5 'O razvedenii lesov v stepnykh uezdakh Tavricheskoi gubernii,' part 2, 28
   July 1843, *RGIA, f.* 387, *op.* 1, *d.* 10408, n.p.

6 'O razvedenii lesov v stepnykh uezdakh Tavricheskoi gubernii,' part 3,
   1843, RGIA, *f.* 387, *op.* 1, *d.* 10409, *ll.* 50–1.

7 'Vedemost' mal'chikov postupivshikh na obratsovuiu ... ,' 1855, *PJBRMA*,
   file 1787, 1.

8 For the decree, along with plans and reports on its implementation, see 'O
   sostavlenii predpolozheniia na chet usileniia razvedeniia kartofelia,' *RGIA,
   f.* 1589, *op.* 1, *d.* 694, passim.

9 Ibid., *ll.* 12–13.

10 'Otchety tavricheskikh gubernatorov ... za 1856,' *RGIA, f.* 1281, *op.* 6, *d.* 97–
    1857, *l.* 264; 'Otchety tavricheskikh gubernatorov ... za 1858,' *RGIA, f.* 1281,
    op. 6, *d.* 52–1859, *l.* 82.

11 K.B.A. Bodlaender, 'Influence of Temperature, Radiation and Photoperiod
    on Development and Yield,' *The Growth of the Potato: Proceedings of the Tenth
    Easter School in Agricultural Science, University of Nottingham, 1963* (London:
    Butterworths, 1963), 209.

12 'Otchety tavricheskikh gubernatorov ... za 1858,' *RGIA, f.* 1281, *op.* 6, *d.* 52–
    1859, *ll.* 82–4.

13 'Ob izbranii na uchebnye fermy mal'chikov iz gosudarstvennykh krest'ian,'
    1851, *RGIA, f.* 383, *op.* 14, *d.* 16143, *l.* 10ob.

14 Department of Agriculture of the Ministry of State Domains to First
    Department of the Ministry of State Domains, *RGIA, f.* 383, *op.* 10, *d.* 9232,
    ll. 3–6.

15 Ibid.

16 Berestova obshchina to Vorontsov, 6 October 1834, *GAOO, f.* 1, *op.* 191, *d.*
    28, n.p.

17 The case is summarized in a report from the Agricultural Desk of the
    Department of Finance in Tavria guberniia to the Civil Governor of Tavria,
    5 November 1834, *GAOO, f.* 1, *op.* 191, *d.* 28, n.p.

18 Berestova obshchina to Vorontsov, 6 October 1834, *GAOO, f.* 1, *op.* 191, *d.*
    28, n.p.

19 Berestova obshchina to Vorontsov, 6 October 1834, *GAOO, f.* 1, *op.* 191, *d.*
    28, n.p.

20 Department of State Domains of the Ministry of Internal Affairs to
    Vorontsov, 15 March 1837, *GAOO, f.* 1, *d.* 191, *op.* 28, n.p.

21 For other examples that explicitly relate land rights to taxes, see the series
    of fifteen petitions protesting land reductions in 1841, *RGIA, f.* 383, *op.* 1,
    d. 190, *ll.* 39–75.

22 Bauman, 'Opisanie kazennago seleniia Tokmaka,' 5–6. According to
    Bauman there were 3,342 male residents in 1844.
23 Bauman, 'Zusammenstellung,' 3–3ob.
24 Ibid., 2.
25 Semple, *Grassland Improvement*, 106.
26 Ibid., 106.
27 Bauman, 'Zusammenstellung,' 2. Note that Volga German colonists
    experienced almost identical problems concerning pasture access, and
    resorted to stinting to force more equitable access – see Long, *From
    Privileged to Dispossessed*, 85.
28 Bauman, 'Zusammenstellung,' 3–3ob.
29 Scattered wage data from 1854, 1857, 1859 and 1860 can be found in
    GAKO, f. 26, *op.* 1, *d.* 20812; *f.* 26, *op.* 1, *d.* 21942; *f.* 26, *op.* 1, *d.* 23043; *f.* 26,
    op. 1, *d.* 23801; *f.* 26, *op.* 1, *d.* 24037; *f.* 26, *op.* 1, *d.* 24040.
30 Verzeichnis über der russische Dienstboth auf dem Vorwerke Iushanlee,'
    1845–1852, *PJBRMA*, 1214, 1–23.
31 *PJBRMA*, 1177, 1–1ob.
32 Khanatskii, ed., *Pamiatnaia knizhka Tavricheskoi gubernii*, 225.
33 Agricultural Department of the Ministry of Internal Affairs to Governor
    General Vorontsov, 27 July 1836, *GAOO, f.* 1, *op.* 191, *d.* 32, n.p. 'The poor
    are victimized' is a liberal translation. The actual phrase is: 'skudnye
    ostaiutsia pred nymi [the rich] kraine obizhennymi,' or literally 'The poor
    stand before them utterly offended.'
34 Bauman, 'Opisanie,' 2.
35 The project itself is not extant, but it is described in a number of the
    documents cited here regarding the Bolshoi Tokmak repartition. The full
    name of the project is '*Proekt pravil khoziaistvennago raspredeleniia zemel' v
    kazennykh seleniiakh iuzhnykh gubernii.*'
36 Bauman, 'Zusammenstellung'; Bauman, 'Opisanie kazennago seleniia
    Tokmaka.'
37 See Chapter 3, p. 63.
38 On the 1880s pattern, see Postnikov, *Krest'ianskoe khoziaistvo*, 193.
39 Bauman, 'Zusammenstellung,' 2.
40 Semple, *Grassland Improvement*, 22.
41 Regarding yields, see Postnikov, *Krest'ianskoe khoziaistvo*, 255. Postnikov gives
    yields per desiatina as follows: winter rye – 4.1 *chet./des.*; spring wheat – 3.2
    chet./des.; barley – 5.2 *chet./des.* Because breakdowns by crop are not
    available for the period 1840 to 1861, it is impossible to make direct
    comparisons, but given the standard practice of planting one chetvert per
    desiatina, the average seed/output ratio for all crops would have been little
    different than the 1/4.09 achieved in the period 1840 to 1861, and would

have been worse than the 1/5.13 obtained in the period 1856 to 1861. Regarding soil exhaustion, see ibid, 190.

42 'Po otnosheniiu Departamenta Sel'skago Khoziaistva o raspredelenii zemel v dache seleniia Bol'shago Tokmaka s vyselivshimisia iz nego derevniami Berdianskago okruga,' 14 April 1847, *RGIA, f.* 383, *op.* 10, *d.* 9108, *ll.* 3–12ob.

43 Ibid.

44 Timofeev does not say which Karakulak, but he was presumably referring to Verkhnii Karakulak, which had a very large proportion of poor land.

45 The report of the village elders is not included with the reports of the regional authorities, but is described in the Ministry of State Domains summary ('Po otnosheniiu Departamenta Sel'skago Khoziaistva o raspredelenii zemel v dache seleniia Bol'shago Tokmaka s vyselivshimisia iz nego derevniami Berdianskago okruga,' 14 April 1847, *RGIA, f.* 383, *op.* 10, *d.* 9108, *ll.* 3–12ob.).

46 'Po otnosheniiu Departamenta Sel'skago Khoziaistva o raspredelenii zemel' v dache seleniia Bol'shago Tokmaka s vyselivshimisia iz nego derevniami Berdianskago okruga,' 14 April 1847, *RGIA, f.* 383, *op.* 10, *d.* 9108, *ll.* 3–12ob.

47 Ibid. The peasants probably had a better appreciation of the water requirements of their livestock than Bauman. Modern experts place great emphasis on water quality, and A.T. Semple specifically criticizes the practice of constructing shallow reservoirs on rangeland, saying it 'wastes water and fails to supply dependable and potable stocks.' Semple, *Grassland Improvement* (Cleveland: CRC Press, 1970), 258.

48 'Po otnosheniiu Departamenta Sel'skago Khoziaistva o raspredelenii zemel'' v dache seleniia Bol'shago Tokmaka s vyselivshimisia iz nego derevniami Berdianskago okruga,' 14 April 1847, *RGIA, f.* 383, *op.* 10, *d.* 9108.

49 'Zusamunstellung der von mir in den Steppen des südlichen Russland gemachten Beobachtungen in Beziehung auf den Ackerbau,' 1847, *PJBRMA*, file 1291, 1–17ob.

50 Note that rye had now entered the commercial market. During the *Mnogozemel'naia* period the price of rye in the Molochna had shown no significant correlation with prices in the rest of the guberniia, but it now reacted to changes elsewhere (see Table 6.4). On the other hand, the correlation between wheat prices in Berdiansk and the rest of the guberniia ($r^2 = 0.46$) is actually below the threshold usually considered to denote statistical significance. This anomalous result probably is because Berdiansk only reported grain prices sporadically in the first years after its

establishment, so that the available data are insufficient to establish a correlation with any degree of certainty. The result for Melitopol (r^2 = 0.56) suggests that, as expected, wheat prices were linked to the larger guberniia market.

51 On state peasant livestock preferences, see Friesen, 'New Russia,' 110; Bauman, 'Opisanie,' 5.
52 The disastrous harvest failures in 1833 to 1834 and 1839 would have mitigated against the per capita holdings rising much further.
53 Skal'kovskii, *Opyt statisticheskago opisaniia*, 368.
54 Detailed maps of the district, dating from the 1840s and 1850s, confirm this. See, e.g., 'Umen'shennyi plan kazennykh dach, sel i dereven' Orekhovskoi volosti, Berdianskago uezda, Tavricheskoi gubernii, sostavlen v 1853 godu,' *GAZO, f.* 263, *op.* 1, *d.* 51, n.p.

Chapter Seven: Consolidation and Alienation

1 Quoted in Goerz, *The Molotschna Settlement*, 28.
2 Bolotenko, 'Administration of the State Peasants,' Appendix III:v.
3 Postnikov, *Krest'ianskoe khoziaistvo*, 166.
4 Loan payment receipts, 1848, *PJBRMA*, file 1352, 1–34ob.
5 'Verzeichnis der Nogaier Schafesfelden für Iuschanlii,' 1848, *PJBRMA*, file 1261, 6–8.
6 'Immenyi spisok,' 1850, *PJBRMA*, file 1477, 20–1; 'Spisok nogaitsam,' 1851, *PJBRMA*, file 1576, 2–5ob.; 'Wie viel Land der Akkermener Dorfsgemeinde zu verpachten wunscht,' 2 Feb. 1853, *PJBRMA*, file 1687, 1–10b.
7 'Otdacha nogaitsami v arendu zemli s tsel'iu uplaty nalogov,' 1851, *PJBRMA*, file 1615, 1–76.
8 'Landpacht–Rechnung,' 1851, *PJBRMA*, file 1557, 1–3.
9 See, e.g., the map of land rented by David Schellenberg in 1853, *PJBRMA*, file 1686, 1–1ob.
10 Sergeev, 'Ukhod tavricheskikh nogaitsev,' 181.
11 'Wie viel Land der Akkermener Dorfsgemeinde zu verpachten wunscht,' 2 Feb. 1853, *PJBRMA*, file 1687, 1–1ob.
12 'Otdacha nogaitsami v arendu zemli s tsel'iu uplaty nalogov,' 1851, *PJBRMA*, file 1615, 1–76.
13 See Alexander Petzholdt, *Reise im westlichen und südlichen Russland im Jahre 1855* (Leipzig: Hermann Fries, 1864), 211–31; A. Bode, *Notizen, gesammelt auf einer Forstreise durch einen Theil des Europaichen Russlands* (Osnabrück: Verlag reprint, 1969 from 1854 original), 291–316.

14 Petzholdt, *Reise*, 212–14.
15 'Otchety tavricheskikh gubernatorov ... za 1853,' 1854, *RGIA, f.* 1281, *o.* 5, *d.* 60a, *l.* 5.
16 'Otchety tavricheskikh gubernatorov ... za 1842,' 1843, *RGIA, f.* 1282, *o.* 4, *d.* 73a, *l.* 41.
17 'Otchety tavricheskikh gubernatorov ... za 1842,' 1843, *RGIA, f.* 1282, *o.* 4, *d.* 73a, *l.* 41.
18 Pinson, 'Russian Policy and the Emigration of the Crimean Tatars,' 38–9.
19 Pinson, 'Russian Policy and the Emigration of the Crimean Tatars,' 46.
20 I. Kh. Kalmykov, R. Kh. Kereitov, and L.I.M. Sikaliev, *Nogaitsy: istoriko-etnograficheskii ocherk* (Cherkessk: Stavropol'skoe Knizhnoe Izdatel'stvo, 1988), 39.
21 Nogai *Murzas* to Ministry of State Domains, 18 July 1857, *RGIA, f.* 383, *op.* 20, *d.* 26953, *ll.* 2–6.
22 'Po otnosheniiu deistvitel'nago statskago sovetnika Rametno,' 18 August 1859, *RGIA, f.* 383, *op.* 20, *d.* 26953, *ll.* 16–17ob.
23 Sergeev, 'Ukhod tavricheskikh nogaitsev,' 201.
24 Ibid., 205.
25 Peter M. Friesen, *The Mennonite Brotherhood in Russia (1789–1910)*, trans. J.B. Toews, et al (Fresno, CA: Board of Christian Literature of the General Council of Mennonite Brethren, 1978), 855.
26 Urry, *None But Saints*, 207.
27 Franz Isaac, *Die Molotschnaer Mennoniten: Ein Beitrag zur Geschichte derselben* (Halbstadt: Braun, 1908), 63–4.
28 Isaac, *Molotschnaer Mennoniten* 31 n1 and 31 n2.
29 Ibid., 56, italics added.
30 Rempel, 'Mennonite Commonwealth,' 2:7.
31 Ibid., 2:7.
32 Franz Isaac, *Die Molotschner Mennoniten*, 32.
33 See, e.g., 'Landpacht-Rechnung,' 1851, *PJBRMA*, file 1557, 1–3ob.
34 'Pachtrechnung,' *PJBRMA* file 1393 (1849), 1–9. Note that the confusion over land costs may stem from the complicated two-tiered payment system. In 1849 leasers were required to pay a flat annual rate per desiatina of about 20 kopecks, an additional tri-annual payment totalling approximately 40 kopecks, and a state tax of approximately 2 kopecks.
35 Similar problems occurred in the Volga German colonies, where loss of access to steppe land pushed many colonists to the brink of economic ruin. See Long, *From Privileged to Dispossessed*, 88–9.
36 Khanatskii, ed., *Pamiatnaia knizhka Tavricheskoi gubernii*, 168–9. For the hydrographic survey prompted by the complaints, see 'Raboty po

snabzheniiu vodoi pereselentsev, proizvedennyia v Tavricheskoi gubernii v 1862 godu,' *ZhMGI* 83 (July 1863).

37 The best source on the subject remains Rempel, 'The Mennonite Commonwealth,' 2: 23–33.

38 Urry, *None But Saints*, 108–37.

Chapter Eight: Conclusion

1 'Otchet o zaniatiiakh tavricheskoi gubernskoi komissii, dlia prigotovitel'nykh rasporiazhenii po priemu gosudarstvennykh imushchestv, s 10 avgusta na 10 sentiabria 1838 goda,' *RGIA, f.* 1589, *op.* 1, *d.* 362, *ll.* 86–89ob.

2 Cornies to Fadeev, 13 September 1833, *PJBRMA*, file.

3 'O pereselenii smolenskikh ... krest'ian,' 1803–1822, *RGIA, f.* 1285, *op.* 1, *d.* 13a, *ll.* 87–8.

4 Cornies to Wiebe, 20 January 1840, *PJBRMA*, file 647.

Bibliography

Archival Collections

Gosudarstvennyi arkhiv Krimskoi oblast (GAKO) Fondy 26, 27, 377.
Gosudarstvennyi arkhiv Zaporozhskoi oblast (GAZO) Fondy 3, 109, 250, 262, 263
Gosudarstvennyi arkhiv Odeskoi oblast (GAOO) Fondy 1, 6, 7, 22.
Gosudarstvennyi arkhiv Khersonskoi oblast (GAKhO) Fondy 14, 22, 198, 254, 320
Gosudarstvennyi arkhiv Dnepropetrovskoi oblast (GADO) Fond 134.
Russkii gosudarstvennyi istoricheskii arkhiv (RGIA) Fondy 380, 381, 382, 383, 387, 571, 1281, 1283, 1285, 1287, 1399
Russkii gosudarstvennyi voenno-istoricheskii arkhiv (RGVIA) Fond 377
Peter J. Braun Russian Mennonite Archive (PJBRMA)

Books

Aksakov, Ivan. *Izsledovanie o Torgovie na Ukrainskikh Iarmarkakh*. St Petersburg, 1858.
Antsupov, I.A. *Gosudarstvennaia Derevnia Bessarabii v XIX veke (1812–1870 gg.)*. Kishinev: Kartia Moldoveniaske, 1966.
Bagalei, D.I. *Kolonizatsiia Novorossiiskago kraia i pervye shagi ego po puti kul'tury*. Kiev: G.M. Kochark-Novitskogo, 1889.
Baker, Alan R.H., and Robin A. Butlin, eds. *Studies of Field Systems in the British Isles*. Cambridge: Cambridge University Press, 1973.
Barnard, Alan. *The Australian Wool Market, 1840–1900*. Melbourne: Melbourne University Press, 1958.
– *Human Capital: The Settlement of Foreigners in Russia, 1762–1804*. Cambridge: Cambridge University Press, 1979.

Bartlett, Roger P., ed. *Land Commune and Peasant Community in Russia: Communal Forms in Imperial and Early Soviet Society.* London: Macmillan, 1990.

Bater, James H., and R.A. French, eds. *Studies in Russian Historical Geography.* 2 vols. London: Academic Press, 1982.

Bitkova, T.G., et al., eds. *Nemtsy v Rossii : Istoriko-kul'ternye aspekty.* Moscow: AN, 1994.

Bloch, Marc. *French Rural History: An Essay on its Basic Characteristics.* Translated by Janet Sonderheimer. London: Routledge and Kegan Paul, 1966.

Booth, Anne, and R.M. Sundrum. *Labour Absorption in Agriculture: Theoretical Analysis and Empirical Investigations.* Oxford: Oxford University Press, 1985.

Brandes, Detlef. *Von den Zaren adoptiert: Die deutschen Kolonisten und die Balkansiedler in Neurussland und Bessarabien 1751–1914.* Munich: Oldenbourg, 1993.

Byres, T.J., ed. *Sharecropping and Sharecroppers.* London: Frank Cass, 1983.

Chang, Claudia, and E. Koster, eds. *Pastoralists at the Periphery: Herders in a Capitalist World,* 79–95. Tucson: University of Arizona Press, 1994.

Clark, Colin, and Margaret Haswell. *The Economics of Subsistence Agriculture,* 4th ed. London: Macmillan, 1970.

Crummey, Robert. *The Old Believers and the World of Antichrist: The Vyg Community and the Russian State, 1694–1855.* Madison: University of Wisconsin Press, 1970.

Druzhinin, N.M. *Gosudarstvennye krest'iane i reforma P.D. Kiseleva,* 2 vols. Moscow: Nauka, 1946, 1958.

Druzhinina, E.I. *Kiuchuk-Kainardzhiiskii mir 1774 goda (ego podgotovka i zakliuchenie).* Moscow: Nauka, 1955.

– *Severnoe Prichernomor'e v 1775–1800 gg.* Moscow: Nauka, 1959.

– *IUzhnaia Ukraina v 1800–1825 gg.* Moscow: Nauka, 1970.

– *IUzhnaia Ukraina v period krizisa feodalizma 1825–1860 gg.* Moscow: Nauka, 1981.

Dyck, Harvey L., ed. and trans. *A Mennonite in Russia: The Diaries of Jacob D. Epp, 1851–1880.* Toronto: University of Toronto Press, 1991.

Elkinton, Joseph. *The Doukhobors: Their History in Russia, Their Migration to Canada.* Philadelphia: Ferris and Leach, 1903.

Ellis, Frank. *Peasant Economics: Farm Households and Agrarian Development.* Cambridge: Cambridge University Press, 1988.

Epp, David H. *Johann Cornies.* Translated by Peter Pauls. Winnipeg: CMBC / The Manitoba Mennonite Historical Society, 1995.

Ffolliott, Peter F., ed. *Dryland Forestry: Planning and Management.* New York: John Wiley and Sons, 1995.

Fisher, Alan W. *The Russian Annexation of the Crimea, 1772–1783.* Cambridge: Cambridge University Press, 1970.

Fitzpatrick, Anne Lincoln. *The Great Russian Fair: Nizhnii Novgorod, 1840–90.* London: Macmillan, 1990.

Francis, E.K. *In Search of Utopia: The Mennonites in Manitoba.* Altona, MB: D.W. Friesen and Sons, 1955.

Friesen, John. *Against the Wind: The Story of Four Mennonite Villages (Gnadenthal, Grünfeld, Neu-Chortitza, and Steinfeld) in Southern Ukraine, 1872–1943.* Winnipeg: Henderson Books, 1994.

Friesen, John, ed. *Mennonites in Russia, 1788–1988: Essays in Honour of Gerhard Lohrenz.* Winnipeg: CMBC, 1989.

Friesen, Peter M. *The Mennonite Brotherhood in Russia, 1789–1910.* Translated by John B. Toews, et. al. Fresno, CA: Conference of Mennonite Brethren Churches. 1980.

Goerz, Heinrich. *The Molotschna Settlement.* Translated by Al Reimer and John B. Toews. Winnipeg: CMBC / Manitoba Mennonite Historical Society, 1993.

Gottman, Jean, ed. *Center and Periphery: Spatial Variation in Politics.* Beverly Hills: Sage. 1980.

Harrison, Robert Pogue. *Forests: The Shadow of Civilization.* Chicago: University of Chicago Press, 1992.

Haxthausen, August von. *The Russian Empire, Its People, Institutions, and Resources.* 2 vols. Translated by Robert Farie. London: Chapman and Hall, 1856.

– *Studies on the Interior of Russia.* Translated by Eleanore L.M. Schmidt. Chicago: University of Chicago Press, 1972.

– *Studien über die innern Zustände, das Volksleben und insbesondere die ländlichen Einrichtungen Russlands,* 3 vols. Hanover: Hahn, 1847.

– *Etudes sur la situation, la vie nationale et les institutions rurales de la Russie,* 2 vols. Hanover: Hahn, 1847.

Herlihy, Patricia. *Odessa: A History, 1794–1914.* Cambridge: Harvard University Press, 1986.

Hoch, Steven L. *Serfdom and Social Control in Russia: Petrovskoe, a Village in Tambov.* Chicago: University of Chicago Press, 1986.

Isaac, Franz. *Die Molotschner Mennoniten. Ein Beitrag zur Geschichte derselben.* Halbstadt: I. Braun, 1908.

Kabuzan, V.M. *Narodonaselenie Rossii v XVIII-pervoi polvine XIX v. (po materialam revizii).* Moscow: Nauka, 1963.

– *Zaselenie Novorossii (Ekaterinoslavskoi i Khersonskoi gubernii), vol. 8 pervoi polovine XIX veka (1719–1858 gg.).* Moscow: Nauka, 1976.

Kahan, Arcadius. *The Plow, the Hammer, and the Knout: An Economic History of Eighteenth-Century Russia.* Chicago: University of Chicago Press, 1985.

Kalmykov, I.Kh., R.Kh. Kereitov, and L.I.M. Sikaliev. *Nogaitsy: Istoriko-etnograficheskoi ocherk.* Cherkessk: Stavropolskoe Knizhnoe Izdatelstvo, 1988.

Khanatskii, K.B., ed. *Pamiatnaia knizhka Tavricheskoi gubernii.* Simferopol: Tipografiia Tavricheskoi gubernskoi pravlenii, 1867.

Khazanov, A.M. *Nomads and the Outside World.* Cambridge: Cambridge University Press, 1984.

Kingston-Mann, Esther, and Timothy Mixter, with the help of Jeffrey Burds, eds. *Peasant Economy, Culture, and Politics of European Russia, 1800–1901.* Princeton: Princeton University Press, 1991.

Klassen, Peter J. *A Homeland for Strangers: An Introduction to Mennonites in Poland and Prussia.* Fresno, CA: Center for Mennonite Brethren Studies, 1989.

Klaus, A.A. *Nashi kolonii.* St Petersburg: Nusval ta, 1869.

Klibanov, A.I. *Istoriia religioznogo sektantstva v rossii (60-e gody XIX v.–1917 g.).* Moscow: Nauka, 1965.

Koch, Fred C. *The Volga Germans: In Russia and the Americas, from 1763 to the Present.* University Park: Pennsylvania State University Press, 1978.

Kochekaev, B.B. *Nogaisko-Russkie Otnosheniia,* vol. 15–18. Alma-Ata: Nauka, 1988.

Köppen, P. *Predvarutel'naia svedeniia o chisle zhitelei v Rossii, po guberniiam i uezdam, v 1854 godu. Na osnovanii dannykh 9-i narodnoi perepiski i drugikh pokazanii.* St Petersburg: Nauka, 1854.

– *Deviataia reviziia. Izsledovanie o chisle zhitelei v Rossii v 1851 godu.* St Petersburg: Nauka, 1857.

Koniukhova, T.A. *Gosudarstvennaia derevnia Litvy i reforma P.D. Kiseleva 1840–1857 gg. (Vilenskaia i Kovenskaia gubernii).* Moscow: Moskovskogo Universiteta, 1975.

Krader, Lawrence. *Social Organization of the Mongol-Turkic Pastoral Nomads.* The Hague: Mouton, 1963.

Lincoln, W. Bruce. *In the Vanguard of Reform: Russia's Enlightened Bureaucrats, 1825–1861.* Dekalb: Northern Illinois University Press, 1982.

Loewen, Harry, and Al Reimer, eds. *Visions and Realities: Essays, Poems and Fiction Dealing with Mennonite Issues.* Winnipeg: Hyperion, 1985.

Long, James W. *From Privileged to Dispossessed: The Volga Germans, 1860–1917.* Lincoln: University of Nebraska Press, 1988.

Malinovskii, L.V. *Nemtsy v Rossii i na Altae; Populiarno-istoricheskie ocherki.* Barnaul: Barnaul State Pedagogical University, 1995.

Maude, Aylmer. *A Peculiar People: The Doukhobors.* New York: Funk and Wagnells, 1904.

McGrew, Roderick E. *Russia and the Cholera, 1823–1832.* Madison: University of Wisconsin Press, 1965.

Melville, Elinor G.K. *A Plague of Sheep: Environmental Consequences of the Conquest of Mexico.* Cambridge: Cambridge University Press, 1994.

Mironov, B.N. *Vnutrennii rynok Rossii vo vtoroi polovine XVIII-pervoi polovine XIX v.* Leningrad: Nauka, 1981.

Novitskii, Orest. *O Dukhobortsakh.* Kiev: Kievopecherskoi lavr, 1832.

– *Dukhobortsy. Ikh istoriia i verouchenie.* 2nd ed. Kiev: Universitetsakaia tipografiia, 1882.

Nuttonson, M.Y. *Ecology and Crop Geography of the Ukraine and the Ukrainian Agro-Climatic Analogues in North America.* Washington, DC: American Institute of Crop Ecology, 1947.

Pallas, P.S. *Travels through the Southern Provinces of the Russian Empire, in the Years 1793 and 1794,* 2 vols. London: S. Strahan. 1802.

Pallot, Judith, and Denis J.B. Shaw. *Landscape and Settlement in Romanov Russia, 1613–1917.* Oxford: Clarendon Press, 1990.

Petrikin, V.I., et al., eds. *Istoriia mist i sil ukrains'koi RSR: Zaporiz'ka oblast.* Kiev: Nauka URSR, 1970.

Pinkerton, Robert. *Russia: Or Miscellaneous Observations on the Past and Present State of that Country and Its Inhabitants.* London: Seeley and Sons, 1833.

Plett, Delbert F. *The Golden Years: The Mennonite Kleine Gemeinde in Russia (1812–1849).* Steinbach, MB: Author, 1985.

Postnikov, V.E. *Iuzhnoe-russkoe krest'ianskoe khoziaistvo.* Moscow: Kushnerev, 1891.

Raeff, Marc. *The Well-Ordered Police State: Social and Institutional Change through Law in the Germanies and Russia, 1600–1800.* New Haven: Yale University Press, 1983.

Redekop, Calvin, Victor A. Krahn, and Samuel J. Steiner, eds. *Anabaptist/Mennonite Faith and Economics.* Lanham, MD: University Press of America, 1994.

– Stephen C. Ainslay, and Robert Siemans, eds. *Mennonite Entrepreneurs.* Baltimore: Johns Hopkins University Press, 1995.

Rhinelander, Anthony L.H. *Prince Michael Vorontsov: Viceroy to the Tsar.* Montreal: McGill-Queen's University Press, 1990.

Riasanovsky, Nicholas. *Nicholas I and Official Nationality in Russia, 1825–1855.* Berkeley: University of California Press, 1967.

Schippan, Michael, and Sonja Striegnitz. *Wolgadeutsche: Geschichte und Gegenwart.* Berlin: Dietz Verlag, 1992.

Schlatter, Daniel. *Bruchstücke aus einigen Reisen nach dem südlichen Russland, in den Jahren 1822 bis 1828.* St Gallen: Huber und Co., 1830.

Scott, James C. *The Moral Economy of the Peasant: Rebellion and Subsistence in Southeast Asia.* New Haven: Yale University Press, 1976.

– *Domination and the Arts of Resistance: Hidden Transcripts.* New Haven: Yale University Press, 1990.

Semevskii, V.I. *Krest'iane v tsarstvovanie Imperatritsy Ekateriny II,* 2 vols. St Petersburg: Stasiulevich, 1881.

Semple, A.T. *Grassland Improvement.* Cleveland: CRC Press, 1970.

Shmidt, A. *Khersonskaia guberniia. Materialy geografii i statistiki Rossii sobrannye ofitserami general'nogo shtaba,* 2 vols. St Petersburg: Voennoi Tipografii, 1863.

Skal'kovskii, A.A. *Khronologicheskoe obozrenie istorii Novorossiiskago kraia 1730– 1823.* Chast II. s 1796 po 1823. Odessa, 1838.

– *O nogaiskikh tatarakh, zhivushchikh v Tabricheskoi gubernii.* St Petersburg, 1843.

– *Prostranstvo i Narodonaselenie Novorossiiskago kraia.* Odessa, 1848.

– *Rostov-na-Donu i torgovlia Zaovskago basseuna 1749–1863.* Odessa, 1866.

Smith, R.E.F., and David Christian. *Bread and Salt: A Social and Economic History of Food and Drink in Russia.* Cambridge: Cambridge University Press, 1984.

Starr, S. Frederick. *Decentralization and Self-Government in Russia, 1830–1870.* Princeton: Princeton University Press, 1972.

Stumpp, Karl. *The German-Russians: Two Centuries of Pioneering.* Translated by Joseph S. Height. Bonn and New York: Edition Atlantic Forum, 1978.

Tarasoff, Koozma J., ed. *The Spirit Wrestlers: Centennial Papers in Honour of Canada's Dukhobor Heritage.* Hull: Canadian Museum of Civilization. 1995.

Unruh, Benjamin Heinrich. *Die niederländisch-niederdeutschen Hintergründe der mennonitischen Ostwanderungen im 16., 18. und 19 Jahrhundert.* Karlsruhe: Heinrich Schneider, 1955.

Urry, James. *None But Saints: The Transformation of Mennonite Life in Russia, 1789–1889.* Winnipeg: Windflower Communications, 1989.

Viola, Lynne. *Peasant Rebels under Stalin: Collectivization and the Culture of Peasant Resistance.* New York: Oxford University Press, 1996.

Wolf, Eric R. *Peasants.* Englewood Cliffs, NJ: Prentice-Hall, 1966.

Woodcock, George, and Ivan Avakumovic. *The Doukhobors.* London: Faber and Faber, 1968.

Worster, Donald. *The Wealth of Nature: Environmental History and the Ecological Imagination.* New York: Oxford University Press, 1993.

Yaney, George L. *The Systemization of Russian Government: Social Evolution in the Domestic Administration of Imperial Russia, 1711–1905.* Urbana: University of Illinois Press, 1973.

Articles in Journals and Edited Collections

Aleksandrov, Vadim Aleksandrovich. 'Land Re-allotment in the Peasant Commune of Late-Feudal Russia.' In Roger Bartlett, ed. *Land Commune and Peasant Community in Russia: Communal Forms in Imperial and Early Soviet Society.* London: Macmillan, 1990.
Aronson, Michael I. 'Geographical and Socioeconomic Factors in the 1881 Anti-Jewish Progoms in Russia.' *Russian Review* 39 (January 1980): 13–31.
Bauman, Wilhelm Bernhard. 'Opisanie kazennago seleniia Tokmaka, v Tavricheskoi gubernii.' *Zhurnal minusterstva gosuderstvenii imushestv (ZhMGI)* 24 (1847): 1–9.
– 'Neskol'ko zametok o khoziaistve v stepiakh iuzhnoi rossii.' *ZhMGI* 29 (1848): 3–14.
– '1848 god v Tavricheskoi gubernii v khoziaistvennom otnoshenii.' *ZhMGI* 31 (1850): 2–10.
Cornies, Johann. 'Kratkii obzor polozheniia Nogaiskikh Tatar, vodvorennykh v Melitopol'skom uezde Tavricheskoi gubernii.' *Teleskop* 33 (1836).
– 'O sostoianii khoziaistva v Molochanskikh Menonistskikh koloniiakh v 1843 godu.' *ZhMGI* 10:1 (1844): 129–44.
Bodlaender, K.B.A. 'Influence of Temperature, Radiation and Photoperiod on Development and Yield.' In J.D. Ivins and F.L. Milthorpe, eds. *The Growth of the Potato: Proceedings of the Tenth Easter School in Agricultural Science.* London: University of Nottingham Press, 1963.
Burds, Jeffrey. 'The Social Control of Peasant Labor in Russia: The Response of Village Communities to Labor Migration in the Central Industrial Region, 1861–1905.' In Esther Kingston-Mann, and Timothy Mixter, with the help of Jeffrey Burds, eds. *Peasant Economy, Culture, and Politics of European Russia, 1800–1921.* 52–100. Princeton: Princeton University Press, 1991.
Burnham, Philip. 'Spatial Mobility and Political Centralization in Pastoral Societies.' In *Pastoral Production and Society: Proceedings of the International Meeting on Nomadic Pastoralism.* Cambridge: Cambridge University Press, 1979.
Buyniak, Victor O. 'Skovoroda in early Dukhobor History – Fact or Myth.' In Koozma J. Tarasoff, ed. *The Spirit Wrestlers: Centennial Papers in Honour of Canada's Dukhobor Heritage,* 9–20. Hull: Canadian Museum of Civilization, 1995.
Byres, T.J. 'Historical Perspectives on Sharecropping.' In T.J. Byres, ed. *Sharecropping and Sharecroppers.* London: Frank Cass, 1983.
Crisp, Olga. 'The State Peasants under Nicholas I.' In Olga Crisp, *Studies in the Russian Economy before 1914.* London: Macmillan, 1976.

Davidson, Bruce R. 'The Development of the Pastoral Industry in Australia During the Nineteenth Century.' In Claudia Chang and E. Koster, eds. *Pastoralists at the Periphery: Herders in a Capitalist World*, 79–95. Tucson: University of Arizona Press, 1994.

Digard, Jean-Pierre. 'The Segmental System: Native Model or Anthropological Construction? Discussion of an Iranian Example.' In Wolfgang Weissleder, ed. *The Nomadic Alternative: Modes and Models of Interaction in the African-Asian Deserts and Steppes.* The Hague: Mouton, 1978.

Dyck, Harvey L. 'Russian Servitor and Mennonite Hero: Light and Shadow in Images of Johann Cornies.' *Journal of Mennonite Studies* 2 (1984): 9–43.

– 'Landlessness in the Old Colony: The *Judenplan* Experiment 1850–1880.' In John Friesen, ed. *Mennonites in Russia 1788–1988: Essays in Honour of Gerhard Lohrenz*, 183–202. Winnipeg: CMBC, 1989.

Fedulova, P.A. 'Klimat.' In V.P. Semenov-Tian-Shanskii, ed. *Rossiia. Polnoe Geograficheskoe Opisanie Nashego Otechestva*, 14, 49–71. St Petersburg: A.F. Devriena, 1910.

Friesen, Leonard G. 'Mennonites and Their Peasant Neighbours in Ukraine before 1900.' *Journal of Mennonite Studies* 10 (1992): 56–68.

– 'Bukkers, Plows and Lobogreikas: Peasant Acquisition of Agricultural Implements in New Russia before 1900.' *Russian Review* 53(3) (1994): 399–418.

Galaty, John G. 'Cultural Perspectives on Nomadic Pastoral Societies.' *Nomadic Peoples* 16 (October 1984): 15–30.

Gohstand, R. 'The Geography of Trade in Nineteenth-Century Russia.' In James H. Bater and R.A. French, eds. *Studies in Russian Historical Geography*, vol. 2: 329–74. London: Academic Press, 1983.

Kahan, Arcadius. 'The "Tsar Hunger" in the Land of the Tsars.' In Arcadins Kahan, *Russian Economic History: The Nineteenth Century.* Chicago: University of Chicago Press, 1989.

Karatygina, V.G. 'Rastitelnyi zhivotnyi mir.' In V.P. Semenov-Tian-Shanskii, ed. *Rossiia. Polnoe Geograficheskoe Opisanie Nashego Otechestva*, 14, 72–125. St Petersburg: A.F. Devriena, 1910.

Karpova, B.G. 'Formy poverkhnosti i stroenie zemnoe kory v peredelakh Novorossii.' In V.P. Semenov-Tian-Shanskii, ed. *Rossiia. Polnoe Geograficheskoe Opisanie Nashego Otechestva*, 14, 1–48. St Petersburg: A.F. Devriena, 1910.

Khazanov, A.M. 'Characteristic Features of Nomadic Communities in the Eurasian Steppes.' In Wolfgang Weissleder, ed. *The Nomadic Alternative: Modes and Models of Interaction in the African-Asian Deserts and Steppes.* The Hague: Mouton, 1978.

Klippenstein, Lawrence. 'The Mennonite Migration to Russia 1786–1806.' In John Friesen, ed. *Mennonites in Russia 1788–1988: Essays in Honour of Gerhard Lohrenz*, 13–42. Winnipeg: CMBC, 1989.

Köppen, O. 'Neskol'ko slov o razvedenii kormovykh trav v Tavricheskoi gubernii.' *Zhurnal minusterstva gosuderstvenii imushestv* (1863): 269–74.

– 'O polevodstve v Tavricheskoi gubernii i o vrednykh na nego vliianiiakh.' *ZhMGI* 83 (1863).

Köppen, P. 'Statisticheskiia dannyia o torgovle skotom v Rossii.' *ZhMGI* 24 (1847): 11–114.

Kotsievskii, A.S. 'Krest'ianskaia kolonizatsiia iuzhnoi ukrainy v pervoi treti XIX v.' *Materialy po istorii sel'skogo khoziaistva i krest'ianstva SSSR* 4 (1964).

Leibhardt, Barbara. 'Interpretation and Causal Analysis: Theories in Environmental History.' *Environmental Review* 12 (Spring 1988): 23–60.

Lewin, Moshe. 'The *Obshchina* and the Village.' In Roger Bartlett, ed. *Land Commune and Peasant Community in Russia: Communal Forms in Imperial and Early Soviet Society,* 20–35. London: Macmillan, 1990.

Malinowski, Lew. 'Passage to Russia: Who Were the Emigrants?' *Journal of the American Society of Germans from Russia* 2 (1979): 27–9.

Pearce, R. 'Sharecropping: Towards a Marxist View.' In T.J. Byres, ed. *Sharecropping and Sharecroppers,* 42–70. London: Frank Cass, 1983.

Pinson, Mark. 'Russian Policy and the Emigration of the Crimean Tatars to the Ottoman Empire, 1854–1862.' *Gurney-Dogu Avrupa Arasturmalari Dergisi* 1 (1972): 37–56.

Redekop, Calvin. 'The Mennonite Romance with the Land.' In Harry Loewen and Al Reimer, eds. *Visions and Realities: Essays, Poems and Fiction Dealing with Mennonite Issues.* Winnipeg: Hyperion, 1985.

Rempel, David G. 'The Mennonite Commonwealth in Russia.' *Mennonite Quarterly Review* 47 (1973): 259–308 and 48 (1974): 5–54.

Rowney, Don Karl, and Walter McKenzie Pintner. 'Officialdom and Bureaucratisation: Conclusion.' In Don Karl Rowney and Walter McKenzie Pintner, eds. *Russian Officialdom: The Bureaucratization of Russian Society from the Seventeenth Century to the Twentieth Century.* Chapel Hill: University of North Carolina Press, 1980.

Salzman, Philip Carl. 'Synthetic and Multicausal Approaches to the Study of Nomadic Peoples.' *Nomadic Peoples* 16 (1984): 31–41.

Sekirinskii, S.A. Iz istorii krestianskoi kolonizatsii Tavricheskoi gubernii v kontse XVIII-seredine XIX v. *Ezhegodnik po agrarnoi istorii costochnoi evropy* (1961): 356–62.

Sergeev, A.A. 'Nogaitsy na Molochnykh vodakh (1790–1832). Istoricheskii ocherk.' *Izvestiia Tavricheskoi Uchenoi Arkhivnoi Kommissii* 48 (1912): 1–144.

– 'Ukhod Tavricheskikh Nogaitsev v Turtsiiu v 1860 gg.' *Izvestiia Tavricheskoi Uchenoi Arkhivnoi Kommissii* 49 (1913): 178–222.

Skal'kovskii, A.A. 'Ovtsevodstvo i torgovlia sherst'iu v Novorossiiskom krae.' *ZhMGI* 24: 3 (1857).

Sprunger, Mary S. 'Dutch Mennonites and the Golden Age Economy: The Problem of Social Disparity in the Church.' In Calvin Redekop, Victor A. Krahn, and Samuel J. Steiner, eds. *Anabaptist/Mennonite Faith and Economics*, 19–40. Lanham, MD: University Press of America, 1994.

Strassoldo, Raimondo. 'Center-Periphery and System-Boundary: Culturological Perspectives.' In Jean Goffman, ed. *Center and Periphery: Spatial Variation in Politics*, 27–62. Beverly Hills: Sage, 1980.

Urry, James. '"All that Glisters ... ": Delbert Plett and the Place of the Kleine Gemeinde in Russian Mennonite History.' *Journal of Mennonite Studies* 4 (1986): 228–50.

– 'The Social Background of the Emergence of the Mennonite Brethern in Nineteenth Century Russia.' *Journal of Mennonite Studies* 6 (1988): 8–35.

– 'Mennonites, Nationalism and the State in Imperial Russia.' *Journal of Modern History* 12 (1994): 65–88.

White, Richard. 'American Environmental History: The Development of a New Historical Field.' *Pacific Historical Review* 54 (1985): 297–335.

Whittington, G. 'Field Systems of Scotland.' In Alan R.H. Baker and Robin A. Butler, eds. *Studies of Field Systems in the British Isles*, 530–79. Cambridge: Cambridge University Press, 1973.

Witte, I.U. 'O sel'skom khoziaistve v Khersonskoi, Tavricheskoi i Ekaterinoslavskoi guberniiakh.' *ZhMVD* (1834): 58–75; 101–22.

Worobec, Christine. 'The Post-Emancipation Russian Peasant Commune in Orel Province, 1861–90.' In Roger Bartlett, ed. *Land Commune and Peasant Community in Russia: Communal Forms in Imperial and Early Soviet Society*. London: Macmillan, 1990.

Dissertations

Bolotenko, George. 'Administration of the State Peasants in Russia before the Reforms of 1838.' PhD Dissertation, University of Toronto, 1979.

Friesen, Leonard George. 'New Russia and the Fissuring of Rural Society.' PhD Dissertation, University of Toronto, 1988.

Fry, Gary Dean. 'The Doukhobors, 1801–1855: The Origins of a Successful Dissident Sect.' PhD Dissertation, The American University, 1976.

Sunderland, Willard. 'Making the Empire: Colonists and Colonization in Russia, 1800–1850s.' PhD Dissertation, Indiana University, 1997.

Index

Kalmykov, Ilarion, 95, 99
Kalmykov, Vasilii, 95, 99
Kapustin, Savelii, 69–70, 94
Karakulak village, 157–8
Karasubazar, 25
Kharkov, 134
Khazanov, A.M., 34
Kherson guberniia, 59
Kherson, 18, 134
Khortitsa Agricultural Society, 132
Khortitsa Mennonite Settlement, 72,
114, 132
Khortitsa village, 109
khutors, 31–2, 148–50, 154, 161–2,
182
Kiev guberniia, 125
Kiselev, P.D., 12, 26, 28, 91–2, 102,
128, 145
Klassen cloth factory, 126, 175
Kleine Gemeinde, 83–4, 110
Köppen, Petr, 40, 66, 95–6, 101–3,
105, 145
Kolosov (District Administrator),
69–70, 95–7, 101–3
Konskaia River, 34
Kuban, 32
Kulman (Nogai sharecropper), 55–6
kurdiuch sheep, 55, 64–5, 72, 135,
139–40
Kurushan River, 7, 33, 52
Kuznetsov (land surveyor), 148

labour absorption rates, 81–2
labour markets, 81–3, 126, 151–3, 176
labourers, 11, 151–3
land allocation and tenure practices,
5, 20, 65, 68; of Doukhobors, 39–
40, 68–70, 80, 95, 102–4; of
German colonists, 42–3, 68, 72, 81–

2, 85; of Mennonites, 16, 42–3, 68,
72, 74–8, 80–1, 85, 120–1, 127,
142, 153–4, 163, 174–6, 181–2, 184;
of Molokans, 41, 68, 71, 80; of
Nogai, 33–6, 50, 57, 85, 147, 171;
of Orthodox state peasants, 23, 58–
9, 67, 76, 85, 149–50, 153–4, 163,
182; of the tsarist state, 18–20, 29–
31, 33, 35–6, 39–42, 67, 91–3, 144–
5, 149
land lease practices, 40, 78–82, 89,
93, 103, 105, 138, 162, 165, 167–9,
173, 175
land redistribution, 142, 154
land repartition, 4, 16, 58, 91–2, 141,
144, 147–61, 163, 165, 167, 180,
184–5
land shortages, 88, 91–2, 149, 179,
183; of Mennonites, 120, 124–5,
182, 184; of Molokans, 41, 80, 91;
of Nogai, 52, 141; of Orthodox
state peasants, 16, 58, 66, 80, 85,
91–3, 104, 147–51, 153, 163, 182;
tsarist state policy, 91, 103–4, 121
Land Survey Department, 20, 25, 48,
67
land surveys, 8, 19–20, 35, 67, 147–9,
154–5
land value, 171
landlessness, 75, 77–8, 81–6, 124–8,
133, 137–9, 142, 153–4, 165, 168–
70, 172, 175–6, 178; crisis, 4, 16,
74, 81, 127, 133, 165, 172–8
landlords, 11, 16
Landskrone village, 121
Langeron, L.A., 94, 98
Large Flemish Congregation, 83–4,
110, 130–2
legal rights of settlers, 18